FAT-FREE

Holiday Recipes

FAT-FREE
Holiday Recipes

SANDRA WOODRUFF, RD

Avery Publishing Group
Garden City Park, New York

Text Illustrator: John Wincek
Interior Color Photographs: John Strange
Front Cover Photograph: Envision/Steven Mark Needham
Back Cover Photographs: John Strange
Cover Design: William Gonzalez
Typesetting: Bonnie Freid
In-House Editor: Joanne Abrams

Cataloging-in-Publication Data

Woodruff, Sandra L.
    Fat-free holiday recipes : delicious fat-free and low-fat
recipes for holidays, family celebrations, and elegant
get-togethers / Sandra Woodruff
    p. cm.
    Includes index.
    ISBN 0-89529-629-2

    1. Holiday cookery. 2. Low-fat–Recipes. I. Title.
TX739.W66 1995

641.5'68
QB194-1766

Printed in the United States of America

10   9   8   7   6   5   4   3   2   1

Contents

This book is dedicated to my favorite taste tester, Wiley Coyote.

Acknowledgments

I am fortunate to know so many people who have been constant sources of inspiration, ideas, and information. It is therefore difficult to even know where to begin with these acknowledgments.

I would like to thank Rudy Shur and Avery Publishing Group for providing the opportunity to publish this book. Special thanks go to my editor, Joanne Abrams, whose efforts have added so much to this book, and who, like everyone at Avery, has been a pleasure to work with.

I am grateful to my friends and family, who have been so supportive over the years—my mother, Wanda Burlison; my father and stepmother, George and Jeanne Woodruff; my dear friends, Mary Jo Weale, Gail Bauman, Lori Turner, Toni Trimarco, and Robert Baker; and, especially, my significant other, Tom Maureau.

Thanks go to Lisa Harris, Sara Goldiner, David Pargman, and Louis Weinreb for sharing their ideas, their enthusiasm, and their insights into Jewish cuisine.

Thanks also go to my colleagues at Tallahassee Community Hospital's Communicare Center, and to the many clients, students, and members of this community who have been both supportive and inspiring over the years.

I am also eternally grateful to Ellie Whitney, PhD, and the talented writers at Nutrition and Health Associates who patiently taught me so much.

Preface

As a nutritionist, I have long been aware of the need to help people eliminate fat from their diet. I also know the importance of creating nutrient-rich dishes made with whole grains and other ingredients that are as close as possible to their natural state. And because of my work as a teacher, I also know that foods must be more than just healthy. They must be visually appealing and absolutely delicious. If not, people simply won't eat them.

Fat-Free Holiday Recipes is the perfect book for people who want to reduce the fat in their diet, maximize their nutrition, and treat their friends and family to delicious holiday and special-occasion dishes. From Spicy Barbecue Meatballs to Onion Dill Dip to Chocolate Raspberry Torte, every recipe has been designed to reduce fat and boost nutrition. Just as important, every recipe has been kitchen-tested to make sure that you enjoy success each and every time you make it, and people-tested to make sure that every dish you create is sure to be a hit.

Fat-Free Holiday Recipes begins by explaining just why dietary fat should be reduced, and just how much fat is allowable in a healthy diet. You'll also learn of the many nonfat and low-fat ingredients that will help you reduce fat without reducing taste, and you'll learn about the nutritional analysis that accompanies each and every recipe in the book.

Following this important information, the book is divided into four parts, each of which focuses on a specific type of party or holiday food, or presents complete menus and recipes for special-occasion meals. Part One offers a cornucopia of low-fat and fat-free finger-food recipes that are perfect for any gathering. Included in this section are recipes for both hot treats, like meatballs and kabobs, and cold treats, like finger sandwiches and dips. Also included are recipes for hot and cold beverages that round out party menus and add to the festivities without adding fat.

Part Two presents menus and accompanying recipes for five traditional holidays, including

Thanksgiving, Christmas, Hanukkah, Passover, and Easter. Each menu is composed of a variety of taste-tempting fat-free and low-fat appetizers, main dishes, side dishes, and desserts. Whenever possible, options have been provided to allow you to tailor the meal to suit your family's tastes. The Thanksgiving menu, for instance, gives you a selection of four stuffings, three cranberry sauces, and six side dishes—in addition to the turkey, of course. In many menus, you'll find low-fat and no-fat versions of traditional holiday foods. In others, you'll find new and exciting recipes for dishes that may become new holiday traditions in your home. Best of all, each menu includes suggested plan-ahead strategies that will allow you to complete many of your preparations in advance, helping you avoid a last-minute rush on the day of your get-together.

Part Three presents menus and recipes for a variety of special occasions, including New Year's Day, Valentine's Day, Saint Patrick's Day, Memorial Day, the Fourth of July, Labor Day, and Halloween. Again, each of these complete menus includes a variety of healthy, easy-to-make dishes that maximize nutrition and taste while minimizing fuss.

Part Four rounds out our collection of holiday and party recipes with a bonanza of fat-free and low-fat dessert and baked-goods recipes. Whether you're searching for a festive quick bread to complement a simple luncheon dish or a dazzling grand finale to a special-occasion dinner, this section will meet your needs. All sweet treats are made without butter, margarine, or oil, and all are so delectable, no one but you will guess just how wholesome they are.

It is my hope that *Fat-Free Holiday Recipes* will prove to you, as well as to your friends and family, that party food does not have to be rich and fattening, and that low-fat food can be satisfying, exciting, and fun. So eat well and enjoy! As you will see, it is possible to do both—every day of the year.

Introduction

Great food adds that special touch to any occasion. Food livens up a party and makes every holiday more enjoyable and memorable. Unfortunately, holidays and parties have long been thought of as a license to indulge in fat, sugar, and salt—ingredients that we now know must be kept to a minimum in a healthful diet. The good news is that the wide availability of low-fat and nonfat products, as well as a greater knowledge of healthy cooking techniques, now means that *good* doesn't have to be *greasy.* Moreover, elegant and delicious dishes that are special enough for any occasion can be just as easy to prepare as traditional special-occasion foods.

As a nutritionist and teacher, I began looking for ways to reduce or totally eliminate dietary fat a long time before anyone heard the term "fat-free." Through years of experimentation and kitchen testing, and with the help of clients and students, I have developed simple ways to do just that. Of course, because of our new awareness of the link between diet and health, many low-fat cookbooks are now available. Unfortunately, these cookbooks don't always use the most healthful ingredients. Often, artificial sweeteners and other highly processed ingredients are used to cut fat and calories. In the process, nutrition is often compromised. Moreover, these books often ignore an important part of everyone's life—holiday gatherings and special-occasion get-togethers. *Fat-Free Holiday Recipes* was designed to fill the gap by providing tried-and-true recipes that will enable you to create healthful, delicious low- and no-fat party menus.

The recipes in this book are far more than just low-fat or no-fat. Besides eliminating or greatly reducing fat, I have improved the nutritional value of recipes by using natural sweeteners like fruits and juices whenever possible. Whole grains and whole grain flours have also been used, providing added fiber and nutritional value. As an added bonus, the use of herbs, spices, and seasonings, as well as a minimal reliance on pro-

1

cessed foods, has helped to keep sodium under control.

Probably the best part of these recipes, though, is their simplicity. Every effort has been made to keep the number of ingredients, pots, pans, and utensils to a minimum. This will save you time and make cleanup a breeze—important considerations for most people today.

At this point, you may be wondering why you should even worry about what you eat during the holidays. After all, an occasional overindulgence will not ruin an otherwise healthy diet. But with great-tasting low-fat holiday favorites just as easy to prepare as their high-fat counterparts, why would you *not* opt for healthier alternatives?

Besides, through the years, I've found that once people make the change to a low-fat diet, they really do prefer the fresher, lighter taste of foods made without fat—every day of the year.

As you will see, watching your fat intake does not have to mean feeling deprived during holidays and special occasions. In fact, this book is filled with ideas for easy and elegant entertaining, whether you are just having a few people over for coffee or holding an open house for fifty. From New Year's Day through Valentine's Day and the Fourth of July and all the way to Christmas and Hanukkah, this book will help you begin new and exciting holiday traditions. I wish you the best of luck and health with all your fat-free cooking!

Getting the Fat Out of Parties

Do you dread social gatherings, fearing what they might do to your intentions to eat well? If so, you may have good reason. It is not uncommon for people to gain ten or even fifteen pounds between the start of the football season and New Year's Eve.

Food and festivity are part of the American way. Food does liven up a party, and there is nothing wrong with enjoying special dishes on special occasions. Unfortunately, traditional party favorites top the list of foods high in fat, sugar, and salt. Fatty dips, spreads, meats, cheeses, crackers, and chips are often the only selections on hors d'oeuvres tables. Have a taste of each, and you could easily consume a full day's worth of fat and calories. Most people fare no better at dinner parties, where the hosts go all out with a fat-laced gourmet menu. After all, it is a party, and your hosts want to serve "the best" to their guests.

Fortunately, many people now realize that delicious, appealing foods do not have to be loaded with fatty ingredients like cream, butter, and egg yolks. Nor does a large portion of meat have to be the centerpiece of a special-occasion meal. Elegant desserts, too, can be prepared with little or no fat, and with a lot less sugar than is usually used. That is why *Fat-Free Holiday Recipes* was written. In these pages, you will find a wide variety of simple and elegant hors d'oeuvres and dinner dishes made with nonfat and low-fat ingredients. You will be delighted by "defatted" versions of old favorites, as well as tempting new creations that will let you party to your heart's content.

Perhaps just as important, this book will show you that contrary to popular belief, putting together a party does not have to be an ordeal. As you will see, the recipes in this book will save you not only fat and calories, but also time and effort. Most of the recipes are very simple to follow, even for beginners, and are designed to create as little mess as possible, saving you cleanup time. The party menus even provide strategies for preparing foods in advance, so that little work will be required at the last minute, allowing you to enjoy your own party.

This section will explain why dietary fat should be decreased, and will guide you in budgeting your daily fat intake. In addition, we'll look at the various healthful ingredients used throughout this book—ingredients that will enable you to prune fat from every meal of the day, as well as from party foods and holiday feasts.

BIG FAT PROBLEMS

Excess fat may well be the number-one dietary problem in America. With more than twice the calories of carbohydrates and protein, fat is a concentrated source of calories. Compare a cup of butter or margarine (almost pure fat) with a cup of flour (almost pure carbohydrates). The butter has 1,600 calories, while the flour has only 400 calories. It's easy to see where most of our calories come from.

Besides being high in calories, fat is also readily converted into body fat when eaten in excess. Carbohydrate-rich foods eaten in excess are also stored as fat, but they must first be converted into fat—a process that burns up some of the carbohydrates. The bottom line is that a high-fat diet will cause 20 percent more weight gain than will a high-carbohydrate diet, even when the two diets contain the same number of calories. So a high-fat diet is a double-edged sword for the weight-conscious person. It is high in calories, and it is high in the kind of nutrient that is most readily stored as body fat.

But high-fat diets pose a threat to much more than our weight. When fatty diets lead to obesity, diseases like diabetes and high blood pressure can result. And specific types of fats present their own unique problems. For example, eating too much saturated fat—found in meat, butter, and palm and coconut oils, among other foods—raises blood cholesterol levels, setting the stage for heart disease. Polyunsaturated fat, once thought to be the solution to heart disease, can also be harmful when eaten in excess. A diet overly rich in corn oil, safflower oil, and other foods high in polyunsaturates can alter body chemistry to favor the development of blood clots, high blood pressure, and inflammatory diseases. Too much polyunsaturated fat can also promote free-radical damage in cells, contributing to heart disease and cancer.

Where do monounsaturated fats fit in? Monounsaturated fats—found in olive oil, canola oil, avocados, and nuts—have no known harmful effects other than being a concentrated source of calories, as all fats are.

Considering the problems caused by excess fat, you may think that it would be best to totally eliminate fat from your diet. But the fact is that we do need some dietary fat. For instance, linoleic acid, a polyunsaturated fat naturally present in grains, nuts, and seeds, is essential for life. The average adult needs a minimum of 3 to 6 grams of linoleic acid per day—the amount present in 1 to 2 teaspoonfuls of polyunsaturated vegetable oil or 1 to 2 tablespoonfuls of nuts and seeds. Linolenic acid, a fat found mainly in fish and green plants, is also essential for good health.

Unfortunately, many people are getting too much of a good thing. The liberal use of foods like mayonnaise, oil-based salad dressings, margarine, and cooking oils has created an unhealthy overdose of linoleic acid in the American diet. And, of course, most people also eat far too much saturated fat. How can we correct this? We can minimize the use of refined vegetable oils and table fats, and eat a diet rich in whole grains, fruits, and vegetables, with moderate amounts of nuts and seeds. This is what *Fat-Free Holiday Recipes* is all about. In the remainder of this section, you'll learn how to budget your daily fat intake, and you'll become acquainted with the healthful foods that will help you prune the fat from your diet and maximize the nutrients. Throughout the rest of the book, you'll learn how to use these foods to create sure-fire crowd pleasers for every holiday from January to December.

BUDGETING YOUR FAT

For most people, close to 40 percent of the calories in their diet come from fat. However, currently it is recommended that fat calories constitute no more than 30 percent of the diet, and, in fact, 20 to 25 percent would be even better in most cases. So the amount of fat you can eat every day is based on the number of calories you need. Because people's caloric needs depend on their weight, age, sex, activity level, and metabolic rate, these needs vary greatly among people. Most adults, though, must consume 13 to 15 calories per pound to maintain their weight. Of course, some people need even fewer calories, while very physically active people need more.

Once you have determined your calorie requirement, you can estimate a fat budget for yourself. Suppose you are a moderately active person who weighs 150 pounds. You will probably need about 15 calories per pound to maintain your weight, or about 2,250 per day. To limit your fat intake to 20 percent of your caloric intake, you can eat no more than 450 calories derived from fat per day (2,250 x .20 = 450). To convert this into grams of fat, divide by 9, as one gram of fat has 9 calories. Therefore, you should limit yourself to 50 grams of fat per day (450 ÷ 9 = 50).

The table at the bottom of this page shows both 20-percent and 25-percent maximum daily fat gram budgets. If you are overweight or underweight, go by the weight you would like to be. And keep in mind that although you have budgeted X amount of fat grams per day, you don't *have* to eat that amount of fat—you just have to avoid going over budget.

ABOUT THE INGREDIENTS

Never before has it been so easy to eat healthfully. Nonfat and low-fat alternatives are available for just about any ingredient you can think of. This makes it possible to create a dazzling array of healthy and delicious treats, including nonfat and low-fat versions of many of your favorite foods. In the pages that follow, we'll take a look at low-fat and nonfat cheeses, fat-free spreads and dressings, fat-free egg substitutes, ultra-lean meats, and other ingredients that will insure success in all your fat-free cooking adventures.

Low-Fat and Nonfat Cheeses

Americans have long had a love affair with cheese. For many years, though, people who wanted to reduce the fat in their diet had to also reduce the cheese, or even eliminate cheese entirely. Fortunately, a wide range of nonfat and low-fat products is now available, making it possible to have your cheese and eat it, too. Let's learn about some of the cheeses that you'll be using in your fat-free holiday recipes.

Maximum Daily Fat Intakes

Weight	Recommended Daily Calorie Intake (13–15 calories per pound)	Fat Grams Allowed (20%)	Fat Grams Allowed (25%)
100	1,300–1,500	29–33	36–42
110	1,430–1,650	32–37	40–46
120	1,560–1,800	34–40	43–50
130	1,690–1,950	38–43	47–54
140	1,820–2,100	40–46	51–58
150	1,950–2,250	43–50	54–62
160	2,080–2,400	46–53	58–67
170	2,210–2,550	49–57	61–71
180	2,340–2,700	52–60	65–75
190	2,470–2,850	55–63	69–79
200	2,600–3,000	58–66	72–83

Cottage Cheese. Although often thought of as a diet food, full-fat cottage cheese has 5 grams of fat per 4-ounce serving, making it far from diet fare. Instead, choose nonfat or low-fat cottage cheese, which may be puréed until smooth and used as a base for dips and spreads. Select brands with 1 percent or less milk fat. Most brands of cottage cheese are high in sodium, with about 400 milligrams per half-cup, so it's best to avoid adding salt whenever this cheese is a recipe ingredient. As an alternative, use unsalted cottage cheese, which is available in some stores.

Another option when buying cottage cheese is dry curd cottage cheese. This nonfat version is made without the "dressing" or creaming mixture. Minus the dressing, cottage cheese has a drier consistency; hence its name, "dry curd." Unlike most cottage cheese, dry curd is very low in sodium. Use it as you would nonfat cottage cheese in casseroles, quiches, dips, spreads, salad dressings, and cheesecakes.

Cream Cheese. Regular full-fat cream cheese contains about 10 grams of fat per ounce, making this popular spread a real menace if you're trying to reduce dietary fat. A tasty alternative is light cream cheese, which has only 5 grams of fat per ounce. Still another reduced-fat alternative is Neufchatel cheese, which contains 6 grams of fat per ounce. And, of course, nonfat cream cheese contains no fat at all. Like light cream cheese and Neufchatel, nonfat cream cheese may be used in dips, spreads, and cheesecakes. Look for brands like Philly Free and Healthy Choice.

Firm and Hard Cheeses. Both low-fat and nonfat cheeses of many types—including Swiss, Cheddar, Monterey jack, and mozzarella—are available in most grocery stores. Reduced-fat cheeses generally have 3 to 5 grams of fat per ounce, while nonfat cheeses contain no fat at all. Compare this with whole-milk varieties, which contain 9 to 10 grams of fat per ounce, and you'll realize your savings in fat and calories.

Nonfat and reduced-fat firm and hard cheeses can be used in casseroles, in sauces, and in any other way their full-fat counterparts are used. Look for brands like Alpine Lace Lo, Cracker Barrel Lite, Healthy Choice, Kraft Light Naturals, Kraft Healthy Favorites, Jarlsberg Lite Swiss, and Weight Watchers.

Parmesan Cheese. Full-fat Parmesan cheese typically contains 8 grams of fat per ounce. Fortunately, as is true of most cheeses, reduced-fat and nonfat versions are available. Keep in mind, though, that a little bit of this flavorful cheese goes a long way, so even if you use regular Parmesan in any of the recipes in this book, the total fat per serving will still be quite low.

Pasteurized Processed Cheese Product. Sold in large blocks, this cheese is designed to melt smoothly, and so is intended as a cooking cheese for use in hot cheese dips and similar dishes. When buying nonfat processed cheese products, look for brands like Healthy Choice.

Ricotta Cheese. Ricotta is a mild, slightly sweet, creamy cheese that may be used in dips, spreads, and traditional Italian dishes like lasagna. As the name implies, nonfat ricotta contains no fat at all. Low-fat ricotta and light ricotta, on the other hand, have 1 to 3 grams of fat per ounce, while whole-milk ricotta has 4 grams of fat per ounce.

Soft Curd Farmer Cheese. This soft, spreadable white cheese makes a good low-fat substitute for cream cheese. Brands made with skim milk have about 3 grams of fat per ounce, compared with cream cheese's 10 grams. Soft curd farmer cheese may be used in dips, spreads, and cheesecakes, and as a filling for blintzes. Some brands are made with whole milk, so read the label carefully. Look for a brand like Friendship Farmer Cheese.

Yogurt Cheese. A good substitute for cream cheese in dips, spreads, and cheesecakes, yogurt cheese can be made at home with any brand of plain or flavored yogurt that does not contain gelatin. Simply place the yogurt in a funnel lined with cheesecloth or a coffee filter, and let it drain into a jar in the refrigerator for eight hours or overnight. When the yogurt is reduced by half, it is ready to use. The whey that collects in the jar may be used in place of the liquid in bread and muffin recipes.

Nondairy Cheese Alternatives. If you choose to avoid dairy products because of a lactose intolerance or for another reason, you'll be glad to know that low-fat cheeses made from soymilk, almond milk, and Brazil nut milk are now available in a variety of flavors. Look for brands like Almondrella, Veganrella, and Tofurella.

Measuring Cheese

Throughout the recipes in this book, I have usually expressed the amount of cheese needed in cups. For instance, a recipe may call for 1 cup of cottage cheese or $\frac{1}{4}$ cup of grated Parmesan. Since you will sometimes buy cheese in chunks and grate it in your own kitchen, or buy packages marked in ounces when the recipe calls for cups, it is useful to understand that the conversion of cheese from ounces (weight) to cups (volume) varies, depending on the texture of the cheese. When using the recipes in *Fat-Free Holiday Recipes,* the following table should help take the guesswork out of these conversions.

Cheese Equivalency Amounts

Cheese	Weight	Equivalent Volume
Cheddar	8 ounces	2 cups shredded or crumbled
Cottage Cheese	8 ounces	1 cup
Cream Cheese	8 ounces	1 cup
Farmer Cheese	8 ounces	1 cup
Mozzarella	8 ounces	2 cups shredded or crumbled
Parmesan	8 ounces	2¼ cups grated
Ricotta	8 ounces	1 cup

Other Low-Fat and Nonfat Dairy Products

Of course, cheese isn't the only dairy product we use in holiday recipes. How about the sour cream in onion dip and the buttermilk in your favorite biscuits? Fortunately, there are low-fat and nonfat versions of these and other dairy products as well.

Buttermilk. Buttermilk adds a rich flavor and texture to baked goods like biscuits, muffins, and cakes, and lends a "cheesy" taste to sauces, cheesecakes, and casseroles. Originally a by-product of butter making, this product should perhaps be called "butterless" milk. Most brands of buttermilk contain from 0.5 to 2 percent fat by weight, but some brands contain as much as 3.5 percent fat. When following the recipes in this book—which call for nonfat buttermilk—choose brands that are no more than 1 percent milk fat.

If you do not have buttermilk on hand, a good substitute can be made by mixing equal parts of nonfat yogurt and skim milk. Alternatively, mix a tablespoon of vinegar or lemon juice with one cup of skim milk, and let it sit for five minutes before using. For a nondairy alternative to buttermilk, mix a tablespoon of vinegar or lemon juice with one cup of soymilk.

Milk. Whole milk, the highest-fat milk available, is 3.5 percent fat by weight and has 8 grams of fat per cup. Instead, choose skim (nonfat) milk, which—with all but a trace of fat removed—has only about 0.5 gram of fat per cup. Another good choice is 1-percent milk, which, as the name implies, is 1 percent fat by weight and contains 2 grams of fat per cup.

Sour Cream. As calorie- and fat-conscious people know, full-fat sour cream can contain almost 500 calories and about 48 grams of fat per cup! Use nonfat sour cream, though, and you'll save 320 calories and 48 grams of fat. Made from cultured nonfat milk thickened with vegetable gums, this product beautifully replaces its fatty counterpart in cold dips, spreads, and sauces. Look for brands like Land O'Lakes Nonfat. Plain nonfat yogurt may also be substituted for sour cream.

Yogurt. Yogurt adds creamy richness and flavor to sauces, baked goods, and casseroles. And, of course, it is a perfect base for many dips and dressings. In your low-fat cooking, select brands with 1 percent or less milk fat. If you must avoid dairy products, look for soy yogurt, which is available in health foods stores and many grocery stores.

Fat-Free Spreads and Dressings

Like cheeses, spreads and dressings were long a major source of fat and calories. Happily, many low-fat and nonfat alternatives to our high-fat favorites are now available. Let's learn a little more about these fat-saving products.

Margarine. None of the recipes in this book uses margarine or butter of any kind—or oil or shortening, for that matter. But if you are used to spreading foods with margarine, you can easily reduce your dietary fat by switching to a nonfat or reduced-fat margarine, and using it sparingly. Every tablespoon of nonfat margarine that you substitute for regular margarine will save you 11 grams of fat.

Mayonnaise. Nonfat mayonnaise is highly recommended over regular mayonnaise, which is almost pure fat. How can mayonnaise be made without all that oil? Manufacturers use more water and vegetable thickeners. Some commonly available nonfat brands are Kraft Free, Miracle Whip Free, and Smart Beat. Reduced-fat mayonnaise is also available, with half to two-thirds less fat and calories than regular mayonnaise. Look for brands like Hellman's Reduced-Fat, Kraft Light, Blue Plate Light, and Weight Watcher's.

Salad Dressings. Now made in a number of flavors, fat-free dressings contain either no oil or so little oil that they have less than 0.5 grams of fat per tablespoon. Use these dressings instead of oil-based versions to dress your favorite salads or as a delicious basting sauce for grilled foods.

Fat Substitutes for Baking

Almost any moist ingredient can be used to replace the fat in cakes, muffins, quick breads, and other baked goods. The recipes in this book use a variety of fat substitutes. Most of these substitutes, including applesauce, fruit purée, fruit juice, nonfat buttermilk, and mashed pumpkin, are readily available in grocery stores. Two additional substitutes—Prune Butter and Prune Purée—can be easily made at home using the recipes found in Part Four.

Egg Whites and Egg Substitutes

Everyone who cooks knows the value of eggs. Eggs are star ingredients in quiches, add lightness to many casseroles, and are indispensable in a wide range of baked goods. Of course, eggs are also high in cholesterol. For this reason, the recipes in this book call for egg whites or fat-free egg substitute. Just how great are your savings in cholesterol and fat when whole eggs are replaced with one of these ingredients? One large egg contains 80 calories, 5 grams of fat, and 210 milligrams of cholesterol. The equivalent amount of egg white or fat-free egg substitute contains 20 to 30 calories, no fat, and no cholesterol. The benefits of these substitute ingredients are clear.

You may wonder why some of the recipes in this book call for egg whites while others call for egg substitute. In some cases, one ingredient does, in fact, work better than the other. For instance, egg substitute is the best choice when making quiches and puddings. In addition, because they have been pasteurized (heat treated), egg substitutes are safe to use uncooked in eggnogs and salad dressings. On the other hand, when recipes require whipped egg whites, egg substitutes simply do not work.

In most recipes, egg whites and egg substitute can be used interchangeably. Yet, even in these recipes, one may sometimes be listed instead of the other due to ease of measuring. For example, while a cake made with three tablespoons of fat-free egg substitute would turn out just as well if made with three tablespoons of egg whites, this would require you to use *one and a half* large egg whites, making measuring something of a nuisance.

Whenever a recipe calls for egg whites, use *large* egg whites. When selecting an egg substitute, be sure to look for a fat-free brand like Egg Beaters. (Some egg substitutes contain vegetable oil.) When replacing egg whites with egg substitute, or whole eggs with egg whites or egg substitute, use the following guidelines:

---

1 large egg = $1\frac{1}{2}$ large egg whites

---

1 large egg = 3 tablespoons egg substitute

---

1 large egg white = 2 tablespoons egg substitute

Ultra-Lean Poultry, Meat, and Vegetarian Alternatives

Because of the high fat and cholesterol contents of meats, many people have sharply reduced their consumption of meat, have limited themselves to white-meat chicken and turkey, or have totally eliminated meat and poultry from their diet. The good news is that whether you are a sworn meat eater, someone who only occasionally eats meat dishes, or a confirmed vegetarian, plenty of lean meats, lean poultry, and excellent meat substitutes are now available.

The most important point to remember when including poultry and meat in meals is to keep portions to a modest 6 ounces or less per day. For perspective, 3 ounces of meat is the size of a deck of cards. Here are some suggestions for choosing the leanest possible poultry and meat.

Turkey

Although both chicken and turkey have less total fat and saturated fat than beef and pork, your very best bet when buying poultry is turkey.

What's the difference between the fat and calorie contents of chicken and turkey? While 3 ounces of chicken breast without skin contain 139 calories and 3 grams of fat, the same amount of turkey breast without skin contains only 119 calories and 1 gram of fat.

Your best defense against fat when preparing and eating poultry is removing the skin and any underlying visible fat. Doing just this eliminates half the fat. If possible, eliminate the skin *before* cooking. Poultry cooked without the skin has been found to have 20 percent less fat than poultry that had the skin removed after cooking. In addition, if you remove the skin after cooking, you will also remove the seasoning.

All of the leanest cuts of turkey come from the turkey breast, so that all have the same amount of fat and calories per serving. Here is what you're likely to find at your local supermarket:

Turkey Cutlets. Turkey cutlets, which are slices of turkey breast, are usually about $\frac{1}{4}$ inch thick and weigh about 2 to 3 ounces each. These cutlets may be used as a delicious and healthy alternative to boneless chicken breast, pork tenderloin slices, and veal.

Turkey Medallions. Sliced turkey tenderloins, these medallions are usually about 1 inch thick and weigh 2 to 3 ounces each. Substitute them for pork medallions in your favorite recipes.

Turkey Steaks. Cut from the turkey breast, these steaks are about $\frac{1}{2}$ to 1 inch in thickness. Turkey steaks may be baked, broiled, grilled, cut into stir-fry or kabob pieces, or ground for burgers.

Turkey Tenderloins. Large sections of fresh turkey breast, tenderloins usually weigh about 8 ounces each. Tenderloins may be sliced into cutlets, cut into stir-fry or kabob pieces, ground for burgers, or grilled or roasted as is.

Whole Turkey Breast. Perfect for people who love roast turkey but want only the breast meat, turkey breasts weigh 4 to 7 pounds each. These breasts may be roasted with or without stuffing.

Ground Turkey. Ground turkey is the perfect ingredient for use in meatballs, chili, burgers—in any dish that uses ground meat. When shopping for ground turkey, you'll find that different products have different percentages of fat. Ground turkey breast, which is only 1 percent fat by weight, is the leanest ground meat you can buy. Ground dark meat turkey made without the skin is 8 to 10 percent fat by weight. Brands with added skin and fat usually contain 15 percent fat. The moral is clear: Always check the labels before making a purchase!

Beef and Pork

Although not as lean as turkey, beef and pork are both considerably leaner today than in decades past. Spurred by competition from the poultry industry, beef and pork producers have changed breeding and feeding practices to reduce the fat content of these products. In addition, butchers are now trimming away more of the fat from retail cuts of meat. The result? On average, grocery store cuts of beef are 27 percent leaner today than they were in the early 1980s, and retail cuts of pork are 43 percent leaner.

Choosing the Best Cuts and Grades. Of course, some cuts of beef and pork are leaner than others. Which are the smartest choices? The table on the next page will guide you in selecting those cuts that are lowest in fat.

While identifying the lowest-fat cuts of meat is an important first step in healthy cooking, be aware that even lean cuts have varying amounts of fat because of differences in *grades*. In general, the higher, and more expensive, grades of meat, like USDA Prime and Choice, have more fat due to a higher degree of *marbling*—internal fat that cannot be trimmed away. USDA Select meats have the least amount of marbling, and therefore the lowest amount of fat. How important are these differences? A USDA Choice piece of meat may have 15 to 20 percent more fat than

a USDA Select cut, and USDA Prime may have even more fat. Clearly, the difference is significant. So when choosing beef and pork for your table, by all means check the package for grade. Then look for the least amount of marbling in the cut you have chosen, and let appearance be the final judge.

Ground Beef. While ground turkey breast is the very best choice when buying ground meat, low-fat ground beef is now available, giving you a second healthy option. One of your best bets is Healthy Choice Ground Beef. A mixture of lean beef and a small amount of oat flour, which is used to hold in moisture, this product is 4 percent fat by weight, giving it about 33 calories and 1 gram of fat per ounce. Other brands of 93- to 96-percent lean ground beef are also on the market. Some use the sea vegetable carrageen instead of oat flour.

Lean Processed Meat

Because of our new fat-consciousness, low-fat sausages, hams, and lunch meats are now available, with just a fraction of the fat of regular processed meats. Many of these low-fat products are used in the recipes in this book.

When a recipe calls for smoked turkey sausage, try a brand like Healthy Choice, which has just 1 gram of fat per ounce. When a recipe calls for ground turkey breakfast sausage, try a brand like Louis Rich. Many stores now make their own fresh turkey sausage, including turkey Italian sausage. When buying these fresh sausages, always check the package and choose the leanest mixture available.

One of the biggest boons to health-conscious party givers are low-fat lunch meats, which allow you to easily prepare a variety of heart-smart hors d'oeuvres and cold cut platters. For recipes that include ham or turkey pastrami, look for Healthy Choice, Butterball, and Oscar Mayer Healthy Favorites—brands with no more than 1 gram of fat per ounce.

Lean Beef and Pork Cuts

Cut (3 ounces, cooked & trimmed)	Calories	Fat
Beef		
Eye of Round	143	4.2 grams
Top Round	153	4.2 grams
Round Tip	157	5.9 grams
Top Sirloin	165	6.1 grams
Pork		
Tenderloin	139	4.1 grams
Ham (95% lean)	112	4.3 grams
Boneless Sirloin Chops	164	5.7 grams
Boneless Loin Roast	165	6.1 grams
Boneless Loin Chops	173	6.6 grams

Vegetarian Alternatives

Nonmeat alternatives to ground meat can be substituted for ground beef or poultry in any of the recipes in this book. One good choice is Harvest Burger. Made from soybeans, Harvest Burger is rich in protein and has only about 1 gram of fat per ounce. Harvest Burger comes packaged as dry nuggets in individual pouches. When rehydrated, the contents of a single pouch is equivalent to one pound of ground meat. Harvest Burger can be shaped into meatballs or patties, and can replace ground meat in dishes like chili.

Texturized vegetable protein (TVP) is yet another alternative to ground meat. Made from defatted soy flour, TVP has about 0.3 grams of fat per ounce. Like Harvest Burger, TVP is packaged as dry nuggets that you rehydrate with water. This product makes an excellent ground meat substitute in chili, tacos, and many other dishes.

Grains and Flours

Just because a food is fat-free does not mean it is good for you. Fat-free products made from refined white flour and refined grains provide few nutrients, and can actually deplete nutrient stores if eaten in excess. Whole grains and whole grain flours, on the other hand, contain a multitude of nutrients such as vitamin E, zinc, magnesium, chromium, potassium, and many other nutrients that are lacking in refined grains. Whole grain products also add fiber to our diets, making our meals more satisfying. You see, fiber—like fat—provides a feeling of fullness. Fiber also helps maintain blood sugar levels, which helps keep hunger at bay.

Fortunately, once accustomed to the heartier taste and texture of whole grains, most people prefer them over tasteless refined grains. Following is a description of some of the whole grain products used in the recipes in this book. Many of these products are readily available in grocery stores, while others may be found in health foods stores and gourmet shops. If you are unable to locate a particular grain or flour in your area, it is probably available by mail order. (See the Resource List on page 241.)

Barley. This grain has a nutty light flavor, making it a great substitute for rice in any dish. Barley flour, made from ground barley kernels, is rich in cholesterol-lowering soluble fiber. Slightly sweet in taste, this flour adds a cake-like texture to baked goods, and can be used interchangeably with oat flour in any recipe.

Brown Rice. Brown rice is whole-kernel rice, meaning that all nutrients are intact. With a slightly chewy texture and a pleasant nutty flavor, brown rice makes excellent pilafs and stuffings. *Brown rice flour*, which is simply finely ground brown rice, has a texture similar to cornmeal and adds a mildly sweet flavor to baked goods. Use it in cookies for a crisp and crunchy texture.

Cornmeal. This grain adds a sweet flavor, a lovely golden color, and a crunchy texture to baked goods. Select whole grain (unbolted) cornmeal for the most nutrition. By contrast, bolted cornmeal is nearly whole grain, and degermed cornmeal is refined.

Oat Bran. Made of the outer part of the oat kernel, oat bran has a sweet, mild flavor and is a concentrated source of cholesterol-lowering soluble fiber. Oat bran helps retain moisture in baked goods, making it a natural for fat-free baking. Look for it in the hot cereal section of your grocery store, and choose the softer, more finely ground products, like Quaker Oat Bran. Coarsely ground oat bran makes excellent hot cereal, but is not the best for baking.

Oats. Loaded with cholesterol-lowering soluble fiber, oats add a chewy texture and sweet flavor to a variety of dishes. *Oat flour* is widely available in health foods stores and many grocery stores, and can also be made at home by grinding quick-cooking rolled oats in a blender. (Look for oats that cook in one minute.) Like oat bran, this flour retains moisture in baked goods, reducing the need for fat.

Unbleached Flour. This is refined white flour that has not been subjected to a bleaching process. Unbleached white flour lacks significant amounts of nutrients compared with whole wheat flour, but does contain more vitamin E than bleached flour.

Whole Grain Wheat. Available in many forms, this grain is perhaps easiest to use in the form of *bulgur wheat.* Cracked wheat that is precooked and dried, bulgur wheat can be prepared in a matter of minutes, and can be used to replace rice in any recipe.

Whole wheat flour, made of ground whole grain wheat kernels, includes the grain's nutrient-rich bran and germ. Nutritionally speaking, whole wheat flour is far superior to refined flour. Sadly, many people grew up eating refined baked goods, and find whole grain products too heavy for their taste. A good way to learn to enjoy whole grain flours is to use part whole wheat and part unbleached flour in recipes, and gradually increase the amount of whole wheat used over

time. (1 cup plus 1 tablespoon unbleached flour can replace 1 cup of whole wheat flour in recipes.)

When muffin, quick bread, cake, and cookie recipes call for whole wheat flour, *whole wheat pastry flour* works best, although regular whole wheat flour may be used with good results. Whole wheat pastry flour produces lighter, softer-textured baked goods than regular whole wheat flour because it is made from a softer (lower-protein) wheat and is more finely ground. Look for whole wheat pastry flour in health foods stores and many grocery stores.

White whole wheat flour is another excellent option for baking. Made from hard white wheat instead of the hard red wheat used to make regular whole wheat flour, white whole wheat flour is sweeter and lighter tasting than its red-wheat counterpart. To substitute white whole wheat flour for other flours, use the following guidelines:

---

1 cup white whole wheat flour =
1 cup unbleached (refined) flour

---

1 cup + 1 tablespoon white whole wheat flour =
1 cup whole wheat pastry flour

---

1 cup + 1 tablespoon white whole wheat flour =
1 cup regular whole wheat flour

Sweeteners

Refined white sugar contains almost no nutrients. In fact, when eaten in excess, refined sugar can actually deplete body stores of essential nutrients like chromium and the B vitamins. Of course, a moderate amount of sugar is usually not a problem for people who eat an otherwise healthy diet. What's moderate? No more than 10 percent of your daily intake of calories should come from sugar. For an individual who needs 2,000 calories a day to maintain his or her weight, this amounts to an upper limit of 12.5 teaspoons (about $\frac{1}{4}$ cup) of sugar a day. Naturally, a diet that is lower in sugar is even better.

The baked-goods and dessert recipes in this book contain 25 to 50 percent less sugar than traditional recipes do. Ingredients like fruit juices, fruit purées, and dried fruits; flavorings and spices like vanilla extract, nutmeg, and cinnamon; and mildly sweet flours like oat and barley have often been used to reduce the need for sugar.

The recipes in this book call for moderate amounts of white sugar, brown sugar, and different liquid sweeteners. However, a large number of sweeteners are now available, and you should feel free to substitute one sweetener for another, using your own tastes, your desire for high-nutrient ingredients, and your pocketbook as a guide. (Some of the newer less-refined sweeteners are far more expensive than traditional sweeteners.) For best results, replace granular sweeteners with other granular sweeteners, and substitute liquid sweeteners for other liquid sweeteners. You can, of course, replace a liquid with granules, or vice versa, but adjustments in other recipe ingredients will have to be made. (For each cup of liquid sweetener substituted for granular sweetener, reduce the liquid by $\frac{1}{4}$ to $\frac{1}{3}$ cup.) Also be aware that each sweetener has its own unique flavor and its own degree of sweetness, making some sweeteners better suited to particular recipes.

Following is a description of some of the sweeteners commonly available in grocery stores, health foods stores, and gourmet shops. Those sweeteners that can't be found in local stores can usually be ordered by mail. (See the Resource List on page 241.)

Apple Butter. Sweet and thick, apple butter is made by cooking down apples with apple juice and spices. Many brands also contain added sugar, but some are sweetened only with juice. Use apple butter as you would honey to sweeten products in which a little spice will enhance the flavor. Spice cakes, bran muffins, and oatmeal cookies are all delicious made with apple butter.

Brown Rice Syrup. Commonly available in health foods stores, brown rice syrup is made by converting the starch in brown rice into sugar. This syrup is mildly sweet—about 30 to 60 percent as sweet as sugar, depending on the brand—and has a delicate malt flavor. Perhaps most important, brown rice syrup retains most of the nutrients found in the rice from which it was made. This sweetener is a good substitute for honey or other liquid sweeteners whenever you want to tone down the sweetness of a recipe.

Brown Sugar. This granulated sweetener is simply refined white sugar that has been coated with a thin film of molasses. Light brown sugar is lighter in color than regular brown sugar, but not lower in calories as the name might imply. Because this sweetener contains some molasses, brown sugar has more calcium, iron, and potassium than white sugar. But like most sugars, brown sugar is no nutritional powerhouse. The advantage to using this sweetener is that it is more flavorful than white sugar so that less can generally be used.

Date Sugar. Made from ground dried dates, date sugar provides copper, magnesium, iron, and B vitamins. With a distinct date flavor, date sugar is delicious in breads, cakes, and muffins. Because it does not dissolve as readily as white sugar does, it's best to mix date sugar with the recipe's liquid ingredients and let it sit for a few minutes before proceeding with the recipe. Because date sugar is less dense than white sugar, it is only about two-thirds as sweet. However, date sugar is more flavorful, and so can often be substituted for white sugar on a cup-for-cup basis.

Fruit Juice Concentrates. Frozen juice concentrates add sweetness and flavor to baked goods while enhancing nutritional value. Use the concentrates as you would honey or other liquid sweeteners, but beware—too much will be overpowering. Always keep cans of frozen orange and apple juice concentrate in the freezer just for baking. Pineapple and tropical fruit blends also make good sweeteners, and white grape juice is ideal when you want a more neutral flavor.

Fruit Source. Made from white grape juice and brown rice, this sweetener has a rather neutral flavor and is about as sweet as white sugar. Fruit Source is available in both granular and liquid forms. Use the liquid as you would honey, and the granules as you would sugar. The granules do not dissolve as readily as sugar does, so mix Fruit Source with the recipe's liquid ingredients and let it sit for a few minutes before proceeding with the recipe.

Fruit Spreads, Jams, and Preserves. Available in a variety of flavors, these products make delicious sweeteners. For best flavor and nutrition, choose a brand made from fruits and fruit juice concentrate, with little or no added sugar, and select a flavor that is compatible with the baked goods you're making. Use as you would any liquid sweetener.

Honey. Contrary to popular belief, honey is not significantly more nutritious than sugar, but it does add a nice flavor to baked goods. It also adds moistness, reducing the need for fat. The sweetest of the liquid sweeteners, honey is generally 20 to 30 percent sweeter than sugar. Be sure to consider this when making substitutions.

Maple Sugar. Made from dehydrated maple syrup, granulated maple sugar adds a distinct maple flavor to baked goods. Powdered maple sugar is also available, and can be used to replace powdered white sugar in glazes.

Maple Syrup. The boiled-down sap of sugar maple trees, maple syrup adds delicious flavor to all baked goods, and also provides some potassium and other nutrients. Use it as you would honey or molasses.

Molasses. Light, or Barbados, molasses is pure sugarcane juice boiled down into a thick syrup. Light molasses provides some calcium, potas-

sium, and iron, and is delicious in spice cakes, muffins, breads, and cookies. Blackstrap molasses is a by-product of the sugar-refining process. Very rich in calcium, potassium, and iron, it has a slightly bitter, strong flavor, and is half as sweet as refined sugar. Because of its distinctive taste, more than a few tablespoons in a recipe is overwhelming.

Sucanat. Granules of evaporated sugarcane juice, Sucanat tastes similar to brown sugar. This sweetener provides small amounts of potassium, chromium, calcium, iron, and vitamins A and C. Use it as you would any other granulated sugar.

Sugarcane Syrup. The process used to make sugarcane syrup is similar to that of making light molasses. Consequently, the syrup has a molasses-like flavor and is nutritionally comparable to the other sweetener.

Throughout our discussion of sweeteners, we have mentioned that some sweeteners are higher in nutrients than others. Just how much variation is there among sweeteners? The table on the next page compares the amounts of selected nutrients found in one-quarter cup of different sweeteners. Pay special attention to how the sweeteners compare with white sugar, the most refined of all the sweeteners.

Other Ingredients

Aside from the ingredients already discussed, a few more items may prove useful as you venture into fat-free cooking. Some ingredients may already be familiar to you, while others may become new additions to your pantry.

Dried Cranberries. These tasty treats—which are simply cranberries that have been sweetened and dried—look like red raisins, and are sometimes referred to as "craisins." Dried cranberries add a festive touch to muffins, cookies, and other baked goods, and provide a nice change of pace from raisins. Look for them in specialty stores,

Comparing Sweeteners

Sweetener (1/4 cup)	Calories	Calcium (mg)	Iron (mg)	Potassium (mg)
Apple Butter	130	10	0.5	176
Brown Rice Syrup	256	3	0.1	140
Brown Sugar	205	47	1.2	189
Date Sugar	88	10	0.4	209
Fruit Juice Concentrate (apple)	116	14	0.6	315
Fruit Juice Concentrate (orange)	113	23	0.3	479
Fruit Preserves	216	8	0	12
Fruit Source (granules)	192	16	0.4	142
Fruit Source (syrup)	176	15	0.4	138
Honey	240	0	0.5	27
Maple Sugar	176	45	0.8	137
Maple Syrup	202	83	1.0	141
Molasses, Blackstrap	170	548	20.2	2,342
Molasses, Light	172	132	4.3	732
Sucanat	144	41	1.6	162
Sugar Cane Syrup	210	48	2.9	340
White Sugar	192	1	0	2

health foods stores, and many grocery stores. If you cannot find dried cranberries, golden raisins are a good substitute.

Other Dried Fruits. A wide variety of dried fruits are available. Dried pineapple, apricots, prunes, dates, and peaches are available in most grocery stores, while health foods and other specialty stores often carry dried mangoes, papaya, cherries, and blueberries. These fruits add interest to muffins, cookies, and other baked goods, and often reduce the need for sugar. If you cannot find the type of dried fruit called for in a recipe, feel free to substitute another type.

Toasted Wheat Germ. This ingredient adds crunch and a nutty flavor to baked goods. A supernutritious food, with only half the fat of nuts, wheat germ provides significant amounts of vitamin E and minerals.

A Word About Salt

Salt, a combination of sodium and chloride, enhances the flavors of many foods. However, most health experts recommend a maximum of 2,400 milligrams per day, the equivalent of about one teaspoon of salt. For this reason, salt is not often used in the recipes in this book. A minimal use of salt-laden processed ingredients, as well as the wise use of herbs and spices, keeps the salt content under control without compromising taste.

ABOUT THE NUTRITIONAL ANALYSIS

The Food Processor II (ESHA Research) computer nutrition analysis system, along with product information from manufacturers, was used to calculate the nutritional information for all the recipes in this book. Nutrients are always listed per one piece, one muffin, one slice of bread, one cookie, one serving, etc.

Sometimes, recipes give you options regarding the ingredients. For instance, you might be able to choose between nonfat cream cheese and reduced-fat cream cheese, nonfat mayonnaise and reduced-fat mayonnaise, or raisins and nuts. This will help you create dishes that suit your tastes. Just keep in mind that the nutritional analysis is based on the first ingredient listed.

In your quest for fat-free eating, you might be inclined to choose fat-free cheese over reduced-fat cheese, and to omit any optional nuts. Be aware, though, that if you are not used to nonfat cheeses, it might be wise to start by using reduced-fat products. Should you opt to omit the nuts? Not necessarily. Nuts are high in fat, but they also contain essential minerals and vitamin E. Some studies have even indicated that people who eat nuts as part of a healthy diet have less heart disease. If you like nuts, feel free to use them in recipes. In fat-free recipes like the ones in this book, you can afford to add a few nuts or to choose the higher-fat ingredient.

WHERE DOES THE FAT COME FROM IN FAT-FREE RECIPES?

You may notice that even though a recipe may contain no oil, butter, cheese, margarine, shortening, nuts, chocolate chips, or other fatty ingredients, it still contains a small amount of fat (less than one gram). This is because many natural ingredients contain some fat. Whole grains, for example, store a small amount of oil in their germ, the center portion of the grain. This oil is very beneficial because it is loaded with vitamin E, an antioxidant. The germ also provides an abundance of other vitamins and minerals. Products made from refined grains and refined flours—ingredients that have been stripped of the germ—do have slightly less fat than whole grain versions, but they also have far less nutrients.

Other ingredients, too, naturally contain small amounts of fat. For instance, fruits and vegetables, like grains, contain some oil. And, again, the oil also provides many important nutrients. Olives, nuts, and lean meats also contribute fat to some recipes. However, when used in small quantities, the amount of fat is insignificant. In fact, the majority of recipes in this book contain less than 0.5 grams of fat per serving. This qualifies them for the FDA designation *fat-free*.

This book is filled with recipes that make entertaining elegant, simple, and satisfying. Whether you are having a few people over for coffee and dessert, a casual dinner party, or an open house, you will find something to meet your needs. So eat well and enjoy! The dishes you are about to make will not only be delicious, but will also be foods that you can feel good about serving to your friends and family.

Part One

Hors D'Oeuvres for All Seasons

Whether you are planning to have a few people over for light hors d'oeuvres or an open house for fifty, this collection of recipes is sure to meet your needs with a wealth of ideas for fat-free and low-fat finger foods and snacks that are so delicious, no one will even guess that they're good for you. A few simple ingredient substitutions make a big fat difference in traditional party favorites. Ultra-lean ground meats, reduced-fat and nonfat cheeses, nonfat sour cream, and nonfat mayonnaise star in meatballs, dips, spreads, and finger sandwiches that are every bit as tempting as their traditional counterparts.

The following pages first present recipes for hot treats—meatballs, kabobs, quiches, hot dips, and other savory snacks that can be passed around on platters or kept warm in a chafing dish for fuss-free serving. This is followed by a tempting variety of finger sandwiches and other cold pick-up snacks, as well as a wide range of recipes for perhaps the most popular and versatile party foods of all—cold dips and spreads. Chilled beverages and hot brews, from an elegant champagne punch to steaming apple cider, round out the selection, guaranteeing that your next party will be a memorable one.

HOT STUFF

Curried Meatballs

1. Combine the meatball ingredients in a medium-sized bowl, and mix thoroughly. Coat a baking sheet with nonstick cooking spray. Shape the meatball mixture into 50 (1-inch) balls, and place the meatballs on the baking sheet.

2. Bake the meatballs at 350°F for about 25 minutes, or until thoroughly cooked. Transfer the meatballs to a chafing dish or Crock-Pot heated casserole to keep warm.

3. Combine the sauce ingredients in a small saucepan, and simmer over medium-low heat just until hot. Pour the sauce over the meatballs, toss gently to mix, and serve.

Yield: 50 appetizers

MEATBALLS

1 pound ground turkey breast
  or 96% lean ground beef

¾ cup quick-cooking oats

2 egg whites

1 onion, finely chopped

1 tablespoon curry powder

1 teaspoon ground ginger

¼ teaspoon ground black pepper

SAUCE

¼ cup honey

¼ cup Dijon mustard

1 tablespoon lemon juice

2 tablespoons water

1–2 teaspoons curry powder

NUTRITIONAL FACTS (PER APPETIZER)		
Calories: 23	Fat: 0.2 g	Protein: 2.6 g
Cholesterol: 6 mg	Fiber: 0.2 g	Sodium: 23 mg

Time-Saving Tip

To avoid a last-minute rush, make the meatballs in advance. Just cook them as directed—without the sauce—and freeze them in freezer bags. The day before the party, thaw the meatballs in the refrigerator. The next day, simply make the sauce and heat it along with the meatballs.

Spicy Barbecue Meatballs

Yield: 60 appetizers

MEATBALLS

1½ pounds ground turkey breast or 96% lean ground beef

¾ cup quick-cooking oats

2 egg whites

1 cup finely chopped onion

1½ teaspoons crushed fresh garlic

¼ cup minced fresh parsley

1 teaspoon dried oregano

1½ teaspoons beef bouillon granules

½ teaspoon ground black pepper

SAUCE

1 can (8 ounces) unsalted tomato sauce

3 tablespoons honey

3 tablespoons spicy mustard

1¼ teaspoons chili powder

½ teaspoon Tabasco pepper sauce

1. Combine the meatball ingredients in a medium-sized bowl, and mix thoroughly. Coat a baking sheet with nonstick cooking spray. Shape the meatball mixture into 60 (1-inch) balls, and place the meatballs on the baking sheet.

2. Bake the meatballs at 350°F for about 25 minutes, or until thoroughly cooked. Transfer the meatballs to a chafing dish or Crock-Pot heated casserole to keep warm.

3. Combine the sauce ingredients in a small saucepan, and simmer over medium-low heat just until hot. Pour the sauce over the meatballs, toss gently to mix, and serve.

NUTRITIONAL FACTS (PER APPETIZER)

Calories: 24	Fat: 0.2 g	Protein: 3.3 g
Cholesterol: 7 mg	Fiber: 0.2 g	Sodium: 35 mg

Spicy Spinach Balls

1. Combine the ground turkey or beef and the herbs and spices in a medium-sized bowl, and mix thoroughly. Set aside for 15 minutes. Add the remaining spinach ball ingredients, and mix well.

2. Coat a baking sheet with nonstick cooking spray. Shape the spinach mixture into 32 (1-inch) balls, and place them on the baking sheet. Bake at 350°F for about 25 minutes, or until browned.

3. Place the marinara sauce in a small saucepan, and simmer over medium-low heat just until hot. Transfer the sauce to a small bowl. Arrange the spinach balls on a serving platter, and serve hot, accompanied by the sauce.

NUTRITIONAL FACTS (PER APPETIZER)		
Calories: 29	Fat: 0.2 g	Protein: 2.6 g
Cholesterol: 5 mg	Fiber: 0.4 g	Sodium: 56 mg

Yield: 32 appetizers

SPINACH BALLS

8 ounces ground turkey breast or 96% lean ground beef

1 teaspoon dried Italian seasoning

1 teaspoon whole fennel seeds

1 teaspoon crushed fresh garlic

½ teaspoon crushed red pepper

¼ teaspoon salt (optional)

1 package (10 ounces) frozen chopped spinach, thawed and squeezed dry

1½ cups cooked brown rice or bulgur wheat

¾ cup finely chopped onion

⅓ cup grated nonfat or reduced-fat Parmesan cheese

2 egg whites

SAUCE

1½ cups fat-free marinara sauce

Mongolian Meatballs

Yield: 60 appetizers

MEATBALLS

1½ pounds ground turkey breast or 96% lean ground beef

¼ cup plus 2 tablespoons oat bran

1 can (8 ounces) water chestnuts, drained and chopped

2 egg whites

1 cup finely chopped scallions

1½ teaspoons crushed fresh garlic

¾ teaspoon ground ginger

1 tablespoon reduced-sodium soy sauce

SAUCE

1 can (8 ounces) unsalted tomato sauce

2 tablespoons Chinese sweet-hot mustard

2 tablespoons reduced-sodium soy sauce

3 tablespoons brown sugar

1. Combine the meatball ingredients in a medium-sized bowl, and mix thoroughly. Coat a baking sheet with nonstick cooking spray. Shape the meatball mixture into 60 (1-inch) balls, and place the meatballs on the baking sheet.

2. Bake the meatballs at 350°F for about 25 minutes, or until thoroughly cooked. Transfer the meatballs to a chafing dish or Crock-Pot heated casserole to keep warm.

3. Combine the sauce ingredients in a small saucepan, and simmer over medium-low heat just until hot. Pour the sauce over the meatballs, toss gently to mix, and serve.

NUTRITIONAL FACTS (PER APPETIZER)

Calories: 22	Fat: 0.2 g	Protein: 3.2 g
Cholesterol: 8 mg	Fiber: 0.3 g	Sodium: 41 mg

Mama Mia Meatballs

Yield: 50 appetizers

1. Combine the meatball ingredients in a medium-sized bowl, and mix thoroughly. Coat a baking sheet with nonstick cooking spray. Shape the meatball mixture into 50 (1-inch) balls, and place the meatballs on the baking sheet.

2. Bake the meatballs at 350°F for about 25 minutes, or until thoroughly cooked. Transfer the meatballs to a chafing dish or Crock-Pot heated casserole to keep warm.

3. Place the marinara sauce in a small saucepan, and simmer over medium-low heat just until hot. Pour the sauce over the meatballs, toss gently to mix, and serve.

MEATBALLS

1¼ pounds ground turkey breast or 96% lean ground beef

½ cup dried Italian bread crumbs

⅓ cup grated nonfat Parmesan cheese

2 egg whites

1 onion, finely chopped

1 teaspoon crushed fresh garlic

½ teaspoon crushed red pepper (optional)

1½ teaspoons whole fennel seeds

1½ teaspoons Italian seasoning

SAUCE

1½ cups fat-free bottled marinara sauce

NUTRITIONAL FACTS (PER APPETIZER)

Calories: 23	Fat: 0.2 g	Protein: 3.2 g
Cholesterol: 8 mg	Fiber: 0.1 g	Sodium: 40 mg

Florentine Stuffed Mushrooms

Yield: 16 appetizers

If you can't find extra-large mushrooms in your grocery store, use 32 medium-sized mushrooms, and place 1½ teaspoons of stuffing in each cap.

1. Remove and discard the mushroom stems. Wash the mushroom caps and pat dry. Set aside.

2. Place the spinach, thyme or oregano, and garlic in a large nonstick skillet. Sauté over medium heat just until the spinach is wilted. (Add a tablespoon of white wine or broth if the skillet is too dry.)

3. Remove the skillet from the heat and allow the spinach to cool slightly. Stir in the scallions, Parmesan cheese, and sour

16 extra-large stuffing mushrooms

3 cups (packed) chopped raw spinach

½ teaspoon dried thyme or oregano

½ teaspoon crushed fresh garlic

2 scallions, finely chopped

¼ cup grated nonfat Parmesan cheese

¼ cup nonfat sour cream

3 cups soft bread crumbs

2 tablespoons white wine or broth

Lemon wedges (garnish)

cream. Add the bread crumbs and toss gently, just until the crumbs are moistened.

4. Place a heaping teaspoonful of stuffing in each mushroom cap. Place 2 tablespoons of white wine or broth in a shallow baking pan, and arrange the mushrooms in the pan.

5. Bake at 400°F for 20 minutes, or until lightly browned on top. Transfer the mushrooms to a serving platter, garnish with the lemon wedges, and serve hot.

NUTRITIONAL FACTS (PER APPETIZER)		
Calories: 40	Fat: 0.4 g	Protein: 2.6 g
Cholesterol: 0 mg	Fiber: 1.5 g	Sodium: 80 mg

Teriyaki Turkey Kabobs

Yield: 32 appetizers

2 pounds boneless skinless turkey breasts

1 can (20 ounces) unsweetened pineapple chunks, undrained

2 tablespoons reduced-sodium soy sauce

2 tablespoons brown sugar

1½ teaspoons freshly grated ginger root, or ½ teaspoon ground ginger

1 teaspoon crushed fresh garlic

32 whole water chestnuts

1. Cut the turkey into 32 chunks, 1 inch each. Set aside.

2. Drain the pineapple chunks. Reserve the juice for immediate use, and wrap and refrigerate the pineapple. Combine the juice, soy sauce, brown sugar, ginger, and garlic in a shallow dish. Place the turkey in this marinade, cover, and refrigerate for several hours or overnight.

3. Create individual kabobs by skewering 1 piece of pineapple, 1 turkey chunk, and 1 water chestnut on each of 32 wooden toothpicks. Place the skewers in a shallow baking pan, and pour ¼ cup of the marinade over the kabobs.

4. Bake at 350°F for about 20 minutes, or until the turkey is fork-tender and no longer pink inside. Drain off any excess liquid, transfer to a serving platter, and serve hot.

NUTRITIONAL FACTS (PER APPETIZER)		
Calories: 44	Fat: 0.3 g	Protein: 7 g
Cholesterol: 19 mg	Fiber: 0.3 g	Sodium: 30 mg

Sausage and Cheese Bites

Yield: 36 appetizers

1. Place the ground sausage in a medium-sized nonstick skillet, and brown over medium-high heat, stirring constantly to crumble. Transfer the cooked sausage to paper towels to drain. Set aside.

2. Combine the oat bran, flour, and baking powder in a medium-sized bowl, and stir to mix well. Add the buttermilk, and stir just until the dry ingredients are moistened. Stir in the sausage and cheese.

3. Coat mini-muffin tins with nonstick cooking spray, and fill ¾ full with the sausage mixture. Bake at 375°F for 15 to 18 minutes, or just until lightly browned. Transfer to a serving platter, and serve hot.

6 ounces (about 1 cup) ground turkey breakfast sausage

1 cup oat bran

1⅓ cups unbleached flour

1 tablespoon plus 1 teaspoon baking powder

1½ cups nonfat buttermilk

1 cup shredded nonfat or reduced-fat Cheddar cheese

NUTRITIONAL FACTS (PER APPETIZER)

Calories: 37	Fat: 0.4 g	Protein: 3.4 g
Cholesterol: 4 mg	Fiber: 0.6 g	Sodium: 81 mg

Flaky Spinach Pies

Yield: 40 appetizers

1. Combine the spinach, ricotta, mozzarella, Parmesan, and oregano in a medium-sized bowl, and stir to mix well. Set aside.

2. Spread the phyllo dough out on a clean dry surface. You should have a 14-x-18-inch sheet that is 20 layers thick. Cut the phyllo dough lengthwise into 4 long strips. Cover the phyllo dough with plastic wrap to prevent it from drying out as you work. (Remove strips as you need them, being sure to re-cover the remaining dough.)

3. Remove 1 strip of phyllo dough, and lay it flat on a clean dry surface. Spray the strip lightly with cooking spray. Top with another phyllo strip, and spray lightly with cooking spray. Spread 2 teaspoons of filling over the bottom right-hand corner of the double phyllo strip. Fold the filled corner up and over to

1 package (10 ounces) frozen chopped spinach, thawed and squeezed dry

1 cup nonfat ricotta cheese

½ cup shredded nonfat or reduced-fat mozzarella cheese

¼ cup grated nonfat or reduced-fat Parmesan cheese

½ teaspoon dried oregano

20 sheets phyllo dough (1 pound)

Olive oil cooking spray

the left, so that the corner meets the left side of the strip. Continue folding in this manner until you form a triangle of dough. Repeat with the remaining dough and filling to make 40 triangles.

4. Coat a baking sheet with nonstick cooking spray. Place the appetizers seam side down on the sheet, and bake at 375°F for 15 to 20 minutes, or until nicely browned. Transfer to a serving platter, and serve hot.

Time-Saving Tip

To speed last-minute party preparations, prepare the pies in advance to the point of baking, and arrange them in single layers in airtight plastic containers, separating the layers with sheets of waxed paper. Freeze until the day of the party. Then arrange the frozen pies on a coated baking sheet, and allow them to sit at room temperature for 45 minutes before baking.

Making Flaky Spinach Pies.

NUTRITIONAL FACTS (PER APPETIZER)		
Calories: 43	Fat: 0.3 g	Protein: 2.8 g
Cholesterol: 0 mg	Fiber: 0.4 g	Sodium: 69 mg

a. Cut the dough into 4 strips.

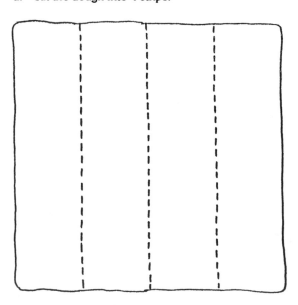

b. Fold the filled corner up and over.

c. Continue folding to form a triangle.

Shrimp and Mushroom Quiche Squares

Yield: 32 appetizers

1. To make the crust, combine the crust ingredients in a small bowl, and stir until well mixed. Coat an 8-x-12-inch pan with nonstick cooking spray, and pat the mixture into an even layer on the bottom of the pan. Set aside.

2. To make the filling, place the mushrooms and wine in a medium-sized nonstick skillet, and sauté over high heat until the mushrooms are tender and all of the liquid has evaporated. Remove the skillet from the heat, and add the remaining filling ingredients except for the Parmesan cheese. Stir to mix well.

3. Pour the filling over the rice crust, spreading evenly. Sprinkle with the Parmesan, and bake at 375°F for 40 to 45 minutes, or until the filling is set and the top is touched with brown. A sharp knife inserted in the center should come out clean.

4. Cool the quiche in the pan for 10 minutes. Cut into squares, transfer to a serving platter, and serve hot.

FILLING

1 cup sliced fresh mushrooms

2 tablespoons dry white wine

6 ounces (about 1 cup) frozen cooked whole salad shrimp, thawed, or 6 ounces diced cooked shrimp

1 cup dry curd or nonfat cottage cheese

¾ cup shredded nonfat or reduced-fat mozzarella cheese

½ cup thinly sliced scallions

1 cup fat-free egg substitute

1 teaspoon crushed fresh garlic

¼ teaspoon ground black pepper

2 tablespoons grated nonfat or reduced-fat Parmesan cheese

CRUST

1½ cups cooked brown rice

1 egg white

NUTRITIONAL FACTS (PER APPETIZER)

| Calories: 20 | Fat: 0.1 g | Protein: 3.8 g |
| Cholesterol: 6 mg | Fiber: 0.1 g | Sodium: 75 mg |

Variations

For a change of pace, substitute any of the following ingredients for the shrimp:

- 1 package (9 ounces) frozen artichoke hearts, thawed and chopped
- 6 ounces (about 1 cup) cooked crab meat combined with 2–3 teaspoons spicy brown mustard
- 1 package (10 ounces) frozen chopped spinach, thawed and squeezed dry

Firey Chicken Fingers

Yield: 32 appetizers

2 pounds boneless skinless chicken
  breasts (5–6 breast halves)

MARINADE

½ cup picante sauce

2 tablespoons honey

1 teaspoon ground cumin

SAUCE

½ cup picante sauce

2 tablespoons honey

½ teaspoon ground cumin

1. Cut the chicken breasts crosswise into 32 strips, 1 inch each. Set aside.

2. Combine the marinade ingredients in a shallow dish. Place the chicken in the marinade, cover, and refrigerate for several hours or overnight.

3. Coat a broiling pan with nonstick cooking spray. Arrange the marinated chicken strips in a single layer on the pan, and baste with the marinade.

4. Broil on the top oven rack for 5 minutes. Turn the strips over, and broil for an additional 3 minutes, or until the chicken is fork-tender and no longer pink inside. Place on a serving platter.

5. Combine the sauce ingredients in a small bowl, and stir to mix well. Serve the chicken hot, accompanied by the bowl of sauce.

NUTRITIONAL FACTS (PER APPETIZER)		
Calories: 41	Fat: 0.5 g	Protein: 7 g
Cholesterol: 16 mg	Fiber: 0.1 g	Sodium: 25 mg

Hot Artichoke Appetizers

1. If the artichoke hearts are large, cut them in quarters. If they are small, cut them in half. You should have about 40 pieces.

2. Combine the marinade ingredients in a blender, and process for 30 seconds, or until smooth. Place the artichoke hearts in a shallow dish, and pour the marinade over them. Cover and refrigerate for several hours or overnight.

3. Cut each ham slice into eight ½-inch strips. Drain the artichoke hearts, and discard the marinade. Wrap a ham strip around each artichoke piece, and secure with a wooden toothpick.

4. Place the wrapped artichokes in a shallow baking dish, and bake at 350°F for 10 to 15 minutes, or until thoroughly heated. Transfer to a serving platter, and serve hot.

Yield: 40 appetizers

3 packages (10 ounces each) frozen artichoke hearts, thawed, or 3 cans (14 ounces each) artichoke hearts, drained

5 4-inch square slices (1 ounce each) lean ham

MARINADE

⅓ cup Dijon mustard

⅓ cup water

¼ cup finely chopped onion

1 tablespoon sugar

NUTRITIONAL FACTS (PER APPETIZER)		
Calories: 11	Fat: 0.3 g	Protein: 1.1 g
Cholesterol: 2 mg	Fiber: 1 g	Sodium: 49 mg

Sensational Broccoli Strudels

1. Combine the broccoli, mozzarella cheese, egg substitute, and mustard in a medium-sized bowl, and stir to mix well. Set aside.

2. Spread the phyllo dough out on a clean dry surface. You should have a 14-x-18-inch sheet that is 12 layers thick. Cover the phyllo dough with plastic wrap to prevent it from drying out as you work. (Remove sheets as you need them, being sure to re-cover the remaining dough.)

3. Remove 1 sheet of phyllo dough, and lay it flat on a clean dry surface with the short end near you. Spray the strip lightly with cooking spray. Top with another phyllo sheet, and spray lightly with cooking spray. Repeat with a third sheet.

Yield: 28 appetizers

1 package (10 ounces) frozen chopped broccoli, thawed and squeezed dry

1 cup shredded nonfat or reduced-fat mozzarella cheese

¼ cup fat-free egg substitute, or 2 egg whites

1 tablespoon Dijon mustard

12 sheets phyllo dough

Nonstick cooking spray

4. Spread $\frac{1}{4}$ of the filling over the lower third of the stacked sheets, leaving a 4-inch margin on each side. Fold the left and right edges inward to enclose the filling, and roll the sheet up from the bottom, jelly-roll style. Repeat with the remaining dough and filling to make 4 rolls.

5. Coat a baking sheet with nonstick cooking spray. Place the rolls seam side down on the sheet, and spray the tops lightly with cooking spray. Bake at 350°F for 25 minutes, or until light golden brown.

6. Remove the rolls from the oven, and allow to cool for 5 minutes. Slice each cooled roll into 7 ($\frac{3}{4}$-inch) slices, transfer to a serving platter, and serve warm.

Time-Saving Tip

Several days before the party, prepare the strudels to the point of baking, and freeze them in freezer bags or airtight containers. Arrange the strudels on a coated baking sheet and allow them to sit at room temperature for 45 minutes before baking.

Making Sensational Broccoli Strudels.

NUTRITIONAL FACTS (PER APPETIZER)		
Calories: 39	Fat: 0.4 g	Protein: 2.8 g
Cholesterol: 0 mg	Fiber: 0.4 g	Sodium: 75 mg

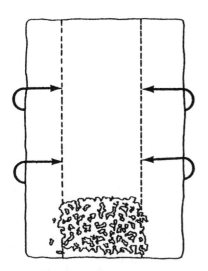

a. Spread the filling over the dough.

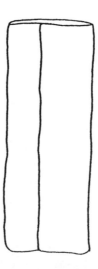

b. Fold the left and right edges inward over the filling.

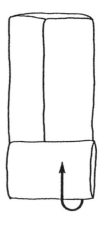

c. Roll the folded sheet up.

Caponata Pizzas

1. Combine all the ingredients except for the bread and cheese in a 1½-quart pot. Cover and cook over low heat, stirring occasionally, for 45 minutes, or until the vegetables are tender and the mixture is thick. Add a few tablespoons of water only if needed to prevent scorching. Remove the pot from the heat and set aside.

2. Arrange the bread slices on a baking sheet, and bake at 400°F for 5 minutes, or until lightly browned. Spread each slice with a tablespoon of the eggplant mixture, and top with 2 teaspoons of the mozzarella cheese. Return the pizzas to the oven, and bake for 7 minutes, or until the cheese is melted.

3. Arrange the pizzas on a serving platter, and serve hot.

Yield: 24 appetizers

2 cups peeled, diced eggplant

½ cup finely chopped onion

½ cup finely chopped celery

½ cup finely chopped green bell pepper

¼ cup chopped black olives

3 tablespoons tomato paste

1 teaspoon crushed fresh garlic

¼ teaspoon crushed red pepper

24 (½-inch) slices French bread

1 cup shredded nonfat or reduced-fat mozzarella cheese

NUTRITIONAL FACTS (PER APPETIZER)		
Calories: 41	Fat: 0.5 g	Protein: 2.6 g
Cholesterol: 1 mg	Fiber: 0.6 g	Sodium: 122 mg

Time-Saving Tip

Avoid a time crunch by preparing the eggplant mixture the day before the party. Cover and chill until you're ready to assemble the pizzas.

Pita Party Pizzas

Yield: 32 appetizers

1/2 cup Italian-style tomato paste with garlic

4 whole wheat or oat bran pita pockets (6-inch rounds)

1 cup shredded nonfat or reduced-fat mozzarella cheese

1/4 cup sliced fresh mushrooms

2 thin slices of onion, separated into rings

1 teaspoon dried Italian seasoning

2 tablespoons grated nonfat or reduced-fat Parmesan cheese

1. Spread 1/4 of the tomato paste on top of each pita pocket. Top with 1/4 of the mozzarella cheese followed by 1/4 of the mushrooms and a few onion rings. Sprinkle with 1/4 of the Italian seasoning and the Parmesan cheese.

2. Place the pita pizzas on a baking sheet, and bake at 450°F for about 10 minutes, or until the cheese is melted and lightly browned. Cut each pizza into 8 pieces, transfer to a serving platter, and serve hot.

NUTRITIONAL FACTS (PER APPETIZER)

Calories: 24	Fat: 0.1 g	Protein: 2 g
Cholesterol: 0 mg	Fiber: 0.5 g	Sodium: 61 mg

Variations

In addition to or instead of the cheese, mushrooms, and onions, top the pizzas with thinly sliced yellow squash, broccoli florets, diced Canadian bacon, or cooked turkey Italian sausage.

Fiesta Quesadillas

Yield: 32 appetizers

3/4 cup shredded nonfat or reduced-fat Monterey jack cheese

3/4 cup shredded nonfat or reduced-fat Cheddar cheese

8 flour tortillas (8-inch rounds)

1/2 cup thinly sliced scallions

1 can (4 ounces) chopped green chilies, drained

2–3 tablespoons chopped jalapeño peppers (optional)

1. Combine the cheeses and set aside.

2. Coat a baking sheet with nonstick cooking spray. Brush one side of each tortilla lightly with water. Lay 4 of the tortillas, moist side down, on the baking sheet. Spread 1/4 of the cheese mixture on each of the 4 tortillas. Top with 1/4 of the scallions, chilies, and jalapeños. Top with the remaining tortillas, placing them moist side up.

3. Bake at 400°F for 7 to 9 minutes, or until the quesadillas are heated through and the cheese is melted. Place the sour cream in a small dish and sprinkle with the scallions. Cut each quesadilla into 8 wedges, transfer to a serving platter, and serve hot, accompanied by the sour cream.

NUTRITIONAL FACTS (PER APPETIZER)		
Calories: 41	Fat: 0.5 g	Protein: 2.9 g
Cholesterol: 1 mg	Fiber: 0.4 g	Sodium: 81 mg

TOPPING

1 cup nonfat sour cream

3 tablespoons thinly sliced scallions

Variation

To make Fiesta Bean Quesadillas, mash 1 cup of drained canned pinto beans with $1\frac{1}{2}$ teaspoons of chili powder. Divide the beans among the tortillas, and spread evenly. Top with the cheese and the remaining ingredients and bake.

NUTRITIONAL FACTS (PER APPETIZER)		
Calories: 51	Fat: 0.5 g	Protein: 3.4 g
Cholesterol: 1 mg	Fiber: 1 g	Sodium: 93 mg

Chili Cheese Bites

1. To make the crust, combine the rice and egg whites in a medium-sized bowl, and stir to mix well. Coat mini-muffin tins with nonstick cooking spray. Place 1 slightly rounded teaspoonful of the rice mixture in each muffin cup, and use the back of a spoon to press the rice against the bottom and halfway up the sides of the cup.

2. To make the filling, combine the filling ingredients in a medium-sized bowl, and stir to mix well. Place 1 tablespoon of filling in each rice crust.

3. Bake at 350°F for 25 minutes, or until the bites are puffed and the filling is set. A sharp knife inserted in the filling should come out clean. Transfer to a serving platter, and serve hot.

Yield: 36 appetizers

CRUST

2 cups cooked brown rice or bulgur wheat

2 egg whites

FILLING

$\frac{2}{3}$ cup dry curd or nonfat cottage cheese

$\frac{2}{3}$ cup shredded nonfat or reduced-fat Cheddar or Monterey jack cheese

$\frac{3}{4}$ cup fat-free egg substitute

1 can (4 ounces) chopped green chilies, drained

1 tablespoon unbleached flour

$\frac{1}{2}$ teaspoon ground cumin

$\frac{1}{8}$ teaspoon ground black pepper

NUTRITIONAL FACTS (PER APPETIZER)		
Calories: 22	Fat: 0.1 g	Protein: 2 g
Cholesterol: 0 mg	Fiber: 0.2 g	Sodium: 27 mg

Mini Reuben Melts

Yield: 24 appetizers

6 slices (1 ounce each) nonfat or reduced-fat Swiss cheese

½ cup fat-free Thousand Island dressing

24 slices cocktail rye bread

24 thin slices (about 8 ounces) 98% lean corned beef or turkey pastrami

¾ cup well-drained sauerkraut

1. Cut each slice of cheese into 4 squares, and set aside. Spread 1 teaspoon of Thousand Island dressing on each piece of bread, and top with 1 slice of corned beef or pastrami, folding the slice as necessary to accommodate the shape of the bread. Top with ½ tablespoon of sauerkraut and 1 square of cheese.

2. Place the Reubens on a baking sheet, and bake at 350°F for 10 minutes, or until the cheese is bubbly and the Reubens are hot. Transfer to a serving platter, and serve hot.

NUTRITIONAL FACTS (PER APPETIZER)

Calories: 47	Fat: 0.3 g	Protein: 5 g
Cholesterol: 5 mg	Fiber: 0.7 g	Sodium: 267 mg

Bacon-Wrapped Shrimp

Yield: 20 appetizers

5 slices turkey bacon

20 large raw shrimp (about 8 ounces), peeled and deveined

1. Cut each piece of bacon in half lengthwise. Then cut each slice crosswise to make 20 pieces. Wrap 1 piece of bacon around each shrimp, and secure with a wooden toothpick.

2. Place the shrimp on a baking sheet, and bake at 350°F for about 20 minutes, or until the shrimp turn pink. Transfer to a serving platter, and serve hot.

NUTRITIONAL FACTS (PER APPETIZER)

Calories: 22	Fat: 0.6 g	Protein: 3.4 g
Cholesterol: 30 mg	Fiber: 0 g	Sodium: 89 mg

Variation

For a different taste—and more crunch—substitute whole water chestnuts for the shrimp.

Crunchy Crab Crostini

1. Combine the crab meat, peppers, scallions, and oregano in a medium-sized bowl. Add the mayonnaise and sour cream, and stir to mix well. Set aside.

2. Slice each roll crosswise into 12 ($\frac{1}{2}$-inch) slices. Arrange the slices on a baking sheet, and bake at 300°F for 15 minutes, or until lightly browned and crisp.

3. Spread each slice with $1\frac{1}{2}$ teaspoons of the crab meat mixture, and top with $\frac{1}{4}$ teaspoon of the Parmesan cheese. Increase the oven temperature to 400°F, and return the appetizers to the oven for 5 minutes, or until the Parmesan is lightly browned.

4. Arrange the crostini on a serving platter, and serve hot.

Yield: 48 appetizers

6 ounces (about 1 cup) cooked crab meat

$\frac{1}{4}$ cup finely chopped red bell pepper

$\frac{1}{4}$ cup finely chopped green bell pepper

$\frac{1}{4}$ cup finely chopped scallions

1 tablespoon minced fresh oregano, or 1 teaspoon dried

2 tablespoons nonfat or reduced-fat mayonnaise

2 tablespoons nonfat sour cream

4 whole wheat submarine-sandwich rolls, each 6 inches long

$\frac{1}{4}$ cup grated nonfat or reduced-fat Parmesan cheese

---

NUTRITIONAL FACTS (PER APPETIZER)

Calories: 18	Fat: 0.3 g	Protein: 1.3 g
Cholesterol: 2 mg	Fiber: 0.4 g	Sodium: 51 mg

Time-Saving Tip

To avoid a last-minute rush, prepare the crab mixture a day ahead of time, and chill until ready to use. You can also bake the bread slices ahead of time and keep them crisp in an airtight container.

Bruschetta Florentine

Yield: 48 appetizers

1 package (10 ounces) frozen chopped spinach, thawed and squeezed dry

1 cup shredded nonfat or reduced-fat mozzarella cheese

¾ cup chopped plum tomatoes (about 2½ medium)

2 tablespoons finely chopped onion

1 tablespoon finely chopped fresh basil

1 teaspoon crushed fresh garlic

4 whole wheat submarine-sandwich rolls, each 6 inches long, or 1 loaf French bread, 24 inches long

1. Combine the spinach, mozzarella cheese, tomatoes, onions, basil, and garlic in a medium-sized bowl, and stir to mix well. Set aside.

2. Slice each roll into 12 (½-inch) slices. If you're using French bread instead of rolls, slice the French bread into 48 (½-inch) slices. Arrange the slices on a baking sheet, and bake at 300°F for 15 minutes, or until crisp and lightly browned.

3. Spread each slice with 1 slightly rounded tablespoon of the spinach mixture. Increase the oven temperature to 400°F, and return the appetizers to the oven for 5 minutes, or until the cheese is melted.

4. Arrange the appetizers on a serving platter, and serve hot.

NUTRITIONAL FACTS (PER APPETIZER)		
Calories: 17	Fat: 0.2 g	Protein: 1.5 g
Cholesterol: 0 mg	Fiber: 0.5 g	Sodium: 52 mg

Time-Saving Tip

Make your party preparations less hectic by preparing the spinach mixture a day ahead of time, and chilling it until ready to use. Crisp the bread slices ahead of time, too, and store them in an airtight container.

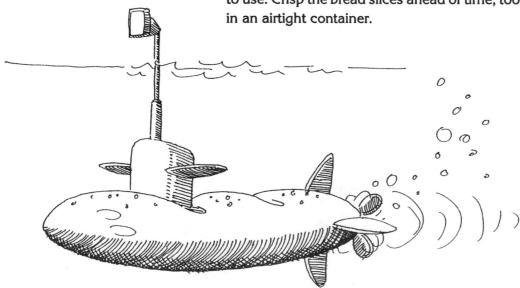

Spiced Artichoke Spread

1. Place all ingredients except 2 tablespoons of the Parmesan cheese in a food processor or blender, and process until chunky.

2. Coat a small casserole dish with nonstick cooking spray. Place the artichoke mixture in the dish, top with the remaining Parmesan, and bake at 350°F for 25 to 30 minutes, or until the cheese is lightly browned.

3. Serve hot with whole grain crackers, flatbread, French bread, or wedges of toasted pita bread.

Yield: 1¼ cups

1 package (10 ounces) frozen artichoke hearts, thawed, or 1 can (14 ounces) artichoke hearts, drained

1 tablespoon plus 1½ teaspoons spicy mustard

1 tablespoon plus 1½ teaspoons nonfat or reduced-fat mayonnaise

⅛ teaspoon cayenne pepper

¼ cup grated nonfat Parmesan cheese

NUTRITIONAL FACTS (PER TABLESPOON)		
Calories: 10	Fat: 0 g	Protein: 0.9 g
Cholesterol: 1 mg	Fiber: 1 g	Sodium: 40 mg

Broccoli Baked Potato Skins

1. If using a conventional oven, bake the potatoes at 400°F for about 45 minutes, or until tender. If using a microwave oven, pierce each potato with a fork before microwaving on high power for about 15 minutes, or until tender. Set aside to cool.

2. Cut the potatoes in half lengthwise. Scoop out and discard the pulp, leaving a ¼-inch-thick shell. Place 1 tablespoon of broccoli in each skin, and top with the cheese.

3. Place the potato skins on a baking sheet, and bake at 450°F for about 15 minutes, or until the cheese is bubbly. Transfer the skins to a serving platter, top each skin with 1 tablespoon of nonfat sour cream and a sprinkling of scallions, and serve hot.

Yield: 12 appetizers

6 small baking potatoes (about 4 ounces each)

¾ cup chopped frozen broccoli, thawed and squeezed dry

¾ cup shredded nonfat or reduced-fat Cheddar cheese

¾ cup nonfat sour cream

¼ cup thinly sliced scallions

NUTRITIONAL FACTS (PER APPETIZER)		
Calories: 59	Fat: 0 g	Protein: 4.2 g
Cholesterol: 1 mg	Fiber: 1 g	Sodium: 75 mg

Variation

To make Spicy Chicken Skins, combine $3/4$ cup of diced cooked chicken breast, 2 tablespoons of picante sauce, and 1 teaspoon of chili powder. Substitute this mixture for the broccoli, top with the cheese, and bake.

NUTRITIONAL FACTS (PER APPETIZER)		
Calories: 75	Fat: 0.4 g	Protein: 7.3 g
Cholesterol: 10 mg	Fiber: 0.7 g	Sodium: 94 mg

Pizza Dip

Yield: 3 cups

4 ounces (about $2/3$ cup) ground turkey Italian sausage

1 cup nonfat or reduced-fat cream cheese, softened to room temperature

$1/2$ cup nonfat sour cream

1 teaspoon dried oregano

1 teaspoon crushed fresh garlic

$1/2$ cup fat-free spaghetti sauce

$1/2$ teaspoon crushed red pepper (optional)

1 cup shredded nonfat or reduced-fat mozzarella cheese

$1/2$ cup sliced scallions

$1/4$ cup sliced black olives

1. Place the ground sausage in a medium-sized nonstick skillet, and brown over medium-high heat, stirring constantly. Transfer the cooked sausage to paper towels to drain. Crumble and set aside.

2. Combine the cream cheese, sour cream, oregano, and garlic in a medium-sized bowl, and stir to mix well. Coat a 9-inch glass pie pan with nonstick cooking spray, and spread the mixture over the bottom of the pan.

3. Combine the spaghetti sauce and the red pepper in a small bowl, and spread over the cheese mixture. Sprinkle the sauce first with the cheese, and then with the sausage, scallions, and olives.

4. Bake at 400°F for 20 minutes, or until the cheese is melted and the mixture is bubbly around the edges. Serve hot with chunks of French or Italian bread, Pita Chips (page 62), or Garlic and Herb Bagel Chips (page 62).

NUTRITIONAL FACTS (PER TABLESPOON)		
Calories: 15	Fat: 0.1 g	Protein: 2.5 g
Cholesterol: 3 mg	Fiber: 0.1 g	Sodium: 59 mg

A Tempting Selection of Hot Hors D'Oeuvres
Top: Spicy Barbecue Meatballs (page 20)
Center Left: Flaky Spinach Pies (page 25)
Center Right: Florentine Stuffed Mushrooms (page 23)
Bottom: Bacon-Wrapped Shrimp (page 34)

A Variety of Festive Cold Hors D'Oeuvres
Top: Salmon Mousse (page 45)
Bottom Left: High Rollers (page 43)
Bottom Right: Creamy Cucumber Dip (page 44)

Thanksgiving Turkey and Fixings
Top: Roast Turkey (page 72)
Center Left: Broccoli Casserole (page 80)
Center Right: Old-Fashioned Cornbread Dressing (page 76)
Bottom: Waldorf Salad (page 77)

Thanksgiving Side Dishes
Top Left: Pineapple-Sweet Potato Casserole (page 81)
Top Right: Cranberry-Wild Rice Stuffing (page 73)
Bottom: Molded Cranberry-Apple Relish (page 82)

Baked Artichoke Dip

Yield: 2 cups

1. Place the cottage cheese, flour, lemon juice, pepper, and garlic in a food processor or blender, and process until smooth. Add the artichoke hearts and all but 2 tablespoons of the Parmesan cheese, and process until the mixture is slightly chunky.

2. Coat a small casserole dish with nonstick cooking spray. Place the artichoke mixture in the dish, top with the remaining Parmesan, and bake at 400°F for 25 minutes, or until the edges are bubbly and the top is lightly browned.

3. Serve hot with whole grain crackers, chunks of sourdough bread, or Pita Chips (page 62).

¾ cup dry curd or nonfat cottage cheese

1 tablespoon unbleached flour

1 tablespoon lemon juice

⅛ teaspoon ground white pepper

½ teaspoon crushed fresh garlic

1 package (10 ounces) frozen artichoke hearts, thawed, or 1 can (14 ounces) artichoke hearts, drained

¼ cup plus 2 tablespoons grated nonfat or reduced-fat Parmesan cheese

---

NUTRITIONAL FACTS (PER TABLESPOON)

Calories: 11	Fat: 0 g	Protein: 1.2 g
Cholesterol: 1 mg	Fiber: 0.6 g	Sodium: 43 mg

Chili Con Queso

Yield: 1¾ cups

1. Place the tomatoes in a medium-sized nonstick saucepan, and heat to boiling over medium-low heat. Place the milk and flour in a jar with a tight-fitting lid, and shake until smooth. Add the flour mixture to the tomatoes, and cook, stirring constantly, until the mixture is thickened and bubbly. Add the cheese, and stir until melted. Stir in the chilies.

2. Transfer the mixture to a chafing dish or Crock-Pot heated casserole to keep warm. Serve with fat-free tortilla chips.

¾ cup Rotelle or Mexican-style canned tomatoes, diced and undrained

¼ cup skim milk

1 tablespoon plus 1½ teaspoons unbleached flour

8 ounces nonfat processed Cheddar cheese product, diced

1 can (4 ounces) chopped green chilies, drained

NUTRITIONAL FACTS (PER TABLESPOON)

Calories: 13	Fat: 0 g	Protein: 2 g
Cholesterol: 0 mg	Fiber: 0.1 g	Sodium: 123 mg

Beef and Bean Dip

Yield: 3¹/₃ cups

6 ounces 96% lean ground beef

1 medium onion, chopped

1 tablespoon chili powder

1 can (1 lb.) pinto beans, drained

¹/₂ teaspoon ground cumin

¹/₂ cup picante sauce

¹/₂ cup shredded nonfat or reduced-
  fat sharp Cheddar cheese

¹/₄ cup thinly sliced scallions

NUTRITIONAL FACTS (PER TBS.)

Calories: 15	Fiber: 0.6 g
Cholesterol: 2 mg	Protein: 2 g
Fat: 0.2 g	Sodium: 35 mg

1. Place the ground beef in a medium-sized nonstick skillet, and brown over medium-high heat, stirring constantly. Drain off any excess fat, and add the onion and 2 teaspoons of the chili powder. Cover and cook over medium heat until the onions are crisp-tender. Set aside.

2. Place the beans, the remaining teaspoon of chili powder, and the cumin in a food processor or blender, and process to the desired consistency. Spread the bean mixture in a layer on the bottom of a 9-inch deep dish pie pan. Top the beans with the ground meat mixture, and add layers of the picante sauce, Cheddar cheese, and scallions, in that order.

3. If using a microwave oven, heat uncovered at 80-percent power for about 5 minutes, or until bubbly. If using a conventional oven, heat uncovered at 400°F for about 20 minutes, or until bubbly. Serve with fat-free tortilla chips.

Baked Clam Dip

Yield: 3¹/₄ cups

2 cans (10 ounces each) chopped
  clams, undrained

1 large round loaf sourdough bread

2 cups nonfat or reduced-fat cream
  cheese, softened

1 tablespoon lemon juice

2 tablespoons finely chopped onion

2 teaspoons white wine
  Worcestershire sauce

NUTRITIONAL FACTS (PER TBS.)

Calories: 19	Fiber: 0 g
Cholesterol: 6 mg	Protein: 3.5 g
Fat: 0.1 g	Sodium: 59 mg

1. Drain the clams, and reserve 2 tablespoons of the liquid.

2. Cut the top from the bread loaf, and set aside. Hollow out the bread, leaving a 1-inch-thick shell. Set aside.

3. Coat a baking sheet with nonstick cooking spray. Cut the removed bread into cubes, and place on the baking sheet. Bake at 350°F for 10 minutes, or until lightly toasted. Set aside.

4. Place the cheese, lemon juice, onion, Worcestershire sauce, and reserved clam juice in a food processor or blender, and process until smooth. Stir in the drained clams. Pour the mixture into the hollowed loaf, cover with the bread top, and wrap in foil.

5. Bake the filled loaf at 350°F for 1 hour and 10 minutes, or until the dip is hot and creamy. Place the loaf on a serving plate, remove the top, and serve hot with whole grain crackers and toasted bread cubes.

COLD STUFF

Chicken Asparagus Rolls

1. Spread the garlic and dill over 1 side of each chicken breast. Top each breast with 4 asparagus spears, roll the chicken around the spears, and secure with a wooden toothpick.

2. Pour the wine or chicken broth into the bottom of a microwave or stove-top steamer, and arrange the chicken rolls in the steamer. Cover and cook on high power or over medium-high heat for 12 to 15 minutes, or until the chicken is opaque and tender. Transfer the steamed chicken rolls to a dish, cover, and refrigerate until ready to serve.

3. Just before serving, trim the ends of each chicken roll, and slice each chicken roll crosswise into 6 pieces. Cut each submarine roll into 12 ($\frac{1}{2}$-inch) slices. Place a chicken roll slice on top of each bread slice.

4. To make the dressing, combine the mayonnaise, sour cream, and mustard. Place the dressing in a small dish, and garnish with the dill. Arrange the chicken rolls on a serving platter and serve with the dressing, instructing guests to spread the dressing on the chicken if desired.

Yield: 24 appetizers

1 teaspoon crushed fresh garlic

1 tablespoon minced fresh dill, or 1 teaspoon dried

4 large boneless skinless chicken breast halves (6 ounces each), pounded to $\frac{1}{4}$-inch thickness

16 fresh asparagus spears, trimmed

$\frac{1}{4}$ cup dry white wine or chicken broth

2 whole wheat submarine-sandwich rolls, each 6 inches long

DRESSING

$\frac{1}{4}$ cup nonfat or reduced-fat mayonnaise

$\frac{1}{4}$ cup nonfat sour cream

2 tablespoons grainy Dijon mustard

1 teaspoon minced fresh dill, or $\frac{1}{3}$ teaspoon dried (garnish)

NUTRITIONAL FACTS (PER APPETIZER)

Calories: 47	Fat: 0.4 g	Protein: 6.6 g
Cholesterol: 14 mg	Fiber: 0.2 g	Sodium: 87 mg

Shrimp Wrapped in Snow Peas

Yield: 64 appetizers

64 large snow peas (about ½ pound)

64 large shrimp (about 1¾ pounds), peeled and cooked

DIPPING SAUCE

3 tablespoons honey

¼ cup Dijon mustard

¾ cup plain nonfat yogurt

1. Combine the sauce ingredients in a small bowl, and stir to mix well. Set aside.

2. Place the snow peas in a microwave or stove-top steamer. Cover and cook on high power or over medium-high heat for 3 minutes, or just until the snow peas are bright green and pliable. Rinse with cool water, and set aside.

3. Wrap a snow pea around each shrimp, and secure with a toothpick. Arrange on a serving platter and serve with the Dipping Sauce.

NUTRITIONAL FACTS
(PER APPETIZER WITH ½ TEASPOON SAUCE)

Calories: 21	Fat: 0.2 g	Protein: 3.4 g
Cholesterol: 27 mg	Fiber: 0.2 g	Sodium: 41 mg

Veggie-Cheese Finger Sandwiches

Yield: 32 appetizers

2 cups nonfat or reduced-fat cream cheese, softened to room temperature

¼ cup finely chopped onion

¼ cup finely chopped green bell pepper

¼ cup grated carrot

2 tablespoons finely chopped fresh parsley

1–2 teaspoons prepared horseradish or spicy mustard

16 slices firm whole wheat, rye, or pumpernickel bread

1. Place the softened cream cheese in a medium-sized bowl. Combine the vegetables, parsley, and horseradish or mustard in a small bowl. Stir the vegetable mixture into the softened cream cheese. Cover and chill for several hours to allow the flavors to blend.

2. Place ¼ cup of filling on each of 8 slices of bread. Top each slice with one of the remaining slices, making 8 sandwiches. Trim the crusts from the bread, and cut each sandwich into 4 fingers. Arrange the sandwiches on a platter and serve.

NUTRITIONAL FACTS (PER APPETIZER)

Calories: 51	Fat: 0.4 g	Protein: 4.5 g
Cholesterol: 2 mg	Fiber: 1.1 g	Sodium: 169 mg

High Rollers

Simple to make and festive in appearance, these appetizers go fast, so be sure to make plenty.

1. Spread each tortilla with 3 tablespoons of cream cheese, extending the cheese to the outer edges. Lay 2 ounces of sliced turkey over the *bottom half only* of each tortilla, leaving a 1-inch margin on each outer edge. Place 1 ounce of sliced Swiss cheese over the turkey, and spread with 1 tablespoon of ranch dressing. Arrange 6 spinach leaves over the Swiss, and sprinkle with 1 tablespoon of olives if desired. Arrange 6 red bell pepper or tomato slices over the olive layer. Top with $\frac{1}{4}$ cup of artichoke hearts.

2. Starting at the bottom, roll each tortilla up tightly. Cut a $1\frac{1}{4}$-inch piece off each end and discard. Slice the remaining tortillas into six $1\frac{1}{4}$-inch pieces. Arrange the rolls on a platter and serve.

Yield: 48 appetizers

8 flour tortillas (10-inch rounds)

$1\frac{1}{2}$ cups nonfat or reduced-fat cream cheese (plain or garlic-and-herb flavor)

1 pound thinly sliced turkey breast

8 ounces thinly sliced nonfat or reduced-fat Swiss cheese

$\frac{1}{2}$ cup fat-free ranch dressing

48 fresh tender spinach leaves

$\frac{1}{2}$ cup finely chopped black olives (optional)

48 very thin slices of red bell pepper or tomato

1 can (14 ounces) artichoke hearts, drained and chopped

NUTRITIONAL FACTS (PER APPETIZER)

Calories: 55	Fat: 0.8 g	Protein: 6 g
Cholesterol: 6 mg	Fiber: 0.7 g	Sodium: 122 mg

Time-Saving Tip

To avoid a last-minute rush, make High Rollers the day before your party, cover the hors d'oeuvres with plastic wrap, and refrigerate. The next day, simply remove the plastic wrap and serve.

Dilly Chicken Salad Finger Sandwiches

Yield: 32 appetizers

1½ cups finely chopped cooked chicken or turkey breast

½ cup finely chopped celery

¼ cup grated carrot

2 tablespoons finely chopped onion

1 tablespoon minced fresh dill, or 1 teaspoon dried

2 tablespoons nonfat or reduced-fat mayonnaise

2 tablespoons nonfat sour cream

16 slices firm whole wheat, rye, or pumpernickel bread

1. In a medium-sized bowl, combine the chicken or turkey with all of the remaining ingredients except the bread. Stir to mix well, adding more nonfat sour cream if the filling seems dry.

2. Place ¼ cup of filling on each of 8 slices of bread. Top each slice with 1 of the remaining slices, making 8 sandwiches. Trim the crusts from the bread, and cut each sandwich into 4 fingers. Arrange the sandwiches on a platter and serve.

NUTRITIONAL FACTS (PER APPETIZER)

Calories: 46	Fat: 0.6 g	Protein: 3.2 g
Cholesterol: 5 mg	Fiber: 1.2 g	Sodium: 101 mg

Time-Saving Tip

Instead of rushing to make finger sandwiches right before your guests arrive, make them several hours in advance. Arrange the finished sandwiches on a serving platter, cover the platter with plastic wrap, and chill until serving time.

Creamy Cucumber Dip

Yield: 2¼ cups

1 medium cucumber, peeled, seeded, and cut in chunks

2 scallions, finely chopped

¼ teaspoon ground white pepper

2 cups nonfat sour cream

1. Place the cucumber in a food processor or blender, and process until finely chopped. Roll the chopped cucumber in a kitchen towel, and squeeze out any excess moisture.

2. Place the sour cream in a medium-sized bowl, and fold in the cucumber and the remaining ingredients. Transfer the dip to a serving dish, cover, and chill for several hours.

3. Serve with raw vegetables and whole grain crackers.

NUTRITIONAL FACTS (PER TABLESPOON)

Calories: 12	Fat: 0 g	Protein: 0.8 g
Cholesterol: 0 mg	Fiber: 0 g	Sodium: 16 mg

Salmon Mousse

For variety, substitute flaked crab meat for the salmon.

Yield: 4 cups

1. Place the water or broth in a small saucepan, and sprinkle the gelatin over the top. Set aside for 5 minutes. Then place over low heat and cook, stirring constantly, just until the gelatin is dissolved. Let cool to room temperature.

2. Drain the salmon, place it in a medium-sized bowl, and separate the meat into fine flakes. Add the cooled gelatin mixture and the remaining ingredients, and stir to mix well. Pour the mixture into an ungreased 4-cup fish-shaped mold, cover, and chill for several hours or overnight.

3. To unmold the mousse, dip the mold in warm—but not hot—water to the depth of the gelatin mixture for 5 to 10 seconds. Remove the mold from the water, and loosen the edges with a sharp knife. Invert the mold onto a serving platter, surround with whole grain crackers and fresh vegetables, and serve cold.

½ cup water or unsalted chicken broth

1 envelope unflavored gelatin

2 cans (6 ounces each) boneless skinless pink salmon

1½ cups nonfat sour cream

½ cup finely chopped celery

¼ cup finely chopped onion

2–3 tablespoons minced fresh dill, or 2–3 teaspoons dried

1 tablespoon lemon juice

NUTRITIONAL FACTS (PER TABLESPOON)

Calories: 13	Fat: 0.3 g	Protein: 1.3 g
Cholesterol: 2 mg	Fiber: 0 g	Sodium: 26 mg

Light Blue Cheese Dip

1. Combine the ingredients in a medium-sized bowl. Transfer the dip to a serving dish, cover, and chill for several hours.

2. Serve with raw vegetables and whole grain crackers.

Yield: 2½ cups

2 cups nonfat sour cream

½ cup crumbled blue cheese

NUTRITIONAL FACTS (PER TABLESPOON)

Calories: 17	Fat: 0.4 g	Protein: 1.1 g
Cholesterol: 1 mg	Fiber: 0 g	Sodium: 35 mg

Smoked Salmon Spread

Yield: 2½ cups

12 ounces smoked salmon

1 cup nonfat or reduced-fat cream cheese, softened to room temperature

2–3 teaspoons prepared horseradish

2 tablespoons finely chopped onion

1 teaspoon lemon juice

½ cup minced fresh parsley

1. Place the salmon in a medium-sized bowl, and separate it into flakes. Add the remaining ingredients except for the parsley, and stir until the mixture is the consistency of a spread.

2. Shape the salmon mixture into a log. Spread the parsley out on waxed paper, and roll the log in the parsley to coat well. Transfer to a serving platter, cover, and refrigerate for several hours. Serve with whole grain crackers and carrot sticks.

NUTRITIONAL FACTS (PER TABLESPOON)

Calories: 16	Fat: 0.4 g	Protein: 2.8 g
Cholesterol: 3 mg	Fiber: 0 g	Sodium: 107 mg

Italian Eggplant Spread

Yield: 1½ cups

2 medium eggplants (about 1 pound each)

2 heads garlic, separated into cloves and peeled

¼ cup chopped sun-dried tomatoes (not packed in oil)

2 tablespoons lemon juice

2 teaspoons olive oil (optional)

1½ teaspoons dried oregano, or 1½ tablespoons fresh

¼ teaspoon ground cumin

¼ teaspoon crushed red pepper

¼ teaspoon salt

1. Cut each eggplant in half lengthwise. Cut 2 deep slits down the length of each half, and insert the garlic cloves and dried tomatoes in the slits.

2. Place the eggplants in a baking pan. Cover and bake at 450°F for 45 to 60 minutes, or until very tender. Cool to room temperature.

3. Scoop out the eggplant flesh, along with the garlic and tomatoes, and place in a food processor or blender with the remaining ingredients. Process until smooth.

4. Transfer the spread to a serving dish, and serve at room temperature with crusty French bread slices or raw vegetables.

NUTRITIONAL FACTS (PER TABLESPOON)

Calories: 12	Fat: 0 g	Protein: 0.5 g
Cholesterol: 0 mg	Fiber: 1.2 g	Sodium: 24 mg

Spicy Mustard Dip

1. Combine the ingredients in a medium-sized bowl. Transfer the dip to a serving dish, cover, and chill for several hours.

2. Serve with raw vegetables, whole grain crackers and bread wedges, and rolled up slices of shaved turkey breast or lean ham.

Yield: 2⅔ cups

2 cups nonfat sour cream

¼ cup finely chopped onion

3 tablespoons spicy brown mustard

½ cup nonfat or reduced-fat mayonnaise

NUTRITIONAL FACTS (PER TABLESPOON)

Calories: 13	Fat: 0 g	Protein: 0.7 g
Cholesterol: 0 mg	Fiber: 0 g	Sodium: 39 mg

Onion Soup Dip

By using only a small amount of onion soup mix and adding scallions, you greatly decrease the sodium content of the dip for a fresher-tasting, healthier snack.

1. Combine the ingredients in a medium-sized bowl. Transfer the dip to a serving dish, cover, and chill for several hours.

2. Serve with raw vegetables or fat-free potato chips.

Yield: 2¼ cups

2 cups nonfat sour cream

3 tablespoons dry onion soup mix

⅓ cup minced scallions

NUTRITIONAL FACTS (PER TABLESPOON)

Calories: 15	Fat: 0 g	Protein: 1 g
Cholesterol: 0 mg	Fiber: 0 g	Sodium: 73 mg

Creamy Light Cheese Spread

Yield: 2 cups

1 cup nonfat ricotta cheese

1 cup nonfat cottage cheese

2 tablespoons honey or maple syrup

½ teaspoon vanilla extract

1. Combine the ingredients in a medium-sized bowl. (For a smoother texture, blend in a food processor or blender.) Transfer the spread to a serving dish, cover, and chill for at least 2 hours.

2. Serve with slices of fruit-nut bread or bagels.

NUTRITIONAL FACTS (PER TABLESPOON)

Calories: 17	Fat: 0 g	Protein: 1.5 g
Cholesterol: 1 mg	Fiber: 0 g	Sodium: 30 mg

Variation

For a different flavor and texture, stir in cinnamon and raisins, drained crushed pineapple, or chopped pecans and grated orange rind.

Commendable Crackers and Chips

One of the most healthful and satisfying complements to a tempting dip or spread is a bowl of low-fat whole grain crackers and chips. The list below includes just some of the lowest-fat brands now available in your grocery and health foods stores. When heartier accompaniments are desired, try thin slices of whole grain bagels or breads, or wedges of toasted whole grain pita bread. These snacks are so delicious—and so nutritious—that you'll find yourself serving them not just at party time, but whenever you're in the mood for a light and healthy snack.

Crackers
Finn Crisp
Hain Fat-Free
Harvest Crips
Health Valley
Hol Grain
Kavli Norwegian Flatbread
Krispy Cakes
Melba Toast
Mini Rice Cakes

Crackers
Pepperidge Farm
   Wholesome Choice
Ry Vita
Rye Krisp
Snackwells
Stoned Wheat Thins
Triscuits (reduced-fat)
Wasa Bread
Wheat Thins (reduced-fat)
Whole Wheat Cracottes

Chips
Guiltless Gourmet Fat-Free
   Tortilla Chips
Louise's Fat-Free Potato Chips
Louise's Reduced-Fat
   Tortilla Chips
Smart Temptations Fat-Free
   Tortilla Chips

Garden Patch Dip

1. Combine the ingredients in a medium-sized bowl. Transfer the dip to a serving dish, cover, and chill for several hours.

2. Serve with raw vegetables and whole grain crackers.

Yield: 2½ cups

2 cups nonfat sour cream

¼ cup finely chopped onion

¼ cup finely chopped green bell pepper

½ cup grated carrot

2 tablespoons finely chopped fresh parsley or dill

1½ teaspoons prepared horseradish (optional)

NUTRITIONAL FACTS (PER TABLESPOON)

Calories: 12	Fat: 0 g	Protein: 0.7 g
Cholesterol: 0 mg	Fiber: 0.1 g	Sodium: 15 mg

Italian Cream Cheese Spread

1. Place the water in a small saucepan, and bring to a boil over high heat. Stir in the tomatoes, cover, and remove from the heat. Set aside for at least 15 minutes, or until the water is absorbed.

2. Combine the cream cheese, olives, scallions, and basil in a medium-sized bowl, and stir to mix well. Stir in the tomatoes. Transfer the spread to a serving dish, cover, and chill for at least 1 hour.

3. Stir before serving with Pita Chips (page 62), Garlic and Herb Bagel Chips (page 62), or wedges of Italian or sourdough bread.

Yield: 1½ cups

¼ cup water

¼ cup chopped sun-dried tomatoes (not packed in oil)

1 cup nonfat or reduced-fat cream cheese, softened to room temperature

¼ cup chopped black olives

¼ cup chopped scallions

1 tablespoon finely chopped fresh basil, or 1 teaspoon dried

NUTRITIONAL FACTS (PER TABLESPOON)

Calories: 13	Fat: 0.1 g	Protein: 2.1 g
Cholesterol: 1 mg	Fiber: 0.1 g	Sodium: 60 mg

Cinnamon Raisin Spread

Yield: 2½ cups

1 cup nonfat or reduced-fat cream cheese, softened to room temperature

1 cup dry curd or nonfat cottage cheese

1 teaspoon ground cinnamon

½ cup dark raisins

1. Place the cheeses in a food processor or blender, and process until smooth. Stir in the cinnamon and raisins. Transfer the spread to a serving dish, cover, and chill for several hours.

2. Serve with sliced whole grain bagels.

NUTRITIONAL FACTS (PER TABLESPOON)

Calories: 15	Fat: 0 g	Protein: 2 g
Cholesterol: 1 mg	Fiber: 0.1 g	Sodium: 40 mg

Apple Cheddar Spread

Yield: 3¼ cups

1 cup nonfat cream cheese or soft curd farmer cheese

1 cup dry curd or nonfat cottage cheese

1½ cups finely chopped tart apples (about 2 medium)

¾ cup shredded nonfat or reduced-fat sharp Cheddar cheese

⅓ cup chopped dates

1. Place the cream cheese or farmer cheese and the cottage cheese in a food processor or blender, and process until smooth. Stir in the apples, Cheddar cheese, and dates. Transfer the spread to a serving dish, cover, and chill for several hours.

2. Serve with whole grain bagel slices, whole grain crackers, celery sticks, and apple wedges.

NUTRITIONAL FACTS (PER TABLESPOON)

Calories: 14	Fat: 0 g	Protein: 1.1 g
Cholesterol: 1 mg	Fiber: 0.1 g	Sodium: 29 mg

Chutney Dip

1. Combine the ingredients in a medium-sized bowl. Transfer the dip to a serving dish, cover, and chill for several hours.

2. Serve with pita bread wedges, whole wheat crackers, celery sticks, apple wedges, and thinly sliced turkey breast.

Yield: 2⅓ cups

2 cups nonfat sour cream or yogurt cheese (page 6)

⅓ cup mango chutney

1 teaspoon curry powder (optional)

NUTRITIONAL FACTS (PER TABLESPOON)

Calories: 16	Fat: 0 g	Protein: 0.8 g
Cholesterol: 0 mg	Fiber: 0 g	Sodium: 29 mg

Broccoli Cheese Dip

1. Combine the sour cream and mayonnaise in a medium-sized bowl, and stir to mix well. Fold in the broccoli and cheese. Transfer the dip to a serving dish, cover, and chill for at least 1 hour.

2. Serve with sliced bagels or vegetable crackers.

Yield: 4 cups

2 cups nonfat sour cream

½ cup nonfat or reduced-fat mayonnaise

1 package (10 ounces) frozen chopped broccoli, thawed and squeezed dry

1 cup shredded nonfat or reduced-fat Cheddar cheese

NUTRITIONAL FACTS (PER TABLESPOON)

Calories: 12	Fat: 0 g	Protein: 1.2 g
Cholesterol: 0 mg	Fiber: 0.1 g	Sodium: 39 mg

Spinach Dip

Yield: 4 cups

1 package (10 ounces) frozen chopped spinach, thawed and squeezed dry

2 cups nonfat sour cream

½ cup nonfat or reduced-fat mayonnaise

1 can (8 ounces) water chestnuts, drained and chopped

½ cup thinly sliced scallions

1 package (1½ ounces) dry vegetable soup mix

A party favorite made healthy. Serve in a hollowed-out loaf of pumpernickel with raw vegetables and whole grain crackers.

1. Combine the ingredients in a large bowl. Transfer the dip to a serving dish, cover, and chill for several hours.

2. Serve with raw vegetables and whole grain crackers, or use as a filling for finger sandwiches or hollowed-out cherry tomatoes.

NUTRITIONAL FACTS (PER TABLESPOON)		
Calories: 13	Fat: 0 g	Protein: 0.7 g
Cholesterol: 0 mg	Fiber: 0.2 g	Sodium: 52 mg

Black Olive Dip

Yield: 2¾ cups

2 cups nonfat sour cream

½ cup chopped black olives

¼ cup finely chopped scallions

1. Combine the ingredients in a medium-sized bowl. Transfer the dip to a serving dish, cover, and chill for at least 2 hours.

2. Serve with fat-free tortilla chips, celery sticks, and carrot sticks.

NUTRITIONAL FACTS (PER TABLESPOON)		
Calories: 13	Fat: 0.2 g	Protein: 0.7 g
Cholesterol: 0 mg	Fiber: 0.1 g	Sodium: 27 mg

Deviled Crab Dip

1. Combine the sour cream and mustard in a medium-sized bowl. Fold in the crab meat and scallions. Transfer the dip to a serving dish, cover, and chill for several hours.

2. Just before serving, sprinkle the dip with paprika. Serve with whole grain crackers or chunks of sourdough bread and raw vegetables.

Yield: 2½ cups

1½ cups nonfat sour cream

1–2 tablespoons spicy brown mustard

1 cup cooked crab meat

¼ cup finely chopped scallions

Paprika (garnish)

NUTRITIONAL FACTS (PER TABLESPOON)

Calories: 13	Fat: 0.1 g	Protein: 1.5 g
Cholesterol: 4 mg	Fiber: 0 g	Sodium: 24 mg

Dilled Shrimp Dip

1. Combine the sour cream and dill in a medium-sized bowl. Fold in the shrimp. Transfer the dip to a serving dish, cover, and chill for several hours.

2. Serve with whole grain crackers and raw vegetables, or use as a filling for hollowed-out cherry tomatoes or cucumbers.

Yield: 2½ cups

1½ cups nonfat sour cream

2 tablespoons minced fresh dill

6 ounces (about 1 cup) frozen cooked whole salad shrimp, thawed, or 6 ounces diced cooked shrimp

NUTRITIONAL FACTS (PER TABLESPOON)

Calories: 13	Fat: 0 g	Protein: 1.5 g
Cholesterol: 8 mg	Fiber: 0 g	Sodium: 22 mg

Savannah Seafood Spread

Yield: 12 servings

1 block (8 ounces) nonfat or reduced-fat cream cheese

¾ cup (4–5 ounces) frozen cooked whole salad shrimp, thawed, or ¾ cup diced cooked shrimp

¾ cup flaked cooked crab meat

SAUCE

¾ cup no-added-salt or low-sodium ketchup

2 tablespoons prepared horseradish

2 tablespoons lemon juice

1. Place the block of cheese in the center of a serving plate. Combine the shrimp and crab meat in a medium-sized bowl, and pile over the cheese. Combine the sauce ingredients in a small bowl, and pour over the seafood.

2. Serve with whole scallions, celery sticks, and whole grain crackers.

NUTRITIONAL FACTS (PER SERVING)

Calories: 57	Fat: 0.3 g	Protein: 8.2 g
Cholesterol: 32 mg	Fiber: 0.4 g	Sodium: 150 mg

Super Stuffed Veggies

It takes a matter of minutes to turn fresh vegetables and any of the dips or sandwich fillings presented in this book into delicious stuffed veggies. Serve these veggies as healthy hors d'oeuvres, or use them to decorate platters of finger sandwiches and canapés. The following ideas should get you started, but do experiment with other vegetables and dips to find the combinations that you like best.

❑ Slice off the tops of cherry tomatoes, scoop out the seeds, and fill with Light Blue Cheese Dip (page 45).

❑ Cut peeled cucumbers into ¾- to 1-inch-thick slices. Scoop out some of the seeds, creating a cucumber cup with a ¼-inch-thick shell. Fill with Dilly Chicken Salad (page 44).

❑ Cut celery into 2- or 3-inch lengths, and fill with Veggie-Cheese spread (page 42).

❑ Boil new potatoes until tender but firm. Cut a thin slice off the bottom of each potato so that it will sit upright, and scoop out some of the flesh, leaving a ½-inch shell. Fill with Onion Dill Dip (page 55).

Pimento Cheese Spread

1. Place the cottage cheese, mayonnaise, mustard, garlic, and pepper in a food processor or blender, and process until smooth. Add the onion and Cheddar cheese, and process to the desired consistency. Stir in the pimentos. Transfer the spread to a serving dish, cover, and chill for several hours.

2. Serve with whole grain crackers, or use as a filling for finger sandwiches or celery.

Yield: 1²/₃ cups

¾ cup dry curd or nonfat cottage cheese

2 tablespoons nonfat or reduced-fat mayonnaise

2 teaspoons spicy mustard

¼ teaspoon crushed fresh garlic

⅛ teaspoon ground white pepper

2 tablespoons finely chopped onion

1 cup shredded nonfat or reduced-fat sharp Cheddar cheese

1 jar (4 ounces) chopped pimentos, drained

NUTRITIONAL FACTS (PER TABLESPOON)

Calories: 11	Fat: 0 g	Protein: 2.1 g
Cholesterol: 1 mg	Fiber: 0.1 g	Sodium: 45 mg

Onion Dill Dip

1. Combine the ingredients in a medium-sized bowl. Transfer the dip to a serving dish, cover, and chill for several hours.

2. Serve with raw vegetables and whole grain crackers.

Yield: 2¼ cups

2 cups nonfat sour cream

2–3 tablespoons minced fresh dill

¼ cup finely chopped onion

NUTRITIONAL FACTS (PER TABLESPOON)

Calories: 14	Fat: 0 g	Protein: 1 g
Cholesterol: 0 mg	Fiber: 0 g	Sodium: 18 mg

Creamy Picante Dip

Yield: 2 cups

1 cup picante sauce

1 cup nonfat sour cream

1. Combine the ingredients in a medium-sized bowl. Transfer the dip to a serving dish, cover, and chill for at least 1 hour.

2. Serve with fat-free tortilla chips.

NUTRITIONAL FACTS (PER TABLESPOON)		
Calories: 9	Fat: 0 g	Protein: 0.7 g
Cholesterol: 0 mg	Fiber: 0.1 g	Sodium: 48 mg

Fresh Fruit Dip

Yield: 2¹/₂ cups

2 cups vanilla yogurt cheese (page 6) or nonfat sour cream

¹/₂ cup crushed fresh fruit (try blueberries, strawberries, cherries, apricots, or raspberries)

You can adjust the sweetness of this dip by choosing either yogurt cheese or sour cream as the base. Yogurt cheese makes a sweet dip, while sour cream makes a tart dip. If desired, add a tablespoon or two of honey when using the sour cream base.

1. Place the yogurt cheese or sour cream in a medium-sized bowl, and fold in the fruit. Transfer the dip to a serving dish, cover, and chill for several hours or overnight.

2. Stir to mix the fruit into the cheese, and serve with graham crackers, bagel slices, and fresh fruit.

NUTRITIONAL FACTS (PER TABLESPOON)		
Calories: 12	Fat: 0 g	Protein: 1 g
Cholesterol: 0 mg	Fiber: 0.1 g	Sodium: 13 mg

Fresh Tomato Salsa

1. Combine the ingredients in a medium-sized bowl. Transfer the salsa to a serving dish, cover, and chill for at least 1 hour.

2. Serve with fat-free tortilla chips.

NUTRITIONAL FACTS (PER TABLESPOON)

Calories: 3	Fat: 0 g	Protein: 0.1 g
Cholesterol: 0 mg	Fiber: 0.2 g	Sodium: 16 mg

Yield: 2 cups

2 large tomatoes, finely chopped

½ cup finely chopped onion

1 can (4 ounces) chopped green chilies, drained

¼ cup minced fresh cilantro

2 tablespoons red wine vinegar

½ teaspoon sugar

Seafood Salsa

1. Combine the ingredients in a medium-sized bowl, and toss to mix well. Transfer the salsa to a serving dish, cover, and chill for at least 1 hour.

2. Serve with fat-free tortilla chips.

NUTRITIONAL FACTS (PER TABLESPOON)

Calories: 6	Fat: 0.1 g	Protein: 1 g
Cholesterol: 6 mg	Fiber: 0.1 g	Sodium: 20 mg

Yield: 2¼ cups

3 ounces (about ½ cup) frozen cooked whole salad shrimp, thawed, or 3 ounces diced cooked shrimp

3 ounces (about ½ cup) flaked cooked crab meat

1 cup diced fresh tomatoes (about 2 medium)

¼ cup finely chopped red bell pepper

¼ cup finely chopped green bell pepper

¼ cup finely chopped onion

2 tablespoons lime juice

2 tablespoons red wine vinegar

½ teaspoon Tabasco pepper sauce

2 tablespoons minced fresh basil, or 2 teaspoons dried

⅛ teaspoon salt

Seven-Layer Bean Dip

Yield: 4 cups

1 can (15 ounces) black beans, drained and rinsed

2–3 teaspoons chopped fresh cilantro

1 teaspoon chili powder

1 small avocado

2 teaspoons lemon juice

2 tablespoons chopped jalapeño peppers

1 medium tomato, seeded and finely chopped

½ cup shredded nonfat or reduced-fat Monterey jack cheese

¼ cup thinly sliced scallions

¼ cup chopped black olives

1. Place the beans, cilantro, and chili powder in a food processor, and process until smooth. Spread the mixture in a 9-inch deep dish pie pan or a shallow serving dish.

2. Peel and finely chop the avocado. Toss with the lemon juice, and set aside.

3. Spread the jalapeño peppers over the bean mixture. Spread the avocados over the jalapeños. Create layers of the remaining ingredients in the order listed.

4. Serve at room temperature or hot. If using a microwave oven, heat uncovered at 80-percent power for about 5 minutes, or until the cheese melts and the edges are bubbly. If using a conventional oven, heat uncovered at 400°F for about 20 minutes. Serve with fat-free tortilla chips.

NUTRITIONAL FACTS (PER TABLESPOON)		
Calories: 12	Fat: 0.3 g	Protein: 0.7 g
Cholesterol: 0 mg	Fiber: 0.6 g	Sodium: 28 mg

Guacamole Dip

Yield: 2½ cups

1 large avocado

1 cup nonfat sour cream

¼ cup finely chopped onion

1 medium plum tomato, seeded and chopped

2–3 teaspoons minced fresh cilantro

2 tablespoons minced jalapeño pepper (optional)

1. Peel and chop the avocado, and combine it with the sour cream in a medium-sized bowl. Stir in the remaining ingredients. Transfer the dip to a serving dish, cover, and chill for several hours.

2. Serve with fat-free tortilla chips.

NUTRITIONAL FACTS (PER TABLESPOON)		
Calories: 19	Fat: 1.5 g	Protein: 1 g
Cholesterol: 0 mg	Fiber: 1 g	Sodium: 24 mg

Mediterranean White Bean Spread

Yield: 3 cups

1. Place the beans in a large pot, add 8 cups of water, and soak for at least 4 hours. Drain off the water, and add 4 cups of fresh water and the whole garlic cloves. Cover and simmer over low heat for 1½ hours, or until the beans are very tender and all of the liquid has been absorbed. (Periodically check the pot during cooking, and add more water if needed.)

2. Allow the beans to cool slightly, and place in a food processor or blender with all of the remaining ingredients except the oregano leaves. Process until smooth.

3. Transfer the dip to a serving dish, and garnish with fresh oregano leaves if desired. Serve at room temperature with French bread or toasted wedges of pita bread.

2 cups dried navy beans or Great Northern beans, sorted

8 cloves garlic, peeled

4 teaspoons olive oil (optional)

Juice and grated rind of 4 lemons

¼ teaspoon salt

Fresh oregano leaves (garnish)

NUTRITIONAL FACTS (PER TABLESPOON)

Calories: 24	Fat: 0 g	Protein: 1.5 g
Cholesterol: 0 mg	Fiber: 1.3 g	Sodium: 11 mg

Spicy Garbanzo Dip

Yield: 2 cups

1. Combine the beans, lemon juice, garlic, cumin, and pepper in a food processor or blender, and process to the desired degree of smoothness. Add the scallions and peppers, and process just enough to mix.

2. Transfer the dip to a serving dish, and garnish with the olives. Serve with wedges of pita bread or whole grain crackers.

1 can (1 pound) garbanzo beans, drained and rinsed

1 tablespoon lemon juice

1 teaspoon crushed fresh garlic

½ teaspoon ground cumin

¼ teaspoon cayenne pepper

¼ cup finely chopped scallions

¼ cup finely chopped red bell pepper

¼ cup finely chopped green bell pepper

¼ cup sliced black olives (garnish)

NUTRITIONAL FACTS (PER TABLESPOON)

Calories: 17	Fat: 0.3 g	Protein: 0.8 g
Cholesterol: 0 mg	Fiber: 0.7 g	Sodium: 22 mg

How to Turn a Cocktail Party Into Dinner

If the host of your next party has not yet switched to a low-fat lifestyle, you will probably be faced with a tempting table of high-fat hors d'oeuvres. Heavy hors d'oeuvres can and should be considered dinner for anyone who's watching his or her waistline. Even then, these appetizing tidbits must be selected properly in order to provide a balanced meal that doesn't quickly outstrip a reasonable allotment of calories and fat. Here are some guidelines:

❑ Begin with an "entrée"—some high-protein appetizers such as cheese cubes or steamed shrimp. Eat in moderation. There's more to come!

❑ A well-balanced meal must include some vegetables, so move on to the vegetable tray for your next course. Try to use a minimal amount of dip, and add some whole grain crackers if available.

❑ Fruit adds refreshing balance to a meal, and has almost no fat, so have a serving or two of melon, pineapple, berries, or other fresh fruits.

❑ For your beverage, pour yourself a glass of club soda or spring water, or choose a diet soft drink. Alcohol is almost as high in calories as those pigs'n'blankets that you love so much!

❑ For dessert, serve yourself a moderate portion of something decadent that you really want. Then enjoy it!

So the next time you're invited to a party, don't despair. You don't have to blow your fat budget in order to enjoy yourself. Just pretend that you've been invited out to dinner, and serve yourself a meal that's high on satisfaction and low on guilt.

Garlic and Sun-Dried Tomato Spread

1. Place the beans in a large pot, add 4 cups of water, and soak for at least 4 hours. Drain off the water, and add 2 cups of fresh water and the whole garlic cloves. Cover and simmer over low heat for 1½ hours, or until the beans are very tender and all of the liquid has been absorbed. (Periodically check the pot during cooking, and add more water if needed.)

2. Add the tomatoes and water to the pot. Cover and simmer for 5 minutes. Cool slightly, and place in a food processor with the remaining ingredients. Process until smooth.

3. Transfer the spread to a serving dish, and serve at room temperature with French bread or toasted wedges of pita bread.

Yield: 2 cups

1 cup dried navy beans or Great Northern beans, sorted

1 head garlic, separated into cloves and peeled

½ cup chopped sun-dried tomatoes (not packed in oil)

½ cup water

1 tablespoon olive oil (optional)

¼ teaspoon salt

⅛ teaspoon ground white pepper

NUTRITIONAL FACTS (PER TABLESPOON)

Calories: 22	Fat: 0 g	Protein: 1.3 g
Cholesterol: 0 mg	Fiber: 1.3 g	Sodium: 20 mg

Lentil Paté

1. Place all the ingredients in a medium-sized pot, and bring the mixture to a boil over high heat. Reduce the heat to low, cover, and simmer for 25 to 30 minutes, or until the lentils are very soft and all of the liquid has been absorbed. (Periodically check the pot during cooking, and add more water if needed.)

2. Cool the mixture slightly, and place in a food processor or blender. Process until smooth. Transfer the mixture to a serving dish, cover, and chill for several hours.

3. Serve with French bread or whole grain crackers.

Yield: 2 cups

1 cup dried brown lentils, sorted

2 cups water

¾ cup chopped onion

1 cup chopped fresh mushrooms

1 teaspoon beef or vegetable bouillon granules

¾ teaspoon dried thyme

¼ teaspoon ground allspice

⅛ teaspoon ground black pepper

NUTRITIONAL FACTS (PER TABLESPOON)

Calories: 23	Fat: 0.1 g	Protein: 1.8 g
Cholesterol: 0 mg	Fiber: 0.8 g	Sodium: 33 mg

Garlic and Herb Bagel Chips

Yield: 8 servings

4 whole wheat or oat bran bagels

2 teaspoons crushed fresh garlic

2 teaspoons dried Italian seasoning

2 tablespoons grated nonfat or
   reduced-fat Parmesan cheese

Olive oil cooking spray

1. Slice the bagels diagonally into $\frac{1}{4}$-inch-thick slices. Coat the inside of a large bowl with the garlic, and sprinkle the Italian seasoning over the garlic coating. Place the bagel chips in the bowl, and toss gently until the chips are coated with the garlic and herbs. Sprinkle the cheese over the chips, and again toss gently to coat.

2. Coat a baking sheet with olive oil cooking spray. Arrange the chips on the sheet in a single layer, and spray the tops of the chips very lightly with the cooking spray. Bake at 350°F for 6 minutes. Turn the chips over and bake for an additional 5 to 8 minutes, or until lightly browned and crisp. Cool to room temperature.

3. Serve the chips with dips and spreads.

NUTRITIONAL FACTS (PER SERVING)

Calories: 95	Fat: 0.4 g	Protein: 3.8 g
Cholesterol: 0 mg	Fiber: 1.6 g	Sodium: 165 mg

Pita Chips

Yield: 12 servings

6 whole wheat or oat bran pita
   pockets (2 ounces each)

$\frac{1}{4}$ cup plus 2 tablespoons grated
   nonfat or reduced-fat Parmesan
   cheese

Dried Italian seasoning (optional)

Garlic powder (optional)

1. Cut each pita bread round into 8 wedges. Separate each wedge into 2 pieces so that you get 16 chips out of each round.

2. Arrange the chips in a single layer on a baking sheet with the inside of the pita bread facing up. Sprinkle the chips with the Parmesan cheese. Sprinkle with a little Italian seasoning or garlic powder if desired. Bake at 400°F for 5 to 8 minutes, or until lightly browned and crisp.

3. Serve the chips with dips and spreads.

NUTRITIONAL FACTS (PER SERVING)

Calories: 85	Fat: 0.3 g	Protein: 3.4 g
Cholesterol: 0 mg	Fiber: 1.3 g	Sodium: 188 mg

BREWS AND BEVERAGES

Hot Apple Cider

For variety, substitute cranberry juice for the apple juice.

Yield: 20 servings

1. Place the water and spices in a large pot, and bring to a boil over high heat. Reduce the heat to low, and simmer for 10 minutes. Strain the mixture, discarding the spices, and return the water to the pot.

2. Add the apple juice to the water, and simmer over low heat until thoroughly heated. Serve warm in mugs.

2 cups water

3 sticks cinnamon

1 tablespoon whole cloves

½ teaspoon whole allspice

2 quarts unsweetened apple juice

NUTRITIONAL FACTS (PER ½-CUP SERVING)

Calories: 46	Fat: 0 g	Protein: 0 g
Cholesterol: 0 mg	Fiber: 0 g	Sodium: 3 mg

Cranberry Wine Spritzer

1. Combine all of the ingredients except the lime slices in a large pitcher, and stir well to blend.

2. Pour into ice-filled glasses, garnish each glass with a lime slice, and serve.

Yield: 22 servings

4 cups chilled white wine

3 cups chilled reduced-calorie cranberry juice cocktail

1 cup chilled orange or pineapple juice

½ cup chilled lime juice

2 cups chilled club soda

22 slices lime (garnish)

NUTRITIONAL FACTS (PER ½-CUP SERVING)

Calories: 64	Fat: 0 g	Protein: 0 g
Cholesterol: 0 mg	Fiber: 0 g	Sodium: 4 mg

Champagne Punch

Yield: 35 servings

$\frac{1}{3}$ cup sugar

$\frac{2}{3}$ cup lime juice

1 quart chilled reduced-calorie cranberry juice cocktail

3 750-milliliter chilled bottles champagne (about 2$\frac{1}{2}$ quarts)

1 quart chilled sugar-free gingerale

Lemon slices (garnish)

1. Stir the sugar into the lime juice until dissolved. Cover and chill.

2. Place the lime juice mixture and all of the remaining ingredients except for the lime slices in a large punch bowl. Garnish with lime slices if desired, and serve.

NUTRITIONAL FACTS (PER $\frac{1}{2}$-CUP SERVING)

Calories: 63	Fat: 0 g	Protein: 0 g
Cholesterol: 0 mg	Fiber: 0 g	Sodium: 5 mg

Light Eggnog

Yield: 10 servings

1 quart skim or 1% low-fat milk

1 cup fat-free egg substitute

$\frac{1}{4}$ cup sugar

$\frac{1}{2}$ cup instant vanilla pudding mix

2–3 teaspoons vanilla extract

$\frac{1}{2}$ teaspoon ground nutmeg

This rich-tasting version has none of the fat of regular eggnog.

1. Place all of the ingredients in a blender, and blend for 30 to 60 seconds, or until smooth. Chill for several hours.

2. Shake or stir eggnog well to blend. Serve in glasses or mugs.

NUTRITIONAL FACTS (PER $\frac{1}{2}$-CUP SERVING)

Calories: 102	Fat: 0.3 g	Protein: 5.2 g
Cholesterol: 4 mg	Fiber: 0 g	Sodium: 211 mg

Variation

To make a sugar-free eggnog that is suitable for people with diabetes, substitute 3 tablespoons of sugar-free instant vanilla pudding mix for the regular vanilla pudding mix, and 6 packets of Equal or Sweet One sweetener for the sugar.

NUTRITIONAL FACTS (PER $\frac{1}{2}$-CUP SERVING)

Calories: 61	Fat: 0.3 g	Protein: 5.2 g
Cholesterol: 4 mg	Fiber: 0 g	Sodium: 142 mg

Part Two

Traditional Holiday Meals

Whenever we think of Thanksgiving, Christmas, Hanukkah, Easter, and other traditional holidays, a flood of images comes to mind. Beautifully decorated fir trees, the flickering candles of a menorah, rainbow-colored eggs—these symbols are all inextricably linked with the holidays that brighten each calendar year. In fact, Christmas probably wouldn't seem like Christmas without an ornamented tree and gaily wrapped gifts. Just as strong as these images are those of the special foods that are traditionally served for each holiday. Thanksgiving turkey and stuffing, for instance, is a must for most of us. Thanksgiving just wouldn't be the same without it.

Yet, when we make the switch to a more healthful diet, we face a dilemma. How can we enjoy lavish meals of holiday favorites, and still prepare low-fat high-nutrient dishes? Part Two answers this question with inventive menus that combine "defatted" traditional dishes with exciting new fare for festive meals that are sure to delight family and friends.

The holiday season begins with a sumptuous Thanksgiving feast. Roast turkey, of course, takes center stage, accompanied by Foolproof Fat-Free Gravy and any one of four savory stuffings. To round out the meal, choose from among three refreshing cranberry sauces, as well as a bevy of vegetable side dishes and salads, including such favorites as Pineapple-Sweet Potato Casserole and Easy Mashed Potatoes. What's for dessert? Offer guests a choice of two classic Thanksgiving treats. Cool and creamy Baked Pumpkin Custard and hot and bubbly Cranapple Crisp are both delicious and made with absolutely no added fat.

Christmas brings two complete holiday menus. The first again features turkey, the perfect low-fat entrée. This time, though, the special-occasion bird makes its appearance as Tarragon Breast of Turkey. Blanketed with Orange-Tarragon Gravy, and flanked by Savory Wheat Stuffing, Orange Whipped Sweet Potatoes, and Celery Crunch Casserole, this bird makes a special meal indeed. Dessert brings Old-Fashioned Rice Pudding, a down-home treat made untraditionally fat-free.

Tired of turkey? Try our second Christmas menu. This meal pairs pork tenderloins with pineapple stuffing for an outrageously luscious main dish. Surrounding the pork roasts are Parmesan Scalloped Potatoes, Glazed Snow Peas and Carrots, and Cran-Raspberry Ring. Creamy

Cherry Cheesecake makes a colorful climax to a festive meal.

Hanukkah poses a special challenge to the fat-free cook. Usually, the Festival of Lights is celebrated with dishes cooked in oil to remind us of the holy oil that burned so long. How can we prepare these time-honored dishes *without* the oil and without sacrificing taste? Two different menus meet the challenge with both traditional holiday treats and new dishes, all defatted and all delicious.

The first menu begins with an appetizer of Smoked Salmon Spread. Next comes Herbed Eye of Round Roast, a satisfying dish braised in wine and herbs for full-bodied flavor. Accompanying the entrée are Potato Latkes, a Hanukkah favorite made remarkably fat-free. Rounding out the meal are a steaming Spinach and Noodle Kugel, refreshing Dilled Cucumber Salad, and chilled Winter Wonder Parfaits.

Our second Hanukkah feast begins with Ruby Borscht, a rosy soup garnished with nonfat sour cream and a sprinkling of dill. Following the soup is Roast Turkey Breast With Sourdough Stuffing and Savory Gravy, accompanied by Green Beans and Mushrooms, Sunshine Carrot Salad, and Cranberry Pear Conserve. Dessert brings fat-free Festive Noodle Pudding, a creamy confection that may be served hot or cold.

As winter turns to spring, celebrate Passover with meals that marry traditional Passover foods with healthful fat-free ingredients. The first Seder menu begins with a Passover must—Chicken Soup with Matzo Balls. Yes, these light and tender matzo balls are truly fat-free! This menu features a main dish of Baked Chicken Paprika, and side dishes of Passover Eggplant Casserole and a delightful Sweet Potato and Carrot Tzimmes. Light-as-air Cocoa Marble Meringues, accompanied by fresh strawberries, lend the perfect finishing touch to this healthy yet satisfying meal.

Our second Seder menu again begins with matzo ball soup. This time, though, the broth is enriched with sweet potatoes for a golden color

and a delightfully different flavor. Braised Beef With Carrots and Prunes, a hearty dish made low-fat by replacing the usual brisket with beef round; Asparagus Vinaigrette; Scalloped Tomato Matzo; and warm Apple Matzo Kugel complete the feast.

Our Easter menus celebrate spring with two selections of fresh and flavorful dishes. The first menu proves that traditional brunch favorites can be warming and satisfying but still light and healthy. Begin the brunch with Sensational Broccoli Strudels, crisp and light appetizers served piping hot. Then present the main course—a ham and cheese casserole made fat-free with egg substitute, nonfat cheese, and lean ham. Round out the meal with Spring Pasta Salad, Blueberry-Orange Muffins, and store-bought bagels. Finally, delight your guests with a culinary masterpiece—creamy Cappuccino Cheesecake.

If you prefer Easter dinner to Easter brunch, our second menu may be just what you're looking for. Creamy Cucumber Dip served with raw vegetables and whole grain crackers makes a light and flavorful beginning. Then comes a marinated tenderloin of pork, fragrant with herbs and spices. Accompanying the entrée are creamy Corn Pudding, Company Carrot-Raisin Salad, and spring-fresh Steamed Asparagus. And the crowning touch to this elegant meal? Chocolate Raspberry Torte, a dessert so rich and extravagant, no one will believe it's fat free!

As you browse through the following menus and recipes to plan your next special-occasion get-together, don't hesitate to mix and match dishes from different menus. Perhaps you love the menu for Easter brunch, but feel that your family would prefer the dessert from Easter dinner. Feel free to make the switch! That is why we have presented so many options—so that you can create meals that will best suit your family's tastes and your own style of entertaining. And don't forget that more holiday and party recipes can be found in Parts One, Three, and Four.

So gather family and friends, and get ready to start some new traditions. Holidays are sure to be even more enjoyable when the dishes you serve are not only festive and enticing, but also satisfying, wholesome, and full of the nutrients that insure good health the whole year round.

Surviving the Holiday Season

November and December are difficult months for those of us who are watching our weight. 'Tis the season for family feasts, office parties, and open houses. For two months, we are faced with every culinary temptation imaginable. In fact, it is not unusual for people to gain ten or even twenty pounds between the start of the football season and January 2.

Fortunately, the situation is far from hopeless. It is possible to enjoy all the festivities—including the special foods that help make the season so enjoyable—and still stay within the boundaries of a reasonable diet. So take heart, and use the following strategies to help maintain some semblance of sanity during the festive season.

❑ *Plan ahead.* If you know that you will be going to a party, work it into your daily meal plan. Save one-third to one-fourth of that day's calorie allotment for a cocktail party, and one-third to one-half of your allotment for a dinner party. Avoid going out for dinner after a cocktail party, as you will almost certainly overshoot your food limit for the day. Heavy hors d'oeuvres should be considered dinner. (To learn about turning a cocktail party into dinner, see the inset on page 60.)

❑ *Don't starve yourself.* Going to a party feeling ravenous will most likely cause you to overeat. Don't starve yourself all day in anticipation of the goodies ahead. Instead, eat a light breakfast and lunch, and save some calories for the evening.

❑ *Eat only special foods.* Don't waste fat and calories on ordinary party and snack foods like chips and dips—foods that you can eat any time of the year. Concentrate on foods that are not usually available, and then eat them only in moderation.

❑ *Eat slowly.* By eating slowly, you will feel more satisfied with less food. (After twenty minutes of eating, the body signals a feeling of fullness to the brain.)

❑ *Remember the law of diminishing returns.* The more you eat of something, the less pleasure you receive. For example, that first bite of cheesecake is the best, because the taste is so new. As you continue to eat, the pleasure diminishes. So eat just a bite or two, and receive 90 percent of the pleasure for only 10 percent of the fat and calories!

❑ *Don't set yourself up for failure.* Make a conscious effort to position yourself away from the hors d'oeuvres. This will prevent you from munching away as you chat with others.

❑ *Beware of the bubbly.* Alcohol contains almost as many calories as fat does. Combine it with creamy or sweet mixers, and you get even more calories. Another problem is that alcohol lowers your inhibitions, possibly making you careless about food choices. What can you do? Sip a wine spritzer, or mix the liquor with water, soda, or a diet beverage. Then alternate alcoholic drinks with glasses of water. Or simply drink club soda or another nonalcoholic beverage instead of the alcohol, and spend more of your calorie budget on delicious holiday foods.

❑ *Enlist the help of others.* No one wants to put on excess pounds during the holidays, so enlist the help of friends, family, and co-workers. You'll then be able to help one another plan more healthful menus and eat within reason.

❑ *Keep things in perspective.* If you lose control at a party or gathering, don't try to make up for it by starving the next day. Instead, get back on track and pick up where you left off. Remember that the most important part of the holidays is time spent with family and friends. Focus on the social aspects, think less about food, and don't punish yourself if you overindulge a little now and then.

Of course, there will be times when *you* are the host of the party. Make the most of this by serving a selection of healthful fat-free and low-fat foods. In Part One, you'll find dozens of ideas for fat- and calorie-smart appetizers. More healthful holidays recipes can be found throughout Parts Two, Three, and Four. Add some trays of fresh fruit and vegetables, as well as plenty of spring water and other low-cal beverages, and you'll set both yourself and your guests up for success instead of failure. Friends and family will appreciate this more than you know.

Thanksgiving

Thanksgiving kicks the holiday season into full swing. For many people, the season brings to mind fond memories of festive feasts—and not-so-fond memories of the resulting extra pounds. Holiday favorites are usually loaded with fat, sugar, and calories. Fortunately, it is possible to reduce the fat and sugar in these foods and still make them every bit as enjoyable as ever. The proof is in the traditional Thanksgiving dinner that follows.

When aiming for fat-free fare, it's hard to go wrong with turkey as a main course. The stuffing and gravy, however, are usually loaded with fat. Here you will find a variety of great-tasting stuffings that are virtually fat-free and full of whole grain goodness. And don't be afraid to pour on Foolproof Fat-Free Gravy! It is delicious over turkey and stuffing, and adds no fat to your meal.

Accompany the main course with Thanksgiving favorites like Waldorf Salad, Pineapple-Sweet Potato Casserole, and Broccoli Casserole. Or try Festive Fruit Salad, Green Bean Casserole, and Easy Mashed Potatoes. Cranberry sauce is a must, and three versions are offered here. Dessert anyone? Try some Baked Pumpkin Custard or Cranapple Crisp. Both contain no added fat and are lower in sugar than traditionally made desserts.

You'll notice that this collection of Thanksgiving dishes is a bit lavish. This is not because we recommend that your Thanksgiving table groan with extra food! Rather, a few extras have been added for variety. Who knows? You may want to prepare a variation of this menu at Christmas time.

Although Thanksgiving dinner is an extravagant meal, the preparations for it need not be overwhelming. Only two dishes must be fully prepared right before serving: the turkey and the mashed potatoes. However, once the turkey is placed in the oven to roast, it will require little of your attention for several hours. And, of course, the mashed potatoes are quite easy to make at the last minute. Or, if you prefer, serve the sweet potato casserole, which can be partially prepared in advance by baking the potatoes the day before. On the day of your dinner, just toss the casserole ingredients together, top with marshmallows, and bake.

If you have chosen a bread-based stuffing, the bread can be cubed and processed into crumbs the day before the dinner, and stored in a plastic bag. Also cut up any vegetables a day in advance, cover, and refrigerate until the next day, when you can finish the stuffing preparations. For a truly make-ahead dish, try Cranberry-Wild Rice Stuffing, which can be assembled up to the point of baking the day before your feast.

Any of the cranberry sauces can easily be made as much as two days in advance. Cover and chill them, and they'll keep beautifully until serving time. Both fruits salads should be prepared several hours in advance, and covered and chilled.

The broccoli and green bean casseroles can both be prepared one day in advance just to the point of adding the topping. On the day of your dinner, simply sprinkle on the topping and pop the casseroles into the oven.

This menu delights guests with a choice of two scrumptious desserts. Baked Pumpkin Custard helps avoid a last-minute rush because it is baked and then chilled for several hours or overnight. Cranapple Crisp must, of course, be assembled and baked right before serving time, and then brought to the table hot and bubbly. Either dessert will be a fitting finale to a deliciously traditional feast.

Thanksgiving Dinner

SERVES 10 TO 12

Roast Turkey (page 72) *with Stuffing* (page 73)

Foolproof Fat-Free Gravy (page 77)

Waldorf Salad (page 77)
or Festive Fruit Salad (page 78)

Green Bean Casserole (page 78)
or Broccoli Casserole (page 80)

Easy Mashed Potatoes (page 80)
or Pineapple-Sweet Potato Casserole (page 81)

Cranberry Sauce (page 82)

Baked Pumpkin Custard (page 84)

Cranapple Crisp (page 84)

Roast Turkey

Yield: 16 servings

12-pound turkey, fresh or defrosted

½ cup water

½ cup dry sherry

BASTING SAUCE

2 tablespoons dry sherry

1 teaspoon crushed fresh garlic

¼ teaspoon ground black pepper

1 teaspoon poultry seasoning

1½ teaspoons paprika

1 teaspoon brown sugar

NUTRITIONAL FACTS
(PER 3-OUNCE SERVING,
SKINLESS WHITE MEAT)

Calories: 119	Fiber: 0 g
Chol.: 73 mg	Protein: 26 g
Fat: 1 g	Sodium: 48 mg

NUTRITIONAL FACTS
(PER 3-OUNCE SERVING,
SKINLESS DARK MEAT)

Calories: 159	Fiber: 0 g
Chol.: 72 mg	Protein: 24 g
Fat: 6 g	Sodium: 67 mg

The method of foil roasting used in this recipe differs from conventional foil-tent roasting in that the bird is totally enclosed in foil for most of the baking time to seal in the moisture. During the last 30 minutes of baking, the foil is removed to allow the skin to brown before serving.

1. Remove the package containing the giblets and neck from the cavities of the turkey. (You may have to release the legs from a band of skin or a wire or plastic lock in order to remove the giblets and neck.) Rinse the turkey, inside and out, and dry it with paper towels. Trim off any excess fat.

2. Transfer the turkey to a rack in a large roasting pan. Return the legs to the wire or plastic lock or band of skin, or loosely tie the legs together with a cord. Fold the wings back and underneath the bird.

3. Pour the water and sherry into the bottom of the roasting pan. Combine the basting sauce ingredients in a small bowl, and brush the sauce over the skin of the bird. Completely enclose the bird in aluminum foil, crimping the foil around the edges of the pan to seal.

4. Bake at 325°F for 3¼ to 4 hours. During the last 30 minutes of cooking, remove the foil and baste with the pan juices.

5. When the turkey is done, a thermometer inserted in the thigh will read 180°F to 185°F, and the drumsticks will move easily in the sockets. Remove the turkey from the oven, and allow it to sit, loosely covered with foil, for 20 minutes before carving.

Savory Stuffings

Nearly every family has its favorite stuffing recipe. The problem is that whether your family's stuffing is savory with sage or sweet with apples and raisins, it's probably also loaded with fat. Fortunately, it is possible to make stuffing that's flavorful and moist while being virtually fat-free. In fact, the following stuffings are so delicious that you may decide to make them part of your daily fare, rather than reserving them for festive occasions.

For safety's sake, it is best to cook the stuffing outside of the bird. Why? Stuffing, improperly handled, is a perfect breeding ground for the harmful bacteria sometimes found in poultry. For this reason, all of the stuffings presented here are baked in casserole dishes. If you choose to bake your stuffing *inside* the bird, omit the broth or Butter Buds liquid used to moisten the stuffing, as the juices from the bird will make the added liquid unnecessary. Always stuff the turkey right before roasting, and be sure to stuff it loosely, leaving a little space at the end for expansion. After spooning in the stuffing, secure the turkey's legs and wings, as explained in the turkey recipe, and cook thoroughly. The internal temperature of the stuffing should reach 165°F. Then remove the stuffing from the bird directly after roasting, and enjoy!

Cranberry-Wild Rice Stuffing

Yield: 12 servings

1 cup uncooked brown rice

½ cup uncooked wild rice

1 medium onion, chopped

1 cup thinly sliced celery (include leaves)

1 bay leaf

1 teaspoon dried rosemary, or 1 tablespoon fresh

3 cups unsalted chicken broth or water

1 teaspoon chicken bouillon granules

¼ teaspoon ground white pepper

1 cup whole berry cranberry sauce

1. Combine all of the ingredients except for the cranberry sauce in a 2½-quart pot. Bring the mixture to a boil over high heat. Reduce the heat to low, cover, and simmer without stirring for 45 to 50 minutes, or until the liquid has been absorbed. Remove the pot from the heat, and set aside, uncovered, for 5 minutes.

2. Coat a 2-quart casserole dish with nonstick cooking spray. Stir the cranberry sauce into the stuffing mixture, and loosely spoon the stuffing into the dish. Cover the dish with aluminum foil, and bake at 350°F for 30 to 45 minutes, or until heated through. Serve hot.

NUTRITIONAL FACTS (PER ½-CUP SERVING)

Calories: 121	Fat: 0.5 g	Protein: 24 g
Cholesterol: 0 mg	Fiber: 2 g	Sodium: 103 mg

Sage and Herb Whole Wheat Stuffing

Yield: 12 servings

12 slices stale whole wheat bread

1 medium onion, finely chopped

1 cup finely chopped celery
    (include leaves)

1 teaspoon dried sage

¾ teaspoon dried thyme

¾ teaspoon dried marjoram

¼ teaspoon ground black pepper

2 egg whites, lightly beaten
    (optional)

⅔ cup chicken broth or Butter
    Buds liquid

1. Take 8 of the 12 slices of bread, and tear them into small pieces. Place the pieces in a food processor or blender, and process into coarse crumbs. Measure the crumbs. There should be 4 cups. (Adjust the amount if necessary.)

2. Take the remaining 4 slices of bread, and cut the bread into ½-inch cubes. Measure the cubes. There should be 4 cups. (Adjust the amount if necessary.)

3. Place the bread crumbs and cubes in a large bowl, and add all of the remaining ingredients except for the chicken broth. Toss to mix well. Slowly add the broth as you continue tossing.

4. Coat a 2-quart casserole dish with nonstick cooking spray. Loosely spoon the stuffing into the dish, and bake uncovered at 325°F for 45 minutes to an hour, or until heated through and lightly browned on top. Serve hot.

NUTRITIONAL FACTS (PER ½-CUP SERVING)

Calories: 92	Fat: 1 g	Protein: 3.7 g
Cholesterol: 0 mg	Fiber: 2.5 g	Sodium: 205 mg

Variations

For a change of pace, add one of the following ingredients to your whole wheat stuffing:

- 1 cup peeled chopped roasted chestnuts
- 1 can (8 ounces) chopped mushrooms, drained, or 1½ cups chopped fresh mushrooms, sautéed in 1 tablespoon of chicken broth

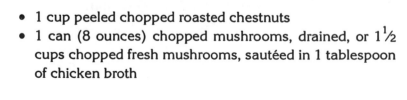

Apple-Raisin Stuffing

Yield: 12 servings

1. Take 6 of the 9 slices of bread, and tear them into small pieces. Place the pieces in a food processor or blender, and process into coarse crumbs. Measure the crumbs. There should be 3 cups. (Adjust the amount if necessary.)

2. Take the remaining 3 slices of bread, and cut them into $\frac{1}{2}$-inch cubes. Measure the cubes. There should be 3 cups. (Adjust the amount if necessary.)

3. Place the bread crumbs and cubes in a large bowl, and add all of the remaining ingredients except for the chicken broth. Toss to mix well. Slowly add the broth as you continue tossing.

4. Coat a 2-quart casserole dish with nonstick cooking spray. Loosely spoon the stuffing into the dish, and bake uncovered at 325°F for 45 minutes to an hour, or until heated through and lightly browned on top. Serve hot.

9 slices stale whole wheat bread

3 large tart apples, peeled and coarsely chopped

$\frac{3}{4}$ cup dark or golden raisins

1 cup finely chopped celery (include leaves)

$\frac{1}{2}$ cup finely chopped onion

1 teaspoon poultry seasoning

$\frac{1}{4}$ teaspoon ground white pepper

$\frac{1}{2}$ cup chopped walnuts or pecans (optional)

2 egg whites, lightly beaten (optional)

$\frac{1}{2}$ cup chicken broth or Butter Buds liquid

NUTRITIONAL FACTS (PER $\frac{1}{2}$-CUP SERVING)

Calories: 119	Fat: 0.7 g	Protein: 3.2 g
Cholesterol: 0 mg	Fiber: 2.9 g	Sodium: 181 mg

Old-Fashioned Cornbread Dressing

Yield: 12 servings

1 cup chopped onion

1 cup thinly sliced celery (include leaves)

1½ teaspoons dried sage

1 teaspoon poultry seasoning

¼ teaspoon ground black pepper

⅔ cup chicken broth or Butter Buds liquid

2 egg whites, lightly beaten (optional)

CORNBREAD

1½ cups whole grain cornmeal

2 teaspoons baking powder

4 egg whites, lightly beaten

1¼ cups nonfat buttermilk

1 teaspoon butter-flavored extract

1. To make the cornbread, combine the cornmeal and baking powder in a large bowl, and stir to mix well. Add the remaining cornbread ingredients, and stir to mix well.

2. Coat a 9-inch square pan with nonstick cooking spray. Spread the batter evenly in the pan, and bake at 400°F for 20 to 25 minutes, or until a wooden toothpick inserted in the center of the bread comes out clean and the bread begins to pull slightly from the sides of the pan. Cool completely.

3. Remove the cornbread from the pan, and crumble into a large bowl. Add the remaining ingredients, and toss to mix well.

4. Coat a 2-quart casserole dish with nonstick cooking spray. Loosely spoon the stuffing into the dish, and bake uncovered at 325°F for 45 minutes to an hour, or until heated through and lightly browned on top. Serve hot.

NUTRITIONAL FACTS (PER ½-CUP SERVING)		
Calories: 77	Fat: 0.8 g	Protein: 3.5 g
Cholesterol: 0 mg	Fiber: 2 g	Sodium: 107 mg

Time-Saving Tip

To make Thanksgiving Day a little less hectic, bake the cornbread 1 to 3 days in advance. Then complete the stuffing preparations the day before or the morning of the dinner, and pop the casserole into the oven 1 hour before serving time.

Variation

To make Country Sausage Stuffing, cook 8 ounces of ground turkey breakfast sausage in a nonstick skillet, stirring constantly to crumble. Drain the sausage, and add it to the stuffing mixture.

NUTRITIONAL FACTS (PER ½-CUP SERVING)		
Calories: 97	Fat: 1.4 g	Protein: 6.3 g
Cholesterol: 8 mg	Fiber: 2 g	Sodium: 308 mg

Foolproof Fat-Free Gravy

1. Defat the pan drippings by placing them in a fat separator cup. (If you don't have a separator cup, pour the drippings into a bowl, add a few ice cubes, and skim off the fat once it rises and hardens.) Combine the fat-free drippings, pepper, poultry seasoning, and bouillon granules in a 1-quart saucepan, and simmer over low heat for 5 minutes.

2. While the gravy is heating, combine the flour and milk in a jar with a tight-fitting lid, and shake until smooth. Slowly add the milk mixture to the simmering broth, stirring constantly with a wire whisk. Continue to cook and stir until the gravy is thick and bubbly.

3. Transfer the gravy to a warmed gravy boat or pitcher, and serve hot with the turkey.

Yield: 2½ cups

2 cups turkey drippings

⅛ teaspoon ground white pepper

¼ teaspoon poultry seasoning

1 teaspoon chicken bouillon granules

¼ cup plus 1 tablespoon unbleached flour

½ cup skim milk

NUTRITIONAL FACTS (PER TABLESPOON)

Calories: 7	Fat: 0 g	Protein: 0.4 g
Cholesterol: 0 mg	Fiber: 0 g	Sodium: 25 mg

Waldorf Salad

1. In a large bowl, combine the apples, celery, raisins, and walnuts, and stir to mix well.

2. In a small bowl, combine the mayonnaise with the sour cream, and stir to mix well. Add the mayonnaise mixture to the apple mixture, and toss to mix.

3. Cover the salad and chill for 1 to 3 hours before serving.

Yield: 12 servings

6 cups diced apples

2½ cups thinly sliced celery

¼ cup plus 2 tablespoons dark raisins

⅓ cup chopped walnuts (optional)

DRESSING

¼ cup plus 2 tablespoons nonfat or reduced-fat mayonnaise

¼ cup plus 2 tablespoons nonfat sour cream

NUTRITIONAL FACTS (PER ⅔-CUP SERVING)

Calories: 63	Fat: 0.2 g	Protein: 1 g
Cholesterol: 0 mg	Fiber: 2 g	Sodium: 94 mg

Festive Fruit Salad

Yield: 12 servings

2 cups nonfat vanilla yogurt

1 can (20 ounces) pineapple chunks in juice, drained, or 2 cups fresh pineapple chunks

2 cans (10 ounces each) mandarin oranges, or 2 cups fresh orange sections, membranes removed

4 large bananas, sliced

¼ cup flaked coconut

1 cup miniature marshmallows

This light and delicious fruit salad has a dressing of yogurt cheese, which you make yourself using nonfat yogurt. Be sure that the yogurt doesn't contain gelatin, as gelatin makes it impossible to extract the "cheese" from the yogurt.

1. To make the yogurt cheese, place a cheesecloth-lined funnel over a jar, and pour the yogurt into the funnel. Place the jar in the refrigerator overnight. The creamy white mixture that remains in the funnel is yogurt cheese. (There should be 1 cup of cheese.)

2. In a large bowl, combine the fruits and marshmallows, tossing to mix. Add the yogurt cheese to the fruit mixture, and toss to mix.

3. Cover the salad and chill for 1 to 3 hours before serving.

NUTRITIONAL FACTS (PER ⅔-CUP SERVING)

| Calories: 85 | Fat: 0.7 g | Protein: 0.8 g |
| Cholesterol: 0 mg | Fiber: 1.5 g | Sodium: 7 mg |

Green Bean Casserole

Yield: 12 servings

3 packages (10 ounces each) frozen French-cut green beans, thawed and drained

1 can (10¾ ounces) condensed low-fat cream of mushroom soup

½ cup nonfat sour cream

¼ teaspoon ground black pepper

1½ medium onions, thinly sliced and separated into rings

4 tablespoons grated nonfat or reduced-fat Parmesan cheese

2 tablespoons Italian bread crumbs

1. In a large bowl, combine the green beans, mushroom soup, sour cream, and pepper, and toss gently to mix.

2. Coat a 2-quart casserole dish with nonstick cooking spray. Place the green bean mixture in the dish, and arrange the onion rings over the top. Combine the Parmesan cheese and bread crumbs in a small bowl, and sprinkle over the onions.

3. Bake at 350°F for 50 minutes, or until the green bean mixture is bubbly and the top is lightly browned. Serve hot.

NUTRITIONAL FACTS (PER ½-CUP SERVING)

| Calories: 51 | Fat: 0.6 g | Protein: 2.8 g |
| Cholesterol: 2 mg | Fiber: 2.5 g | Sodium: 170 mg |

Trimming the Fat
From Your Thanksgiving Feast

If you look back at holiday dinners past, it's easy to see why we all gain weight during this festive time of year. At Thanksgiving alone, the parade of tempting dishes often begins even before dinner with several appetizers, perhaps accompanied by wine. Then comes the turkey and possibly a ham. With the turkey is served three or four different starches—stuffing, mashed potatoes, sweet potatoes, and rolls, for instance—as well as two or more vegetables and, of course, cranberry sauce. Naturally, the turkey, stuffing, and potatoes are topped with fat-laden gravy. And the whole meal is topped with a selection of rich desserts. Even if you insist on fairly small portions, you're likely to use up an entire day's calorie allotment on a dinner like this. You're also likely to feel uncomfortably full at meal's end.

However, it really is possible to enjoy Thanksgiving and other holidays and still eat healthfully. Realize that holiday meals can be a lot simpler than they usually are, but every bit as enjoyable and well-balanced. For instance, roast turkey with stuffing and gravy, along with one other starch—either sweet potatoes or mashed potatoes, for instance—a salad, a vegetable, and dessert make a well-balanced and satisfying meal.

What can you do about all those fat-laden holiday recipes? Keep them, but give them slimming makeovers. Here are some ideas for trimming the fat from your Thanksgiving feast:

❑ Turkey is an ideal low-fat main course. To help keep it this way, buy a fresh unbasted turkey instead of the pre-basted kind, which has been injected with a mixture of oil and salty broth. (Read the label to see if it's been pre-basted.) Then examine the turkey for extra fat, and trim it away.

❑ Baste your turkey with broth, sherry, or white wine instead of fat. During cooking, cover the turkey with foil to retain moistness. Then uncover the bird during the last 30 minutes so that it turns a beautiful brown.

❑ When making your gravy, pour the pan juices into a fat separator cup. This specially designed device has a spout that goes to the bottom of the cup, allowing you to pour off just the broth while the fat, which has risen to the top, stays in the cup. If you don't have a separator cup, pour the juices into a bowl, and add a few ice cubes. The fat will then rise to the top and harden, where it can be easily skimmed off.

❑ Moisten your dressing with broth instead of fat. For added nutrition, try using whole wheat bread instead of white. Then, instead of using salt for flavor, add lots of celery, onion, and other vegetables, as well as herbs and spices.

❑ Get the fat out of side dishes and casseroles. For example, make your mashed potatoes with butter-flavored sprinkles and skim milk, nonfat yogurt, or nonfat sour cream. When making casseroles, use nonfat cheeses, nonfat sour cream, and low-fat cream soups. Lighten your salads with nonfat mayonnaise, nonfat sour cream, and fat-free salad dressings.

❑ Modify your holiday dessert recipes. For instance, use evaporated skim milk in pumpkin pies; substitute egg whites for whole eggs; and reduce the sugar by 25 percent. Choose fruit-based desserts like cobblers and fruit crisps over gooey cakes and pastries.

As you can see, it's not difficult to make a Thanksgiving dinner that is both satisfying and healthful. By trimming the fat from your favorite holiday dishes—and by trimming away any extra dishes, as well—you will surprise both yourself and your family with a memorable feast that is also low in fat and high in nutrition.

Broccoli Casserole

Yield: 12 servings

1½ cups shredded nonfat or reduced-fat sharp Cheddar cheese

2 packages (10 ounces each) frozen chopped broccoli, thawed and drained

⅓ cup finely chopped onion

⅓ cup fat-free egg substitute

1¾ cups dry curd or nonfat cottage cheese

2 tablespoons unbleached flour

¼ teaspoon ground white pepper

3 tablespoons finely ground fat-free cracker crumbs

1. Set aside ½ cup of the grated Cheddar cheese. Combine the rest of the cheese and all of the remaining ingredients except for the cracker crumbs in a large bowl, and stir to mix well.

2. Coat a 2½-quart casserole dish with nonstick cooking spray. Place the broccoli mixture in the dish, sprinkle with the cracker crumbs, and spread the reserved cheese over the top.

3. Bake at 350°F for 50 minutes, or until the top is golden brown. Let sit for 5 minutes before serving.

NUTRITIONAL FACTS (PER ⅔-CUP SERVING)		
Calories: 68	Fat: 0.2 g	Protein: 10 g
Cholesterol: 3 mg	Fiber: 1.8 g	Sodium: 147 mg

Easy Mashed Potatoes

Yield: 12 servings

8 medium potatoes

½ cup nonfat dry milk powder

3 tablespoons butter-flavored sprinkles

¼ teaspoon ground white pepper

1. Peel the potatoes, and cut them into chunks. Place the potatoes in a 4-quart pot, and add water just to cover. Bring the potatoes to a boil over high heat. Reduce the heat to medium, cover, and cook for 10 minutes, or until the potatoes are soft.

2. Drain all but about ⅔ cup of water from the pot, reserving the drained water. Add the dry milk powder, butter-flavored sprinkles, and pepper to the potatoes, and mash them with a potato masher until smooth. If the potatoes are too stiff, add a little of the reserved cooking liquid. Serve immediately.

NUTRITIONAL FACTS (PER 1/2-CUP SERVING)		
Calories: 96	Fat: 0.1 g	Protein: 2.8 g
Cholesterol: 0 mg	Fiber: 1.5 g	Sodium: 86 mg

Variation

For a different taste, make Easy Mashed Potatoes with nonfat sour cream or plain nonfat yogurt instead of nonfat dry milk. Just omit the dry milk, and drain all of the liquid from the potatoes. Add ¾ cup of nonfat sour cream or yogurt, and mash as directed. If the potatoes seem too stiff, return a little of the reserved cooking liquid to the pot.

Pineapple-Sweet Potato Casserole

Yield: 12 servings

1. To cook the sweet potatoes in a conventional oven, bake them at 400°F for about 45 minutes, or until tender. To cook in a microwave oven, prick each potato in several places with a fork, and microwave at high power for about 15 minutes, or until tender. Set aside to cool; then peel and cut into bite-sized pieces.

2. Place the potato pieces in a large bowl and toss with all of the remaining ingredients except the marshmallows. Coat a 2½-quart casserole dish with nonstick cooking spray, and place the sweet potato mixture in the dish. Top with the marshmallows.

3. Bake at 350°F for 35 to 40 minutes, or until the sweet potato mixture is bubbly and the top is lightly browned. If the top starts to brown too quickly, loosely cover the dish with aluminum foil during the last 10 minutes of baking. Serve hot.

3 pounds sweet potatoes (about 6 medium-large)

2 cans (8 ounces each) crushed pineapple in juice, undrained

¼ teaspoon ground cinnamon

4 teaspoons butter-flavored sprinkles

⅓ cup chopped pecans or golden raisins (optional)

1¾ cups miniature marshmallows

NUTRITIONAL FACTS (PER ½-CUP SERVING)

Calories: 143	Fat: 0.2 g	Protein: 2 g
Cholesterol: 0 mg	Fiber: 2.5 g	Sodium: 65 mg

Time-Saving Tip

Instead of using fresh potatoes, use 3 pounds of canned sweet potatoes. Just drain and slice the potatoes, and use them as you would the cut-up baked potatoes.

Cranberries Three Ways

Cranberry sauce recipes are as varied as stuffing recipes. Perhaps you like your sauce enlivened with orange juice and rind. Or perhaps you like your cranberries jelled in a festive mold. Whatever your preferences may be, you're sure to find a dish that will please both you and your guests among the recipes presented below.

Molded Cranberry-Apple Relish

Yield: 12 servings

1 package (4-serving size) sugar-free black raspberry gelatin mix

¼ cup light brown sugar

1½ cups boiling water

1½ cups fresh or frozen cranberries, stemmed and coarsely chopped

1 medium apple, peeled and finely chopped

½ cup finely chopped celery

⅓ cup chopped pecans (optional)

1. Combine the gelatin mix and brown sugar in a large heat-proof bowl. Add the boiling water, and stir until the mix is dissolved. Cover and chill for about 45 minutes, or until the mixture has thickened to the consistency of raw egg whites.

2. Stir the remaining ingredients into the gelatin mixture. Pour the mixture into an ungreased 6-cup mold, cover, and chill for 6 to 8 hours, or until very firm.

3. To unmold the relish, dip the mold in warm—but not hot—water for 5 to 10 seconds. Beware: If the water is too hot or the mold remains in the water too long, the gelatin will start to melt. Remove the mold from the water and loosen the edges of the mixture with a knife. Place a serving platter upside down over the mold, and invert the mold onto the platter. Slice and serve chilled.

NUTRITIONAL FACTS (PER ⅓-CUP SERVING)

| Calories: 30 | Fat: 0.1 g | Protein: 0.5 g |
| Cholesterol: 0 mg | Fiber: 0.9 g | Sodium: 23 mg |

Cranberry-Apricot Sauce

Yield: 18 servings

1. Place the apricots and their juice in the bowl of a food processor or in a blender, and process until coarsely chopped.

2. Combine the chopped apricots and brown sugar in a 2½-quart pot, and stir to mix well. Place over medium heat, and bring to a boil, stirring constantly. Stop stirring, and allow the mixture to boil for 2 minutes with the pot uncovered.

3. Add the cranberries to the pot, and stir to mix. Simmer the mixture over medium heat, with the cover of the pot on but ajar, for 7 to 10 minutes, or until the cranberry skins pop open. Stir occasionally.

4. Allow the mixture to cool to room temperature. Transfer to a serving bowl, cover, and chill for at least 4 hours before serving.

1 can (1 pound) apricots in juice or light syrup, undrained

½ cup light brown sugar

12 ounces (3 cups) fresh or frozen cranberries, stemmed

NUTRITIONAL FACTS
(PER 3-TABLESPOON SERVING)

Calories: 45	Fiber: 1.2 g
Cholesterol: 0 mg	Protein: 0 g
Fat: 0 g	Sodium: 3 mg

Orange-Cranberry Sauce

Yield: 12 servings

1. Combine the orange juice, orange rind, and brown sugar in a 2-quart pot, and stir to mix well. Place over medium heat, and bring to a boil, stirring constantly. Stop stirring, and allow the mixture to boil for 5 minutes with the pot uncovered.

2. Add the cranberries to the pot, and stir to mix. Simmer the mixture over medium heat, with the cover of the pot on but ajar, for 7 to 10 minutes, or until the cranberry skins pop open. Stir occasionally.

3. Allow the mixture to cool to room temperature. Transfer to a serving bowl, cover, and chill for at least 4 hours before serving.

1 cup orange juice

½ tablespoon freshly grated orange rind, or ½ teaspoon dried

½ cup light brown sugar

12 ounces (3 cups) fresh or frozen cranberries, stemmed

NUTRITIONAL FACTS
(PER 3-TABLESPOON SERVING)

Calories: 57	Fiber: 1.2 g
Cholesterol: 0 mg	Protein: 0 g
Fat: 0 g	Sodium: 3 mg

Baked Pumpkin Custard

Yield: 8 servings

1½ cups canned or mashed cooked pumpkin

1 can (12 ounces) evaporated skim milk

1¾ cups fat-free egg substitute

⅓ cup orange juice

1½ teaspoons vanilla extract

½ cup light brown sugar

1½ teaspoons pumpkin pie spice

1. Place all of the ingredients in a blender or food processor, and process until smooth.

2. Coat a 2-quart soufflé dish with nonstick cooking spray. Pour the mixture into the dish, and place the dish in a pan filled with 1 inch of hot water.

3. Bake at 350°F for about 1 hour and 15 minutes, or until a sharp knife inserted in the center of the custard comes out clean. Chill for at least 8 hours or overnight and serve.

NUTRITIONAL FACTS (PER ⅔-CUP SERVING)		
Calories: 131	Fat: 0.2 g	Protein: 8.6 g
Cholesterol: 0 mg	Fiber: 0.9 g	Sodium: 131 mg

Cranapple Crisp

Yield: 8 servings

FRUIT FILLING

8 cups thinly sliced peeled apples

½ cup fresh or frozen cranberries, coarsely chopped

⅓ cup light brown sugar

¼ cup golden raisins

1 tablespoon cornstarch

1 tablespoon apple juice concentrate, thawed

TOPPING

⅔ cup quick-cooking oats

3 tablespoons whole wheat flour

¼ cup light brown sugar

¼ teaspoon ground cinnamon

2 tablespoons frozen apple juice concentrate, thawed

1. To make the topping, in a small bowl, combine the oats, flour, sugar, and cinnamon, and stir to mix well. Add the juice concentrate, and stir until moist and crumbly. Set aside.

2. In a large bowl, combine the filling ingredients, and toss to mix well. Coat a 2½-quart casserole dish with nonstick cooking spray. Place the filling mixture in the dish, and sprinkle with the topping.

3. Bake at 375°F for 30 minutes. Cover the dish loosely with foil, and bake for an additional 15 minutes, or until the filling is bubbly and the topping is golden brown. Serve warm.

NUTRITIONAL FACTS (PER ¾-CUP SERVING)		
Calories: 178	Fat: 0.7 g	Protein: 1.7 g
Cholesterol: 0 mg	Fiber: 4 g	Sodium: 7 mg

Christmas

As visions of sugarplums dance in our heads, so perhaps do less-pleasant visions of heavy, diet-busting holiday roasts, side dishes, and desserts. Ready for a change of pace? Then delight guests with one of our two light and delicious Christmas dinners.

Our first menu is a flavorful twist on the Thanksgiving turkey dinner. As supper finishes cooking, serve Apple Cheddar Spread with whole grain crackers and fresh apple slices. A chilled glass of white wine would be the perfect accompaniment. Begin dinner with a delicate butterhead lettuce salad topped with crunchy croutons and a creamy blue cheese dressing. Then present an impressive main course—Tarragon Breast of Turkey coupled with a savory bulgur wheat stuffing and topped with Orange-Tarragon Gravy. On the side, mildly spiced Orange Whipped Sweet Potatoes and a tasty Celery Crunch Casserole add a pleasing contrast of colors. Last but not least is creamy Old-Fashioned Rice Pudding. Studded with plump raisins and sprinkled with ground nutmeg, this delectable dessert is sure to bring to mind memories of Christmas past.

With so much to do over the holidays, time is always in short supply. Luckily, much of this meal can be fully or partially prepared ahead of time so that you can relax and enjoy your dinner.

Prepare both Apple Cheddar Spread and Lite Blue Cheese Dressing a day in advance to let the flavors mingle. Also rinse the greens for your salad the day before your dinner. If you shake off any excess water, wrap the greens in paper towels, and store them in an airtight container or plastic bag, they will be crisp and fresh on the day of your dinner. And the Crunchy Croutons? These flavorful nuggets can be made several days before Christmas and stored in an airtight container until needed.

This menu's stuffing and side dishes can all be made the day before the dinner. Prepare Savory Wheat Stuffing to the point of baking, and refrigerate the casserole until you're ready to place it in the oven. Fully prepare Orange Whipped Sweet Potatoes, and, again, refrigerate the dish until it's time to reheat. Also prepare Celery Crunch Casserole—in this case, to the point of adding the topping. Chill the casserole until about forty-five minutes before your guests sit down to eat, add the topping, and pop the dish into the oven.

This menu's final no-fuss dish, Old-Fashioned Rice Pudding, is best made the day before your dinner to allow the dessert to set. Chill it until serving time.

But perhaps you're all turkeyed out after Thanksgiving. In that case, our second Christmas menu may be just what you're looking for.

Begin the festivities with an elegant appetizer of warm artichoke hearts marinated in a tangy mustard sauce and wrapped in ultra-lean ham. Then serve your main dish, which pairs the leanest and most tender cut of pork available with a pineapple-bread stuffing to create an entrée that is as attractive as it is delicious. Accompanying the pork and stuffing is a creamy yet fat-free version of Scalloped Potatoes, festive Glazed Snow Peas and Carrots, and colorful molded Cran-Raspberry Ring. For dessert, indulge in guilt-free Creamy Cherry Cheesecake. Made with nonfat cheeses, this deceptively rich confection has the smoothness of traditional cheesecake with none of the traditional fat.

This menu, like our first one, will enable you to get a head start on meal preparations. The day before your dinner, begin making your appetizer by placing the artichokes in the marinade. On the morning of your party, assemble the dish to the point of baking. Then pop these savory morsels into the oven just as guests arrive.

Also prepare the bread crumbs and cubes for your stuffing the day before your dinner, and store them in plastic bags until needed. At the same time, chop the vegetables for the stuffing, and store them in the refrigerator. Then, on the evening before or the morning of the party, prepare the tenderloins to the point of baking, cover, and chill. Remove your entrée from the refrigerator about thirty minutes before baking, and place it in the oven until done.

Parmesan Scalloped Potatoes must be assembled just before baking. However, this simple recipe is a snap to put together, and requires little attention once in the oven. You can, of course, cut up the vegetables for the Glazed Snow Peas and Carrots the day before your dinner. Just cover the peas and carrots and store them in the refrigerator until you're ready to complete the dish.

Both the Cran-Raspberry Ring and the Creamy Cherry Cheescake are boons to the make-ahead cook. In fact, both *must* be made the day before your party. Unmold the Cran-Raspberry Ring onto a platter directly before serving, and arrange the grapes around the ring. When it's time to serve the cheesecake, just release the sides from the springform pan. Serving a crowd-pleasing dessert was never simpler!

A Merry Christmas Dinner
Top Left: Parmesan Scalloped Potatoes (page 96)
Top Right: Glazed Snow Peas and Carrots (page 96)
Bottom: Pork Tenderloins With Pineapple Stuffing (page 95)

Hanukkah, A Feast for the Festival of Lights
Top Left: Green Beans and Mushrooms (page 110)
Top Right: Festive Noodle Pudding (page 112)
Bottom: Roast Turkey Breast With Sourdough Stuffing (page 108)

Passover Seder, A Time of Remembrance
Top Left: Asparagus Vinaigrette (page 122)
Top Right: Golden Matzo Ball Soup (page 121)
Bottom: Braised Beef With Carrots and Prunes (page 121)

A Glorious Easter Dinner
Top Left: Company Carrot-Raisin Salad (page 133)
Top Right: Fresh-Steamed Asparagus With Honey Mustard Sauce (page 134)
Bottom: Rosemary Roasted Tenderloin (page 132)

Christmas Dinner
Menu One

SERVES 8 TO 10

Apple Cheddar Spread (page 50) *with*
Sliced Apples and Whole Grain Crackers

Buttercrunch Salad (page 88) *with*
Lite Blue Cheese Dressing (page 88)

Tarragon Breast of Turkey (page 90) *with*
Orange-Tarragon Gravy (page 91)

Savory Wheat Stuffing (page 91)

Orange Whipped Sweet Potatoes (page 90)

Celery Crunch Casserole (page 92)

Old-Fashioned Rice Pudding (page 93)

Buttercrunch Salad

Yield: 10 servings

12 cups buttercrunch or Boston lettuce (about 4 heads)

1 pint cherry tomatoes

1 medium red onion, thinly sliced and separated into rings

½ cup sliced black olives

Crunchy Croutons (page 89)

1. Place the lettuce in a large salad bowl. Add the cherry tomatoes, onion, and black olives, and toss to mix. Arrange the Crunchy Croutons over the top.

2. Serve with Lite Blue Cheese Dressing.

NUTRITIONAL ANALYSIS
(PER 1-CUP SERVING, WITH CROUTONS)

Calories: 57	Fat: 1.4 g	Protein: 2.4 g
Cholesterol: 0 mg	Fiber: 2 g	Sodium: 137 mg

Lite Blue Cheese Dressing

Yield: 2 cups

½ cup crumbled blue cheese

1 cup dry curd or nonfat cottage cheese

¼ cup nonfat or reduced-fat mayonnaise

¼ cup nonfat buttermilk or nonfat yogurt

¼ cup white wine vinegar or red wine vinegar

1 teaspoon crushed fresh garlic

¼ teaspoon ground white pepper

¼ teaspoon salt (optional)

1. Place ¼ cup of the blue cheese and all of the remaining ingredients in a food processor or blender, and process until smooth. Stir in the remaining blue cheese.

2. Transfer the dressing to a small bowl, cover, and chill for several hours or overnight before serving.

NUTRITIONAL FACTS (PER TABLESPOON)

Calories: 13	Fat: 0.5 g	Protein: 1.2 g
Cholesterol: 2 mg	Fiber: 0 g	Sodium: 48 mg

Crunchy Croutons

1. Rub the inside of a large bowl with the garlic. Place the bread cubes in the bowl, spray lightly with the cooking spray, and sprinkle with the Parmesan cheese. Toss the cubes to coat with the garlic and Parmesan.

2. Coat a large baking sheet with nonstick cooking spray. Arrange the bread cubes in a single layer on the sheet, and bake at 350°F for about 10 minutes, or until the croutons are lightly browned and crisp.

3. Cool the croutons to room temperature, and store in an airtight container until ready to use.

Yield: 2¼ cups

1½ teaspoons crushed fresh garlic

3 cups French bread cubes

Olive oil cooking spray

1 tablespoon grated nonfat or reduced-fat Parmesan cheese

NUTRITIONAL FACTS (PER 3-TABLESPOON SERVING)

Calories: 21	Fat: 0.2 g	Protein: 0.8 g
Cholesterol: 0 mg	Fiber: 0.2 g	Sodium: 47 mg

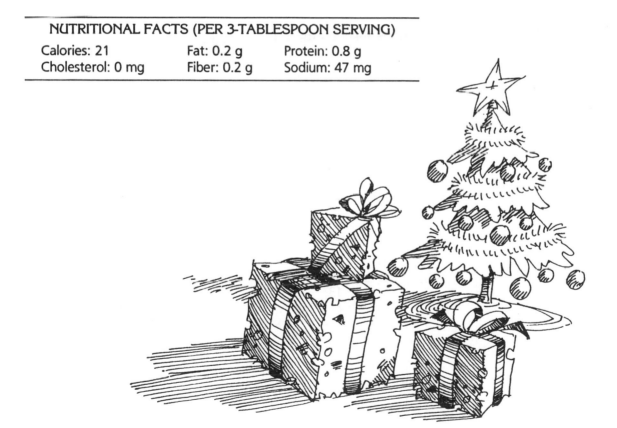

Tarragon Breast of Turkey

Yield: 12 servings

7-pound turkey breast (with bones)

½ cup dry white wine or sherry

BASTING SAUCE

2½ tablespoons frozen orange juice concentrate, thawed

1 teaspoon crushed fresh garlic

1 tablespoon finely chopped fresh tarragon, or 1 teaspoon dried

½ teaspoon chicken bouillon granules

NUTRITIONAL FACTS
(PER 3-OUNCE SERVING)

Calories: 125   Fiber: 0 g
Chol.: 73 mg   Protein: 26 g
Fat: 1 g   Sodium: 86 mg

1. Remove any excess skin from the turkey breast, leaving only enough to cover the top and sides. Rinse the turkey with cool water, and pat dry with paper towels. Place on a rack in a roasting pan.

2. Combine the basting sauce ingredients in a small bowl. Brush half of the sauce over the top and sides of the turkey breast, and reserve the remaining half for later use. Pour the wine or sherry into the bottom of the pan. Cover the pan with aluminum foil, crimping the foil around the edges of the pan to seal.

3. Bake at 325°F for 1½ hours. Carefully remove the foil (steam will escape), and baste the meat with the remaining sauce. Bake uncovered for an additional 45 minutes, or until the skin is golden brown and a meat thermometer inserted in the breast registers 170°F.

4. Transfer the turkey breast to a serving platter. Cover the turkey loosely with aluminum foil, and let sit for 15 minutes before slicing. Serve with Orange-Tarragon Gravy.

Orange Whipped Sweet Potatoes

Yield: 10 servings

3 pounds sweet potatoes (about 6 medium-large)

2 cups orange juice

¼ teaspoon ground nutmeg

¼ teaspoon ground ginger

NUTRITIONAL FACTS
(PER ½-CUP SERVING)

Calories: 120   Fiber: 2.5 g
Cholesterol: 0 mg   Protein: 1.9 g
Fat: 0.3 g   Sodium: 14 mg

1. Peel the potatoes, and cut them into chunks. Place the potatoes and the orange juice in a 4-quart pot. Cover the pot, and bring the potatoes to a boil over medium-high heat. Reduce the heat to low, and cook for about 25 minutes, or until the potatoes are soft. Stir occasionally.

2. Drain all but about ½ cup of the cooking liquid from the pot, reserving the drained liquid. Add the nutmeg and ginger, and mash the potatoes with a potato masher or beat them with an electric mixer until smooth. If the potatoes are too stiff, add a little of the reserved cooking liquid. Serve immediately.

Savory Wheat Stuffing

Yield: 10 servings

1. Combine all of the ingredients except for the egg whites in a 3-quart pot, and stir to mix well. Bring the mixture to a boil over medium-high heat. Stir once, and remove from the heat. Cover and set aside for 45 minutes, or until the liquid has been absorbed and the mixture has cooled.

2. Coat a 2½-quart casserole dish with nonstick cooking spray. Stir the egg whites into the wheat mixture, and spoon the mixture into the dish. Bake at 325°F for 1 hour, or until the mixture is hot and lightly browned. Serve hot.

2 cups bulgur wheat

4 cups water

¾ cup finely chopped onion

¾ cup finely chopped celery (include leaves)

½ cup chopped dried apricots

½ cup dark raisins

2 teaspoons chicken bouillon granules

1 teaspoon poultry seasoning

1 teaspoon dried savory

3 egg whites, lightly beaten

NUTRITIONAL FACTS (PER ¾-CUP SERVING)

Calories: 150	Fat: 0.5 g	Protein: 5.4 g
Cholesterol: 0 mg	Fiber: 6.2 g	Sodium: 209 mg

Orange-Tarragon Gravy

Yield: 2 cups

1. Combine the flour and orange juice in a jar with a tight-fitting lid, and shake until smooth. Set aside.

2. Pour turkey drippings from the roast turkey into a fat separator cup. (If you don't have a separator cup, pour the drippings into a bowl, add a few ice cubes, and skim off the fat once it hardens.) Pour the fat-free drippings into a 2-cup measure, and add enough water to bring the volume up to 1½ cups.

3. Pour the drippings mixture into a 1-quart saucepan, and add the bouillon and seasonings. Bring the mixture to a boil over medium heat. Slowly stir the flour mixture into the gravy, and continue to cook and stir for 1 minute, or until the gravy is thickened and bubbly. Transfer the gravy to a gravy boat, and serve hot.

¼ cup unbleached flour

½ cup orange juice

Roast turkey drippings

1 teaspoon chicken bouillon granules

¾ teaspoon finely chopped fresh tarragon, or ¼ teaspoon dried

⅛ teaspoon ground white pepper

NUTRITIONAL FACTS (PER TABLESPOON)

Calories: 8	Fat: 0 g	Protein: 0.1 g
Cholesterol: 0 mg	Fiber: 0 g	Sodium: 31 mg

Celery Crunch Casserole

Yield: 10 servings

¾ cup evaporated skim milk

3 tablespoons plus 1 teaspoon
  unbleached flour

1 slice whole wheat bread

3 cups sliced celery

1 cup chicken broth

1 can (8 ounces) sliced water
  chestnuts, drained

1 can (4 ounces) sliced mushrooms,
  drained

¼ cup sliced almonds (optional)

¼ cup grated nonfat or reduced-fat
  Parmesan cheese

1. Combine the evaporated milk and flour in a jar with a tight-fitting lid, and shake until smooth. Set aside.

2. Tear the bread slice into small pieces. Place in a food processor or blender, and process into crumbs. Measure the crumbs. You should have ½ cup. (Adjust the amount if necessary.) Set aside.

3. Place the celery and 1 tablespoon of water in a large nonstick skillet. Cook and stir over medium-high heat for about 2 minutes, or until the celery is crisp-tender. Add the chicken broth, and bring the mixture to a boil. Shake the flour mixture, and slowly add it to the celery mixture, stirring constantly. Continue to cook and stir for another minute or 2, or until the mixture is thickened and bubbly. Stir in the water chestnuts, the mushrooms, and, if desired, the almonds.

4. Coat a 2-quart casserole dish with nonstick cooking spray, and place the vegetable mixture in the dish. Combine the bread crumbs and Parmesan cheese in a small bowl, and sprinkle over the mixture.

5. Bake at 350°F for about 35 minutes, or until the mixture is bubbly around the edges and the top is golden brown. Serve hot.

NUTRITIONAL FACTS (PER ½-CUP SERVING)		
Calories: 56	Fat: 0.3 g	Protein: 3.5 g
Cholesterol: 2 mg	Fiber: 1.5 g	Sodium: 238 mg

Old-Fashioned Rice Pudding

Yield: 10 servings

½ cup plus 2 tablespoons uncooked short grain white rice

¾ cup pear or apricot nectar

½ cup water

1 quart skim milk

½ cup sugar

½ cup nonfat dry milk powder

1 cup fat-free egg substitute

2 teaspoons vanilla extract

½ cup dark raisins

¼ teaspoon ground nutmeg

1. Combine the rice, nectar, and water in a 4-quart pot, and bring the mixture to a boil over high heat. Reduce the heat to low, stir once, and cover. Simmer for 15 minutes, or until the rice is almost tender and most of the liquid has been absorbed.

2. Add the milk, sugar, and nonfat dry milk to the rice mixture, and cook over medium heat, stirring constantly, until the mixture just begins to boil. Reduce the heat to low. Stir ½ cup of the hot rice mixture into the egg substitute. Then return the mixture to the pot. Cook and stir for 2 to 3 minutes, or until the pudding thickens slightly. (Do not let it boil.) Remove the pot from the heat, and stir in the vanilla extract and raisins.

3. Coat a 2½-quart casserole dish with nonstick cooking spray, and pour the pudding into the dish. Sprinkle the nutmeg over the top, and place the dish in a pan filled with 1 inch of hot water.

4. Bake at 350°F for 1 hour and 10 minutes, or until a sharp knife inserted midway between the rim of the dish and the center comes out clean. Cool to room temperature. Cover and chill for several hours or overnight before serving.

NUTRITIONAL FACTS (PER ¾-CUP SERVING)		
Calories: 178	Fat: 0.3 g	Protein: 8.4 g
Cholesterol: 2 mg	Fiber: 0.6 g	Sodium: 115 mg

Variations

- If you wish, you can substitute short grain brown rice for the white rice. Simply increase the water to ½ cup plus 2 tablespoons, and cook the rice for 45 to 50 minutes, or until tender.

- For variety, substitute dried cranberries or dried pitted cherries for the raisins.

Christmas Dinner
Menu Two

SERVES 8 TO 10

Hot Artichoke Appetizers (page 29)

Pork Tenderloins
With Pineapple Stuffing (page 95)

Glazed Snow Peas and Carrots (page 96)

Parmesan Scalloped Potatoes (page 96)

Cran-Raspberry Ring (page 97)

Creamy Cherry Cheesecake (page 98)

Pork Tenderloins With Pineapple Stuffing

1. To make the stuffing, tear 4 of the 6 slices of bread into pieces. Place the pieces in a food processor or blender, and process into coarse crumbs. Measure the crumbs. There should be 2 cups. (Adjust the amount if necessary.) Cut the remaining bread into $\frac{1}{2}$-inch cubes, and measure the cubes. There should be 2 cups. (Adjust the amount if necessary.)

2. Place the bread crumbs and cubes in a medium-sized bowl, and add the crushed pineapple, water chestnuts, onion, celery, and seasonings. Toss to mix well. Add the egg whites, and toss to mix well. Set aside.

3. Combine all of the basting sauce ingredients in a small bowl, and stir to mix well. Set aside.

4. Trim the tenderloins of any visible fat and membranes. Rinse with cool water, and pat dry with paper towels. Split each of the tenderloins lengthwise, cutting not quite all the way through, so that each tenderloin can be spread open like a book. Spread $\frac{1}{3}$ of the stuffing mixture over half of each tenderloin, extending the stuffing all the way to the outer edges of the meat. Fold the facing half of each tenderloin over the stuffing-spread half, and use a heavy string to tie the meat together at $2\frac{1}{2}$-inch intervals.

5. Coat a 13-x-16-inch roasting pan with nonstick cooking spray, and lay the tenderloins in the pan, spacing them about 2 inches apart. Bake at 350°F for about 50 minutes, or until the meat is no longer pink inside, occasionally basting with the prepared sauce.

6. Remove the pan from the oven, cover loosely with aluminum foil, and let sit for 5 to 10 minutes before slicing $\frac{1}{2}$ inch thick. Serve immediately.

Yield: 12 servings

3 pork tenderloins, 1 pound each

PINEAPPLE STUFFING

6 slices cracked wheat or multigrain bread

$\frac{1}{2}$ cup crushed pineapple in juice, drained

$\frac{1}{2}$ cup chopped water chestnuts

$\frac{1}{2}$ cup finely chopped onion

$\frac{1}{2}$ cup finely chopped celery

$\frac{3}{4}$ teaspoon dried sage

$\frac{1}{2}$ teaspoon poultry seasoning

2 egg whites, lightly beaten

BASTING SAUCE

3 tablespoons unsweetened pineapple juice

3 tablespoons brown sugar

1 tablespoon spicy mustard

NUTRITIONAL FACTS (PER 4-OUNCE SERVING)		
Calories: 196	Fat: 4.7 g	Protein: 26 g
Cholesterol: 67 mg	Fiber: 1.2 g	Sodium: 147 mg

Glazed Snow Peas and Carrots

Yield: 10 servings

1 teaspoon crushed fresh garlic

1½ teaspoons freshly grated ginger
   root, or ½ teaspoon ground ginger

4 cups (about 1 pound) snow peas or
   sugar snap peas

4 cups (about 4 large) diagonally
   sliced carrots

¼ cup dry sherry or chicken broth

GLAZE

¼ cup chicken broth

2 tablespoons lemon juice

1 tablespoon reduced-sodium soy
   sauce

2 teaspoons sugar

2 teaspoons cornstarch

1. Combine the glaze ingredients in a small bowl, and stir to mix well. Set aside.

2. Coat a large skillet with nonstick cooking spray, and preheat over medium heat. Place the garlic and ginger in the skillet, and stir-fry for 30 seconds. Add the peas and carrots to the skillet, and pour the sherry or chicken broth over the top. Reduce the heat to medium-low, cover, and cook for 8 to 10 minutes, or until the vegetables are crisp-tender. Stir occasionally.

3. Reduce the heat under the skillet to low. Stir the glaze mixture, and pour over the vegetables. Stirring constantly, cook the vegetable mixture for a minute or 2, until the glaze has thickened. Serve immediately.

NUTRITIONAL FACTS (PER ⅔-CUP SERVING)		
Calories: 46	Fat: 0.2 g	Protein: 1.9 g
Cholesterol: 0 mg	Fiber: 2.4 g	Sodium: 89 mg

Parmesan Scalloped Potatoes

Yield: 10 servings

¼ cup unbleached flour

2 tablespoons finely chopped fresh
   parsley, or 2 teaspoons dried

⅛ teaspoon ground white pepper

2 pounds baking potatoes (about 6
   medium)

2 small yellow onions, thinly sliced
   and separated into rings

½ cup grated nonfat or reduced-fat
   Parmesan cheese

2 cups evaporated skim milk

1. Combine the flour, parsley, and pepper in a small bowl, and set aside.

2. Scrub the potatoes, and slice them thinly (slightly less than ¼ inch). Measure the potatoes. There should be 6 cups. (Adjust the amount if necessary.)

3. Coat an 8-x-12-inch baking dish with nonstick cooking spray. Arrange 2 cups of the potatoes in a single layer over the bottom of the dish, slightly overlapping the slices. Lay half of the onion rings over the potatoes, and sprinkle the onions with half of the flour mixture and 2 tablespoons of the Parmesan. Repeat these layers, and top with the remaining 2 cups of potatoes. Pour the milk over the potatoes, and sprinkle with the remaining ¼ cup of Parmesan.

4. Cover the dish with aluminum foil, and bake at 350°F for 45 minutes. Remove the foil, and bake for 30 additional minutes, or until the potatoes are tender and the top is golden brown. Remove the dish from the oven, and let sit for 5 minutes before serving.

NUTRITIONAL FACTS
(PER $\frac{3}{4}$-CUP SERVING)

Calories: 168   Fiber: 2.6 g
Cholesterol: 5 mg Protein: 8.1 g
Fat: 0.3 g   Sodium: 103 mg

Cran-Raspberry Ring

1. To make the first layer, combine the sugar and gelatin in a medium-sized heat-proof bowl, and stir to mix well. Place the juice in a small pot, and heat to boiling. Pour the hot juice over the gelatin mixture, and stir until dissolved. Cool to room temperature, and stir in the fruits. Pour the mixture into a 6-cup ring mold, and chill for several hours, or until firm.

2. To make the second layer, place the gelatin in a medium-sized heat-proof bowl. Place the juice in a small pot, and heat to boiling. Pour the hot juice over the gelatin, and stir until dissolved. Cool to room temperature, and stir in the sour cream. Pour the mixture over the first layer in the mold, and chill for several hours, or until firm.

3. To unmold the ring, dip the mold in warm—but not hot—water for 5 to 10 seconds. Beware: If the water is too hot or the mold remains in the water too long, the gelatin will start to melt. Remove the mold from the water and loosen the edges of the mixture with a knife. Place a serving platter upside down over the mold, and invert the mold onto the platter. Arrange some of the grapes in the center of the ring, and the rest around the outer edges of the ring. Slice and serve chilled.

Variation

For a change of pace, substitute strawberry or cherry gelatin for the raspberry gelatin, and strawberries or pitted sweet cherries for the raspberries.

Yield: 10 servings

FIRST LAYER

$\frac{1}{4}$ cup sugar

1 package (4-serving size) sugar-free raspberry gelatin mix

1$\frac{1}{4}$ cups cranberry juice cocktail

1 cup finely chopped fresh or frozen cranberries, stemmed

1 cup finely chopped fresh or frozen raspberries

SECOND LAYER

1 package (4-serving size) sugar-free raspberry gelatin mix

1 cup cranberry juice cocktail

1 cup nonfat sour cream

1$\frac{1}{4}$ pounds seedless green grapes

NUTRITIONAL FACTS
(PER $\frac{1}{2}$ CUP GELATIN
PLUS $\frac{1}{3}$ CUP GRAPES)

Calories: 123   Fiber: 1.2 g
Cholesterol: 0 mg Protein: 3 g
Fat: 0.4 g   Sodium: 62 mg

Creamy Cherry Cheesecake

Yield: 12 servings

CRUST

8 large (2½-x-5-inch) fat-free graham crackers

2 tablespoons sugar

2 tablespoons fat-free egg substitute

FILLING

15 ounces nonfat ricotta cheese

12 ounces nonfat or reduced-fat cream cheese

½ cup fat-free egg substitute

⅓ cup unbleached flour

¾ cup sugar

2 teaspoons vanilla extract

1 tablespoon lemon juice

TOPPING

1½ cups canned light (low-sugar) cherry pie filling

If you are unable to find fat-free graham crackers, feel free to substitute regular graham crackers. All are relatively low in fat.

1. To make the crust, break the crackers into pieces. Place the broken crackers in the bowl of a food processor or in a blender, and process into fine crumbs. Measure the crumbs. There should be 1¼ cups. (Adjust the amount if necessary.)

2. Return the crumbs to the food processor, and add the sugar and the egg substitute. Process until the mixture is moist and crumbly.

3. Coat a 9-inch springform pan with nonstick cooking spray. Use the back of a spoon to press the crumbs over the bottom of the pan and ½ inch up the sides. Periodically dip the spoon in sugar to prevent sticking.

4. Bake the crust at 350°F for 8 minutes, or until the edges feel firm and dry. Cool the crust to room temperature.

5. Place all of the filling ingredients in a food processor, and process until smooth. Pour the filling into the crust, and bake at 325°F for about 55 minutes, or until the center feels firm when lightly touched. Turn the oven off, and let the cake cool in the oven with the door ajar for 1 hour. (The top will crack slightly during cooling.)

6. Spread the cherry filling over the top of the cooled cake to within ¾ inch of the edges. Refrigerate overnight, cut into wedges, and serve.

NUTRITIONAL FACTS (PER SERVING)

| Calories: 205 | Fat: 0.4 g | Protein: 12.6 g |
| Cholesterol: 10 mg | Fiber: 0.7 g | Sodium: 299 mg |

Hanukkah

Eight days of Hanukkah means lots of friends, family, and good food. The two Hanukkah menus presented here provide something for everyone with both traditional holiday treats and some new dishes, all made *without* the traditional fat.

The first menu begins with an appetizer of homemade Smoked Salmon Spread surrounded by store-bought mini whole grain bagels. Leave room, though, for a hearty main course—Herbed Eye of Round Roast. This satisfying dish is slowly braised in wine and herbs to create a full-bodied flavor without fat.

Accompanying the entrée are Potato Latkes, which are cooked with nonstick cooking spray rather than oil, butter, or chicken fat, and topped with Chunky Applesauce. Other side dishes include a delicious fat-free Spinach and Noodle Kugel and a refreshing Dilled Cucumber Salad.

Winter Wonder Parfaits are the answer to that ever-important question, "What's for dessert?" With layers of angel food cake, nonfat vanilla ice cream, and a festive berry sauce, these parfaits are as beautiful as they are delicious.

Of course, with gifts to buy and wrap, time is probably at a premium. To avoid a last-minute rush, prepare the Spinach and Noodle Kugel to the point of baking the day before, and refrigerate the casserole until you're ready to pop it into the oven. Smoked Salmon Spread and Dilled Cu-cumber Salad can also be prepared the day before, and Chunky Applesauce can be made even further in advance and either refrigerated or frozen.

The sauce for the Winter Wonder Parfaits can be made several days in advance, and then refrigerated until it's time to assemble the desserts. In fact, the only dish that must be fully prepared directly before serving is the roast. Fortunately, this roast nearly makes itself, and will require little of your time.

Our second Hanukkah menu is a delight to the eye as well as the taste buds. The celebration begins with a lovely Ruby Borscht, topped with nonfat sour cream and a sprinkling of fresh dill. Serve a crusty loaf of warm sourdough bread alongside, if desired. The main course, Roast Turkey Breast With Sourdough Stuffing and Savory Gravy, also makes a striking appearance, as do the accompanying dishes of Green Beans and Mushrooms, Sunshine Carrot Salad, and Cranberry-Pear Conserve. For dessert, bring out Festive Noodle Pudding. Loaded with apples, cranberries, and raisins, and crowned with nuts, this creamy pudding is sure to become a family tradition.

Get an early start on this meal by making the Ruby Borscht the day before the holiday. Refrigerate it until it's time to reheat it on the stove. This rosy soup is even better the next day.

The turkey for this menu's spectacular entrée

can be deboned the day before. Also prepare the bread crumbs and cubes and the vegetables for the stuffing in advance, and store them until the day of the dinner, when you will complete the roast preparations.

Rinse and cut the green beans for Green Beans and Mushrooms a day ahead of time. If you purchase mushrooms that are already sliced, this dish can be put together in no time at all.

Both Sunshine Carrot Salad and Cranberry-Pear Conserve should be made in advance to allow the flavors to mingle. Prepare these dishes at least several hours before your dinner, or as early as the previous day.

Finally, fully prepare Festive Noodle Pudding a day in advance, cover the baking dish with aluminum foil, and chill until the afternoon of your dinner. Then bring the pudding to room temperature, or warm it in a 350°F oven for 20 minutes, and serve.

Hanukkah Dinner
Menu One

SERVES 10 TO 12

*Smoked Salmon Spread (page 46) with
Assorted Mini Bagels*

Herbed Eye of Round Roast (page 102)

*Potato Latkes (page 103) with
Chunky Applesauce (page 103)*

Spinach and Noodle Kugel (page 104)

Dilled Cucumber Salad (page 104)

Winter Wonder Parfaits (page 105)

Herbed Eye of Round Roast

Yield: 12 servings

3¼-pound beef eye of round roast

1 tablespoon crushed fresh garlic

½ teaspoon coarsely ground black pepper

½ cup condensed beef broth, undiluted

¼ cup dry red wine or tomato juice

2 bay leaves

1 teaspoon dried marjoram

1 teaspoon dried thyme

1 medium yellow onion, chopped

1. Trim any visible fat from the meat. Rinse the meat, and pat it dry with paper towels. Spread the garlic over both sides of the meat, and sprinkle both sides with pepper.

2. Coat a large cast iron skillet or Dutch oven with nonstick cooking spray, and preheat over medium-high heat. Place the meat in the skillet, and brown it for 2 minutes on each side.

3. Remove the skillet from the heat, and pour the broth and the wine or tomato juice into the bottom of the skillet. Add the bay leaves, and sprinkle the marjoram, thyme, and onion over the top of the roast. Cover the skillet tightly, and bake at 325°F for 45 minutes to 1 hour, or until a meat thermometer inserted in the roast registers 135°F for rare, 145°F for medium-rare, or 155°F for medium doneness.

4. Transfer the roast to a serving platter. Cover the roast loosely with aluminum foil, and let sit for 15 minutes before slicing thinly.

5. Pour the pan juices through a strainer into a fat separator cup. (If the meat was well trimmed, there may be no fat.) Pour the fat-free drippings into a warmed gravy boat or pitcher, and serve hot with the roast.

NUTRITIONAL FACTS (PER 3-OUNCE SERVING)

Calories: 157	Fat: 4.9 g	Protein: 25 g
Cholesterol: 59 mg	Fiber: 0 g	Sodium: 85 mg

Potato Latkes

1. Scrub the potatoes, but leave them unpeeled. Coarsely grate the potatoes into a large bowl of ice water. Let sit for 5 minutes. Drain off the water, and roll the grated potatoes in a clean kitchen towel to remove excess water. Coarsely grate the onions.

2. Place the grated potatoes and onions in a large bowl, and add the remaining ingredients. Stir to mix well.

3. Coat a large nonstick skillet or griddle with nonstick cooking spray, and place it over medium-high heat. For each pancake, spoon $\frac{1}{4}$ cup of the batter onto the skillet, and spread to form a $3\frac{1}{2}$-inch pancake. Cook for 6 minutes on each side over medium-low heat, or until golden brown on the outside and tender on the inside. As the pancakes are done, transfer them to a serving plate and keep warm in a preheated oven.

4. Serve warm with Chunky Applesauce or nonfat sour cream.

Yield: 24 pancakes

$2\frac{1}{2}$ pounds large baking potatoes

1 medium Spanish onion

4 egg whites

2 tablespoons unbleached flour

$\frac{1}{2}$ teaspoon salt

$\frac{1}{4}$ teaspoon ground white pepper

NUTRITIONAL FACTS (PER PANCAKE)

Calories: 50	Fiber: 1.1 g
Cholesterol: 0 mg	Protein: 1.1 g
Fat: 0 g	Sodium: 48 mg

Chunky Applesauce

1. Peel the apples, and cut them into $\frac{1}{2}$-inch chunks. Place the apple chunks and juice concentrate in a 3-quart pot, and stir to combine. Cover and cook over medium-low heat, stirring occasionally, for about 30 minutes, or until the apples are soft.

2. Using a potato masher, mash the mixture to the desired consistency. Serve warm or cold, sprinkling the sauce with a little cinnamon if desired.

Yield: 12 servings

4 pounds Granny Smith apples (14 to 16 medium)

$\frac{1}{2}$ cup frozen apple juice concentrate, thawed

Ground cinnamon (optional)

NUTRITIONAL FACTS (PER $\frac{1}{3}$-CUP SERVING)

Calories: 78	Fiber: 2.0 g
Cholesterol: 0 mg	Protein: 0.2 g
Fat: 0.3 g	Sodium: 2 mg

Spinach and Noodle Kugel

Yield: 12 servings

8 ounces wide no-yolk egg noodles

2 cups dry curd or nonfat cottage cheese

1½ cups grated nonfat or reduced-fat mozzarella cheese

2 packages (10 ounces each) frozen chopped spinach, thawed and squeezed dry

½ cup evaporated skim milk

1 cup fat-free egg substitute

¼ teaspoon ground black pepper

¼ cup grated nonfat or reduced-fat Parmesan cheese

1. Cook the noodles al dente according to package directions. Drain and return to the pot.

2. Add the remaining ingredients, except for the Parmesan, to the noodles, and toss gently to mix. Coat an 8-x-12-inch baking dish with nonstick cooking spray. Transfer the noodle mixture to the dish, and top with the Parmesan.

3. Bake at 350°F for 50 to 60 minutes, or until the filling is set and the top is golden brown. A sharp knife inserted in the center of the kugel should come out clean. Let sit for 5 minutes before serving.

NUTRITIONAL FACTS (PER ¾-CUP SERVING)

Calories: 148	Fat: 0.5 g	Protein: 16 g
Cholesterol: 5 mg	Fiber: 1.6 g	Sodium: 209 mg

Dilled Cucumber Salad

Yield: 12 servings

5 medium cucumbers, peeled and thinly sliced

1½ medium onions, thinly sliced and separated into rings

DRESSING

¼ cup plus 2 tablespoons white wine vinegar

¼ cup water

4½ teaspoons sugar

½ teaspoon salt

4½ teaspoons minced fresh dill, or 1½ teaspoons dried

1. Place the cucumbers and onions in a shallow dish. Combine the dressing ingredients in a small bowl, and pour over the vegetables. Toss to mix well.

2. Cover the salad and chill for several hours or overnight, stirring occasionally, before serving.

NUTRITIONAL FACTS (PER ½-CUP SERVING)

Calories: 24	Fat: 0.2 g	Protein: 0.8 g
Cholesterol: 0 mg	Fiber: 1.3 g	Sodium: 47 mg

Winter Wonder Parfaits

1. To make the sauce, combine the orange juice and sugar in a 2-quart pot. Bring to a boil over medium heat, stirring constantly. Add the cranberries, and bring to a second boil. Reduce the heat to medium-low, and cook, stirring occasionally, for 7 to 9 minutes, or until the cranberry skins have popped open and the mixture has thickened. Add the strawberries, and again bring to a boil. Cook for 2 minutes, stirring occasionally, just until the strawberries begin to break down. Remove the sauce from the heat, and refrigerate until needed.

2. When ready to assemble the parfaits, place $1\frac{1}{2}$ teaspoons of the sauce in the bottom of each of twelve 10-ounce balloon wine glasses or parfait glasses. Crumble 1 slice of the cake, and place half of the slice over the sauce. Top with $\frac{1}{3}$ cup of the ice cream, and a rounded tablespoon of the sauce. Repeat the cake, ice cream, and sauce layers, and serve immediately.

Yield: 12 servings

2 quarts nonfat vanilla ice cream

1 angel food cake (12 ounces), cut into 12 slices

SAUCE

$\frac{1}{2}$ cup plus 2 tablespoons orange juice

$\frac{1}{2}$ cup plus 2 tablespoons sugar

2 cups fresh or frozen cranberries, stemmed

$2\frac{3}{4}$ cups fresh or frozen sliced strawberries

NUTRITIONAL FACTS (PER SERVING)		
Calories: 264	Fat: 0.4 g	Protein: 8.4 g
Cholesterol: 2 mg	Fiber: 1.5 g	Sodium: 299 mg

Hanukkah Dinner
Menu Two

SERVES 10 TO 12

Ruby Borscht (page 107)

*Roast Turkey Breast
With Sourdough Stuffing (page 108)*

Savory Gravy (page 109)

Green Beans and Mushrooms (page 110)

Sunshine Carrot Salad (page 110)

Cranberry-Pear Conserve (page 111)

Festive Noodle Pudding (page 112)

Ruby Borscht

1. Combine the beets, carrots, onion, celery, broth or water, brown sugar, bouillon granules, and pepper in a 4-quart pot, and bring to a boil over high heat. Reduce the heat to low, cover, and simmer for 20 minutes, or until the vegetables are tender.

2. Add the cabbage, and simmer uncovered for 15 minutes, or until the cabbage is tender. Remove the pot from the heat and stir in the vinegar.

3. Ladle the soup into individual serving bowls. Top each serving with a rounded tablespoon of sour cream and a sprinkling of dill, and serve.

NUTRITIONAL FACTS (PER 1-CUP SERVING)

Calories: 67	Fat: 0.4 g	Protein: 2.6 g
Cholesterol: 0 mg	Fiber: 2.3 g	Sodium: 335 mg

Yield: 12 servings

4 cups coarsely shredded peeled beets (about 1¼ pounds)

2 cups diced peeled carrots (about 2 large)

1½ cups chopped onion

1 cup thinly sliced celery

7 cups unsalted beef broth or water

3–4 tablespoons brown sugar

1 tablespoon beef bouillon granules

¼ teaspoon coarsely ground black pepper

2 cups thinly sliced cabbage

¼ cup white wine vinegar

TOPPINGS

1½ cups nonfat sour cream

2 tablespoons minced fresh dill

Roast Turkey Breast
With Sourdough Stuffing

Yield: 12 servings

7-pound turkey breast (with bones)

SOURDOUGH STUFFING

1-pound loaf sourdough bread

1¼ cups finely chopped onion

1 cup finely chopped celery

1 cup chopped fresh mushrooms

1¼ teaspoons poultry seasoning

1¼ teaspoons dried savory

¼ teaspoon ground black pepper

4 egg whites

1¼ cups chicken broth

NUTRITIONAL FACTS
(PER 3 OUNCES MEAT
PLUS ⅔ CUP STUFFING)

Calories: 278	Fiber: 1.6 g
Chol.: 97 mg	Protein: 39 g
Fat: 2.5 g	Sodium: 337 mg

Your butcher can debone the turkey breast for you, or you can debone the breast yourself by following the instructions provided below.

1. To debone the turkey breast, place the breast, skin side down, on a large cutting board. Use a small sharp knife to cut along the bones, starting at the ribs, to release the meat. As you cut around the wishbone and backbone, be careful not to cut through the skin. Discard the bones, and lay the meat flat, skin side down. You should now have a butterfly-shaped piece of meat that is approximately 10 by 14 inches in size. Trim away any jagged edges, rinse with cool water, and pat dry. (Debone the breast up to 24 hours in advance, if desired, and refrigerate the meat until you're ready to fully prepare the dish.)

2. To make the stuffing, tear ¾ of the bread into small pieces. Place the pieces in a food processor or blender, and process into coarse crumbs. Measure the crumbs. There should be 6 cups. (Adjust the amount if necessary.) Cut the remaining bread into ½-inch cubes, and measure the cubes. There should be 6 cups. (Adjust the amount if necessary.)

3. Place the bread crumbs and cubes in a large bowl, and add the onion, celery, mushrooms, seasonings, and egg whites. Toss to mix well.

4. Set aside 3 cups of stuffing to stuff the turkey breast. Add ¼ cup of chicken broth to the remaining stuffing, and toss to mix well. Coat a 2-quart casserole dish with nonstick cooking spray, and place the stuffing in the dish. Bake uncovered at 325°F for 1 hour, or until lightly browned on top. (Place the casserole in the oven 1 hour before the turkey is done.)

5. To stuff the turkey breast, lay the breast flat, skin side down, on a clean surface, and spread the 3 cups of reserved stuffing over half the breast, spreading the stuffing from the center all the way to the outer edges. Fold the other breast half over the stuffing to cover, and use a heavy string to tie the breast together in 3 places.

6. Place the breast on a rack in a large roasting pan, and pour the remaining cup of chicken broth into the pan. Cover the pan loosely with aluminum foil, and bake at 325°F for 1 hour and 10 minutes. Uncover the pan, and bake for 30 additional minutes, or until the skin is golden brown and a meat thermometer inserted in the breast registers 170°F. Occasionally baste with the pan juices during cooking. (Note that the juices which remain in the pan will be used to make Savory Gravy.)

7. Transfer the turkey breast to a serving platter. Cover the turkey loosely with aluminum foil, and let sit for 15 minutes before slicing. Serve with Savory Gravy.

Savory Gravy

1. Combine the flour and milk in a jar with a tight-fitting lid, and shake until smooth. Set aside.

2. Pour the turkey drippings from the roast turkey breast into a fat separator cup. (If you don't have a separator cup, pour the drippings into a bowl, add a few ice cubes, and skim off the fat once it rises and hardens.) Pour the fat-free drippings into a 2-cup measure, and add enough water to bring the volume up to $1\frac{3}{4}$ cups.

3. Pour the drippings mixture into a $1\frac{1}{2}$-quart saucepan, and add the bouillon granules and seasonings. Bring the mixture to a boil over medium heat, reduce the heat to low, and simmer for 5 minutes.

4. Slowly stir the flour mixture into the gravy, and continue to cook and stir until the mixture is thickened and bubbly. Transfer the gravy to a warmed gravy boat or pitcher, and serve hot with the stuffed turkey breast.

Yield: $2\frac{1}{4}$ cups

$\frac{1}{4}$ cup plus $1\frac{1}{2}$ teaspoons unbleached flour

$\frac{1}{2}$ cup skim milk

Roast turkey drippings

1 teaspoon chicken bouillon granules

$\frac{1}{4}$ teaspoon poultry seasoning

$\frac{1}{4}$ teaspoon dried savory

$\frac{1}{8}$ teaspoon ground black pepper

NUTRITIONAL FACTS (PER TABLESPOON)		
Calories: 7	Fat: 0 g	Protein: 0.4 g
Cholesterol: 0 mg	Fiber: 0 mg	Sodium: 30 mg

Green Beans and Mushrooms

Yield: 12 servings

2 pounds fresh green beans

2 cups sliced fresh mushrooms

¼ cup water

1½ teaspoons chicken bouillon granules

1 teaspoon dried thyme

¼ teaspoon ground black pepper

1. Rinse the beans with cool water. Trim the ends, and cut into 1-inch pieces. Place the beans and the remaining ingredients in a 3-quart pot, and stir to mix well.

2. Bring the beans to a boil over medium heat. Reduce the heat to low, cover, and, stirring occasionally, simmer for 12 to 15 minutes, or until the beans are just tender. (Add a tablespoon or 2 of water if the pot becomes too dry.) Serve immediately.

Time-Saving Tip

To make this dish totally fuss-free, substitute 2 pounds of frozen (thawed) cut green beans for the fresh green beans.

NUTRITIONAL FACTS (PER ½-CUP SERVING)		
Calories: 29	Fat: 0.2 g	Protein: 1.7 g
Cholesterol: 0 mg	Fiber: 2.7 g	Sodium: 132 mg

Sunshine Carrot Salad

Yield: 12 servings

4 cups grated carrots (about 8 medium-large)

1 can (20 ounces) pineapple chunks in juice, drained, or 2 cups fresh pineapple chunks

2 cans (11 ounces each) mandarin orange sections in juice or light syrup, drained

1 cup golden raisins

DRESSING

¾ cup nonfat sour cream

½ cup nonfat or reduced-fat mayonnaise

1. Combine the carrots, pineapple chunks, oranges, and raisins in a large bowl, and toss gently to mix. Combine the dressing ingredients in a small bowl, and spread over the carrot mixture. Toss gently to mix well.

2. Cover the salad and chill for at least 2 hours before serving.

NUTRITIONAL FACTS (PER ½-CUP SERVING)		
Calories: 106	Fat: 0.3 g	Protein: 2.2 g
Cholesterol: 0 mg	Fiber: 2 g	Sodium: 139 mg

Cranberry-Pear Conserve

Yield: 12 servings

1. Combine all of the ingredients in a 2-quart pot, and bring to a boil over medium-high heat. Reduce the heat to low, and simmer uncovered, stirring occasionally, for about 10 minutes, or until the cranberry skins have popped open and the mixture has thickened.

2. Cover the conserve and chill for several hours or overnight. Serve as an accompaniment to the turkey.

3 cups diced fresh pears (about 3 medium)

2 cups fresh or frozen cranberries, stemmed

¾ cup pear nectar

¼ cup light brown sugar

¼ cup golden raisins

¼ teaspoon ground cinnamon

¼ teaspoon ground nutmeg

¼ teaspoon ground ginger

NUTRITIONAL FACTS (PER ¼-CUP SERVING)

Calories: 60	Fat: 0.2 g	Protein: 0.4 g
Cholesterol: 0 mg	Fiber: 1.7 g	Sodium: 2 mg

Festive Noodle Pudding

Yield: 12 servings

8 ounces medium or wide eggless noodles

2 cups dry curd or nonfat cottage cheese

1 cup nonfat or reduced-fat cream cheese, softened to room temperature

1½ cups fat-free egg substitute

½ cup sugar

2 teaspoons vanilla extract

2 cups chopped apples (about 3 medium)

½ cup plus 2 tablespoons coarsely chopped fresh or frozen cranberries, stemmed

½ cup golden raisins

TOPPING

3 tablespoons sugar

2 tablespoons chopped walnuts

1. Cook the noodles al dente according to package directions. Drain, rinse with cool water, and drain again. Set aside.

2. Combine the cottage cheese, cream cheese, egg substitute, sugar, and vanilla extract in a large bowl, and stir to mix well. Add the drained noodles, apples, cranberries, and raisins, and toss gently to mix.

3. Coat an 8-x-12-inch pan with nonstick cooking spray, and spread the noodle mixture evenly in the pan. Combine the topping ingredients in a small bowl, and sprinkle over the noodle mixture.

4. Bake uncovered at 350°F for about 1 hour and 10 minutes, or until a sharp knife inserted halfway between the edge of the pan and the center comes out clean. Cool for 20 minutes, cut into squares, and serve warm or at room temperature.

NUTRITIONAL FACTS (PER SERVING)		
Calories: 210	Fat: 1.2 g	Protein: 13 g
Cholesterol: 5 mg	Fiber: 1.3 g	Sodium: 145 mg

Variation

For variety, omit the apples and instead use 2 cups of frozen pitted sweet cherries, cut in half, or 2 cups of drained pineapple tidbits.

Passover

Matzo—a cracker-like unleavened bread—takes center stage during the week of Passover. Fortunately, matzo has always been fat-free, and is wonderfully versatile as well. In the two Seder menus presented in this section, you'll find this and other traditional Passover foods married with healthful fat-free ingredients to make untraditionally light and delicious holiday dishes.

In our first Seder menu, clear Chicken Soup With Matzo Balls begins the meal. Be prepared for a surprise. These matzo balls are made light and tender with absolutely *no* egg yolks or oil! The main course, Baked Chicken Paprika, starts with skinless chicken, and is well seasoned with garlic, onions, tomato juice, and paprika. Add nonfat sour cream if you like. Passover Eggplant Casserole and Sweet Potato and Carrot Tzimmes are the colorful fat-free accompaniments. What's for dessert? Cocoa Marble Meringues. These crisp, light cookies are perfect paired with a cup of after-dinner coffee. For a beautiful presentation, serve with a platter of fresh whole strawberries.

Give yourself time to enjoy this special holiday by getting a head start on your menu preparations. You can easily prepare Chicken Soup with Matzo Balls the day before. Just cover the soup, chill it, and reheat before serving. Also skin the chicken for your entrée a day in advance so that the dish can be quickly assembled and popped into the oven about one and a half hours before dinner is served. Once it begins baking, this dish will need little of your time.

Prepare the eggplant mixture for the Passover Eggplant Casserole a day in advance, and assemble and bake the dish before serving time. The Sweet Potato and Carrot Tzimmes can be fully prepared the day before, if desired, and reheated in just twenty minutes before dinner begins. Or cut up the sweet potatoes, carrots, and prunes the day before, and assemble and bake the dish on the day of your dinner.

The Cocoa Marble Meringues can also be baked the day before your Seder, and stored in an airtight container to keep them crisp. If you've chosen to accompany the meringues with strawberries, the fruit can, of course, be cleaned, dried, and refrigerated on the morning of your gathering, and kept chilled until serving time.

Our second Passover menu offers another collection of crowd-pleasing dishes, many of which are Passover favorites given fat-free makeovers for a healthy and satisfying holiday dinner.

Our second menu, like our first, begins with a Passover must—matzo ball soup. This version features a tasty broth enriched with sweet potatoes, as well as matzo balls made light and tender with whipped egg whites instead of egg yolks and oil.

The soup course is followed by a hearty main

dish—Braised Beef with Carrots and Prunes. Beef round replaces the traditional brisket in this recipe to cut the fat by almost 75 percent. On the side are Asparagus Vinaigrette, a simple but savory dish, and flavorful Scalloped Tomato Matzo. For dessert, enjoy warm Apple Matzo Kugel. Moistened with fresh apples and apple juice instead of butter or margarine, this dessert is bursting with flavor.

To save time on the day of your dinner, much of this meal can be made ahead, while the rest can be easily assembled during the hours before your guests arrive. Golden Matzo Soup, for instance, can be prepared the day before your dinner. Cover the soup and chill it, and reheat just before serving.

The entrée of braised beef can be easily assembled in the hours before guests arrive, and then placed in the oven, where it will require little attention until it's time to make the gravy. Or, if you choose, make this dish the day before your dinner, and reheat it right before serving.

Scalloped Tomato Matzo, one of the menu's two accompaniments, must be assembled and baked directly before serving time. But if you slice the onions and assemble the ingredients in advance, this dish can be whipped together in a matter of minutes.

Asparagus Vinaigrette is the perfect make-ahead dish, as it should be fully prepared the day before your Seder to allow the flavors to blend. Arrange these flavorful vegetables in a serving bowl, and chill until dinner begins.

Our second Seder's dessert can be made the day before your dinner, if desired, and refrigerated until an hour before serving. Cover it with aluminum foil and reheat it for fifteen to twenty minutes if you'd like to serve it warm. For even less fuss, serve it at room temperature. It will be equally delicious!

Passover Seder
Menu One

SERVES 6 TO 8

Chicken Soup
With Matzo Balls (page 116)

Baked Chicken Paprika (page 117)

Passover Eggplant Casserole (page 118)

Sweet Potato and Carrot Tzimmes (page 118)

Cocoa Marble Meringues (page 119)

Fresh Strawberries

Chicken Soup With Matzo Balls

Yield: 8 servings

6 cups unsalted chicken stock

1 medium Spanish onion, chopped

1 stalk celery, thinly sliced

2 teaspoons chicken bouillon granules

$\frac{1}{8}$ teaspoon ground white pepper

$\frac{1}{8}$ teaspoon ground nutmeg

2 tablespoons finely chopped fresh parsley, or 2 teaspoons dried

1 recipe Fluffy Fat-Free Matzo Balls, prepared (below)

1. Place the chicken stock, onion, celery, bouillon granules, pepper, and nutmeg in a $2\frac{1}{2}$-quart pot. Bring to a boil over high heat. Then reduce the heat to low and cover the pot. Simmer for 30 minutes, or until the vegetables are very tender.

2. Use a slotted spoon to transfer the vegetables from the pot to a blender or food processor. Add 1 cup of the hot broth, and process, with the lid slightly ajar to let steam escape, for 30 seconds, or until the mixture is smooth. Return the blended mixture to the pot.

3. Add the parsley and matzo balls to the soup, and simmer, covered, for 10 minutes. Ladle the soup into individual serving bowls, placing 2 matzo balls in each bowl, and serve hot.

NUTRITIONAL FACTS
(PER $\frac{3}{4}$ CUP BROTH AND 2 MATZO BALLS)

| Calories: 62 | Fat: 0.3 g | Protein: 4.2 g |
| Cholesterol: 0 mg | Fiber: 0.8 g | Sodium: 434 mg |

Fluffy Fat-Free Matzo Balls

Yield: 8 servings

6 egg whites, warmed to room temperature

$\frac{1}{2}$ teaspoon salt

1 cup plus 2 tablespoons matzo meal

1 teaspoon chicken bouillon granules, or $\frac{1}{2}$ teaspoon salt (optional)

1. Place the egg whites in the bowl of an electric mixer, and sprinkle with the salt. Beat at high speed until stiff peaks form when the beaters are removed. Remove the beaters, and gently fold in the matzo meal, 3 tablespoons at a time. Cover the mixture, and chill for 15 minutes.

2. Half fill a 6-quart stock pot with water, and bring to a rapid boil over high heat. Add the chicken bouillon granules or salt if desired. Coat your hands with nonstick cooking spray, and gently shape the chilled matzo meal mixture into 16 ($1\frac{1}{4}$-inch) balls. Drop the balls into the boiling water, reduce the heat to medium-low, and cover the pot. Simmer for 20 minutes, or until the matzo balls are firm.

3. Remove the matzo balls with a slotted spoon, and add immediately to your chicken soup, or store in a covered container for 1 to 2 days.

Variation

Cook the matzo balls in unsalted chicken or vegetable stock instead of water.

NUTRITIONAL FACTS
(PER SERVING)

Calories: 48	Fiber: 0.3 g
Cholesterol: 0 mg	Protein: 3.6 g
Fat: 0 g	Sodium: 175 mg

Baked Chicken Paprika

1. Rinse the chicken parts and pat them dry with paper towels. Sprinkle the pieces with salt, and rub the garlic over both sides.

2. Coat a large skillet with nonstick cooking spray, and place over medium-high heat. Place the chicken parts in the skillet 3 pieces at a time, and brown for 2 minutes on each side. Add a tablespoon of water to the skillet if the chicken begins to stick.

3. Coat a 9-x-13-inch pan with nonstick cooking spray, and arrange half of the onion rings over the bottom of the pan. Pour the tomato juice in the pan, and lay the chicken in a single layer over the onions and tomato juice. Sprinkle the paprika over the chicken, and cover with the remaining onion rings.

4. Cover the pan tightly with foil, and bake at 350°F for 1 hour. Remove the foil, and bake for 15 more minutes, or until the chicken is tender and no pink is found when the meat is cut. Transfer the chicken to a serving platter, and keep warm.

5. Pour the pan juices into a fat separator cup. (If you don't have a separator cup, pour the juices into a bowl, add a few ice cubes, and skim off the fat once it rises and hardens.) If desired, drizzle the defatted juices over the chicken, and serve the chicken immediately. If preferred, pour the defatted juices into a 1-quart pot, and place over medium heat. Add the sour cream, and cook and stir until the mixture is smooth and heated through. Transfer the gravy to a warmed gravy boat or pitcher, and serve hot with the chicken.

Yield: 8 servings

7 pounds chicken breasts (with bone) and leg quarters, skinned

½ teaspoon salt

2 tablespoons crushed fresh garlic

4 medium yellow onions, thinly sliced and separated into rings

⅓ cup tomato juice

2 tablespoons ground paprika

1 cup nonfat sour cream (optional)

NUTRITIONAL FACTS
(PER 3-OUNCE SERVING,
WHITE MEAT)

Calories: 165	Fiber: 1.1 g
Chol.: 72 mg	Protein: 27.3 g
Fat: 3.3 g	Sodium: 235 mg

NUTRITIONAL FACTS
(PER 3-OUNCE SERVING,
DARK MEAT)

Calories: 171	Fiber: 1.1 g
Chol.: 79 mg	Protein: 25 g
Fat: 5.1 g	Sodium: 253 mg

Passover Eggplant Casserole

Yield: 8 servings

1 medium eggplant, peeled and cut into 1/2-inch cubes

1 large onion, thinly sliced

1 small green bell pepper, chopped

3 large plum tomatoes, diced

1½ cups unsalted tomato sauce

1 teaspoon dried tarragon, or 1 tablespoon fresh

½ teaspoon salt

¼ teaspoon ground black pepper

1 cup matzo farfel, or 2 matzos, broken into small pieces

1½ cups nonfat ricotta cheese (optional)

1. Place the eggplant, onion, green pepper, tomatoes, tomato sauce, tarragon, salt, and pepper in a 4-quart pot. Cover and simmer over low heat, stirring occasionally, for about 15 minutes, or until the eggplant is tender.

2. Coat a 2-quart casserole dish with nonstick cooking spray. Spread half of the vegetable mixture over the bottom of the dish. Arrange the matzo farfel or broken matzos over the vegetables, and top with the cheese, if desired. End with a layer of the remaining vegetable mixture.

3. Bake uncovered at 350°F for 25 minutes, or until bubbly around the edges. Serve hot.

NUTRITIONAL FACTS (PER ¾-CUP SERVING)

Calories: 61	Fat: 0.2 g	Protein: 2 g
Cholesterol: 0 mg	Fiber: 2.1 g	Sodium: 144 mg

Sweet Potato and Carrot Tzimmes

Yield: 10 servings

4 cups thinly sliced peeled sweet potatoes (about 3 medium)

4 cups thinly sliced peeled Granny Smith apples (about 5 medium)

1 cup thinly sliced carrots (about 2 medium)

¾ cup small pitted prunes, halved

2 tablespoons orange juice

2 tablespoons honey

2 tablespoons brown sugar

1½ teaspoons dried grated orange rind, or 1½ tablespoons fresh

1½ teaspoons potato starch

1. Coat a 2½-quart casserole dish with nonstick cooking spray. Spread half of the potatoes over the bottom of the dish. Top with half of the apples, half of the carrots, and, finally, half of the prunes. Repeat the layers.

2. In a small bowl, combine the orange juice, honey, brown sugar, orange rind, and potato starch, and stir to mix. Pour the orange juice mixture over the tzimmes. Cover the pan with foil, and cut four 1-inch slits in the foil to allow steam to escape.

3. Bake at 350°F for 1 hour and 15 minutes, or until the layers are tender. Serve hot.

NUTRITIONAL FACTS (PER ⅔-CUP SERVING)

Calories: 155	Fat: 0.4 g	Protein: 1.6 g
Cholesterol: 0 mg	Fiber: 4.1 g	Sodium: 16 mg

Cocoa Marble Meringues

These light and airy treats are best made on a nonhumid day, as humidity can cause them to become slightly sticky. If this happens, return the meringues to a 250°F oven for 7 to 8 minutes, cool to room temperature, and store in an airtight container.

1. Place the nuts on a small baking sheet, and bake at 350°F for 10 minutes, or until lightly browned with a toasted fragrance. Cool to room temperature.

2. Place 3 tablespoons of the toasted nuts in a mini-food processor, and process until finely ground. Set aside. (If you do not have a mini-food processor, try fitting the bottom portion of your blender in a pint jar to form a mini-blender. Or grind the nuts with a mortar and pestle.)

3. Place the egg whites in the bowl of an electric mixer, and beat on high until foamy. Add the cream of tartar and salt, and continue beating until soft peaks form. Still beating, slowly add first the sugar, 1 tablespoon at a time, and then the vanilla extract. Gently fold in the ground nuts and, if desired, the coarsely chopped nuts.

4. Transfer ¼ of the egg white mixture to a separate bowl, and gently fold in the cocoa powder. Return the cocoa mixture to the original bowl, and gently fold the 2 mixtures together just enough to produce a marbled effect.

5. Line a large baking sheet with aluminum foil. (Do not grease the sheet or coat it with cooking spray.) Drop heaping teaspoonfuls of the meringue onto the baking sheet, placing them about 1½ inches apart.

6. Bake at 250°F for 45 minutes, or until the meringues feel firm to a light touch. Turn the oven off, and let the meringues cool in the oven for 2 hours with the door closed. Remove the pan from the oven and peel the meringues from the foil. Serve immediately, or store in an airtight container.

Yield: 42 meringues

3 tablespoons coarsely chopped almonds, walnuts, or pecans

⅓ cup coarsely chopped almonds, walnuts, or pecans (optional)

4 egg whites, warmed to room temperature

¼ teaspoon cream of tartar

¼ teaspoon salt

¾ cup sugar

2 teaspoons vanilla extract

2 tablespoons cocoa powder

NUTRITIONAL FACTS
(PER COOKIE)

Calories: 19	Fiber: 0.1 g
Cholesterol: 0 mg	Protein: 0.5 g
Fat: 0.3 g	Sodium: 18 mg

Passover Seder
Menu Two

SERVES 6 TO 8

Golden Matzo Ball Soup (page 121)

Braised Beef
With Carrots and Prunes (page 121)

Asparagus Vinaigrette (page 122)

Scalloped Tomato Matzo (page 123)

Apple Matzo Kugel (page 123)

Golden Matzo Ball Soup

1. Place the chicken stock, sweet potato or squash, onion, celery, and bouillon in a 2½-quart pot. Bring to a boil over high heat. Then reduce the heat to low and cover the pot. Simmer for 30 minutes, or until the vegetables are very tender.

2. Use a slotted spoon to transfer the vegetables from the pot to a blender or food processor. Add 1 cup of the hot broth, and process, with the lid slightly ajar, for 30 seconds, or until the mixture is smooth. Return the blended mixture to the pot.

3. Add the matzo balls to the soup, and simmer, covered, for 10 minutes. Ladle the soup into individual serving bowls, placing 2 matzo balls in each bowl, and serve hot.

Yield: 8 servings

5 cups unsalted vegetable or chicken stock

1¼ cups peeled and diced sweet potato or butternut squash

1 medium yellow onion, chopped

1 stalk celery, thinly sliced

2 teaspoons vegetable or chicken bouillon granules

1 recipe Fluffy Fat-Free Matzo Balls, prepared (page 116)

NUTRITIONAL FACTS
(PER ¾ CUP BROTH AND 2 MATZO BALLS)

Calories: 81	Fat: 0.4 g	Protein: 4.4 g
Cholesterol: 0 mg	Fiber: 1.2 g	Sodium: 437 mg

Braised Beef With Carrots and Prunes

1. Trim any visible fat from the meat. Rinse the meat, and pat it dry with paper towels. Sprinkle both sides with pepper.

2. Coat a large cast-iron skillet or Dutch oven with nonstick cooking spray, and preheat over medium-high heat. Place the meat in the skillet, and brown it for 2 minutes on each side. Remove the skillet from the heat, and spread the onions on the meat. Pour the beef broth in the bottom of the skillet, cover the skillet tightly, and bake at 325°F for 2 hours.

3. Remove the skillet from the oven, and carefully remove the cover. (Steam will escape.) Place the carrots and prunes around the meat, and sprinkle the meat, carrots, and prunes with the cinnamon, salt, and lemon juice. Cover the skillet tightly, and return it to the oven for another 30 minutes, or until the meat

Yield: 8 servings

2½-lb. top round roast or London broil

½ teaspoon coarsely ground pepper

1 medium yellow onion, chopped

½ cup beef broth

6 large carrots (about 1¼ pounds), peeled and cut into ¼-inch slices

1 cup pitted prunes

½ teaspoon ground cinnamon

½ teaspoon salt

1 tablespoon lemon juice

3 tablespoons brown sugar

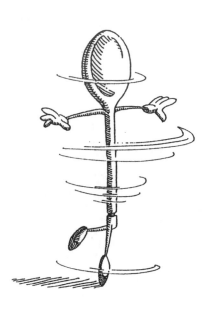

and carrots are tender. Transfer the meat, carrots, and prunes to a serving platter, and keep warm.

4. To make the gravy, pour the meat drippings into a fat separator cup. (If you don't have a separator cup, pour the drippings into a bowl, add a few ice cubes, and skim off the fat once it rises and hardens.) Pour the fat-free drippings into a 1-cup measure, and add enough water to bring the volume up to $\frac{3}{4}$ cup.

5. Return the drippings mixture to the skillet, and add the brown sugar. Bring the mixture to a boil over medium heat, and cook and stir for 1 minute, or until the sugar is dissolved. Transfer the gravy to a warmed gravy boat or pitcher, and serve hot with the meat and vegetables.

NUTRITIONAL FACTS (PER SERVING)

Calories: 283	Fat: 4.6 g	Protein: 28 g
Cholesterol: 59 mg	Fiber: 5.1 g	Sodium: 344 mg

Asparagus Vinaigrette

Yield: 8 servings

2 packages (10 ounces each) frozen cut asparagus, thawed, or 4 cups 1-inch asparagus pieces, steamed

$\frac{1}{4}$ cup finely chopped onion

$\frac{1}{2}$ cup diced red bell pepper

DRESSING

2 tablespoons white wine vinegar

2 tablespoons lemon juice

1 tablespoon grainy Dijon mustard

1 tablespoon olive oil (optional)

$\frac{3}{4}$ teaspoon dried oregano

1 tablespoon sugar

$\frac{1}{4}$ teaspoon salt

1. Combine the vegetables in a shallow dish. Combine the dressing ingredients in a small bowl until the sugar dissolves, and pour over the vegetables. Toss to mix well.

2. Cover the salad and chill for several hours or overnight before serving.

NUTRITIONAL FACTS (PER $\frac{1}{2}$-CUP SERVING)

Calories: 30	Fat: 0.3 g	Protein: 2.2 g
Cholesterol: 0 mg	Fiber: 1.6 g	Sodium: 89 mg

Scalloped Tomato Matzo

1. In a large bowl, combine the tomatoes, salt, and pepper.

2. Coat an 8-inch square pan with cooking spray. Cover the bottom of the pan with half of the onions. Lay 1 matzo over the onions, and top with half of the tomatoes. Place another matzo over the tomatoes, and cover with the remaining tomatoes. Crumble the remaining matzo into small pieces, and sprinkle over the top. Separate the remaining onion into rings, and arrange over the matzo.

3. Bake uncovered at 350°F for 40 minutes, or until the tomatoes are bubbly and the onion rings are browned. Serve hot.

Yield: 8 servings

2 cans (1 pound each) unsalted stewed tomatoes, undrained
$\frac{1}{2}$ teaspoon salt
$\frac{1}{4}$ teaspoon ground black pepper
1 large Spanish onion, thinly sliced
3 matzos

NUTRITIONAL FACTS (PER $\frac{3}{4}$-CUP SERVING)

Calories: 81	Fat: 0.3 g	Protein: 2 g
Cholesterol: 0 mg	Fiber: 2.5 g	Sodium: 152 mg

Apple Matzo Kugel

1. Combine topping ingredients in a small bowl, and set aside.

2. Place the matzo farfel in a large bowl. Add the apple juice, and stir to mix well. Set aside for 5 minutes.

3. Add the egg substitute, sugar, cinnamon, and salt to the matzo mixture, and stir gently to mix well. Stir in the apples and raisins and, if desired, the walnuts.

4. Coat an 8-inch square pan with nonstick cooking spray, and spread the mixture evenly in the pan. Sprinkle with the topping, and bake at 350°F for 40 minutes, or until a sharp knife inserted in the center comes out clean. Let sit for 15 minutes before cutting into squares. Serve warm or at room temperature.

Yield: 9 servings

2 cups matzo farfel, or 3$\frac{1}{2}$ matzos, broken into small pieces
1 cup apple juice
1 cup fat-free egg substitute
$\frac{1}{4}$ cup plus 2 tablespoons sugar
$\frac{1}{2}$ teaspoon ground cinnamon
$\frac{1}{4}$ teaspoon salt
2$\frac{1}{2}$ cups finely chopped tart apples (about 4 medium)
$\frac{1}{2}$ cup golden raisins
$\frac{1}{4}$ cup chopped walnuts (optional)

TOPPING

1 tablespoon plus 1 teaspoon finely ground walnuts
1 tablespoon plus 1 teaspoon sugar

NUTRITIONAL FACTS (PER $\frac{2}{3}$-CUP SERVING)

Calories: 184	Fat: 1 g	Protein: 5.1 g
Cholesterol: 0 mg	Fiber: 1.9 g	Sodium: 110 mg

Easter

Looking for an alternative to that traditional salty Easter ham and all the fatty trimmings? In this section, you'll find *two* delightful alternatives: a light, no-fuss Easter brunch, and a simple but elegant Easter dinner.

Our first menu proves that traditional brunch favorites can be healthy while still being deliciously satisfying. Start off with Sensational Broccoli Strudels. Crisp and light, these piping-hot treats make a striking first impression. Then present the main course—a Ham and Cheese Bake made with fat-free egg substitute, nonfat cheese, and a small amount of lean ham. Hearty and flavorful, this casserole has less than one gram of fat per serving. Spring Pasta Salad, Blueberry-Orange Muffins, a selection of hot store-bought bagels, and your choice of fresh fruit juice round out this filling yet fat-free meal. But save room for dessert—Cappuccino Cheesecake. Creamy and rich-tasting, this fabulous confection adds that perfect finishing touch.

To leave yourself time for that Easter-egg hunt, prepare much of this menu ahead of time. Sensational Broccoli Strudels are a boon to the make-ahead chef, as they can be prepared several days in advance. Just assemble them to the point of baking, and freeze them in single layers in an airtight container. On Easter morning, remove the strudels from the freezer, place them on a baking sheet, and allow them to sit for forty-five minutes before baking.

Prepare the filling for the Ham and Cheese Bake as early as the night before, and refrigerate the filling until you're ready to assemble the dish. Then pop the casserole into the oven one hour before serving.

Spring Pasta Salad *should* be prepared ahead of time to allow the flavors to blend, so make this salad as early as the day before your brunch. Also bake the Blueberry-Orange Muffins the day before, and reheat them just before serving for that fresh-from-the-oven taste.

Cappuccino Cheesecake must be baked at least eight hours in advance. Decorate it right before serving, and present it as your pièce de résistance.

But perhaps you've decided to make an Easter dinner instead of a brunch. If so, our holiday feast is sure to please family and friends alike. Simple, yet special enough for any occasion, this menu captures the essence of spring with its fresh, light, and flavorful dishes.

Creamy Cucumber Dip served with fresh vegetables and whole grain crackers makes for a great beginning. Then comes a marinated tenderloin of pork, fragrant with rosemary and garlic. Corn Pudding, the perfect accompaniment, is made thick and rich with puréed corn instead of cream. Company Carrot-Raisin Salad and Fresh-Steamed Asparagus with a warm Honey Mustard Sauce add balance and color while continuing the spring theme. And the crowning touch? Stunning Chocolate Raspberry Torte. Rich, chocolatey, and moist, this delightful dessert is amazingly simple to make. And your guests won't believe it's fat-free!

Most of the preparations for this dinner can be made well ahead of time, leaving you free to enjoy Easter Sunday with your guests. The day before the dinner, prepare the Creamy Cucumber Dip, and cut up the raw vegetables that will accompany it. The vegetables will stay fresh and crisp if kept chilled in plastic bags or airtight containers.

Place the pork tenderloin in the marinade the day before so that it will be ready to roast an hour or so before your dinner. At the same time,

prepare the Creamy Corn Pudding to the point of baking, and store it in a covered container in the refrigerator. When ready to bake, transfer the pudding to a casserole dish. Once the roast and pudding are in the oven, they will require little attention.

The Company Carrot-Raisin Salad can be prepared as early as a day in advance, as can the sauce for the asparagus. Last-minute preparations for the asparagus should take only minutes of your time.

The cakes for the Chocolate Raspberry Torte can also be baked the day before your dinner. Then assemble the dessert a few hours before your guests arrive, and chill it until serving time. Only you will know how easy it was to prepare this elegant and impressive dessert!

Easter Brunch

SERVES 6 TO 8

Sensational Broccoli Strudels (page 29)

Ham and Cheese Bake (page 128)

Spring Pasta Salad (page 128)

Blueberry-Orange Muffins (page 129)

*Assorted Bagels
With Nonfat Cream Cheese*

Fresh Fruit Juice

Cappuccino Cheesecake (page 130)

Ham and Cheese Bake

Yield: 8 servings

2 cups shredded nonfat or reduced-fat Cheddar cheese

2 cups dry curd or nonfat cottage cheese

2 cups fat-free egg substitute

8 ounces 98% lean ham, diced (about 1½ cups)

¾ cup sliced scallions

2 tablespoons unbleached flour

1 teaspoon Tabasco pepper sauce

4–5 medium potatoes, scrubbed (unpeeled)

1. Combine all of the ingredients except for the potatoes in a large bowl, and stir to mix well. Set aside.

2. Coat a 13-x-9-inch baking dish with nonstick cooking spray. Slice the potatoes ¼ inch thick, and line the bottom and the sides of the pan with the slices to form a crust. Pour the egg mixture over the potatoes.

3. Bake, uncovered, at 375°F for 1 hour, or until the filling is set and the top is touched with brown. Allow to sit for 5 to 10 minutes before cutting into squares and serving.

NUTRITIONAL FACTS (PER 1¼-CUP SERVING)		
Calories: 235	Fat: 0.9 g	Protein: 30 g
Cholesterol: 20 mg	Fiber: 2.6 g	Sodium: 485 mg

Spring Pasta Salad

Yield: 10 servings

12 ounces tricolor rotini pasta

2 cups 1-inch pieces asparagus spears (about 8 ounces)

2 cups snow peas (about 8 ounces)

1 cup diagonally sliced carrots (about 2 medium)

DRESSING

¼ cup plus 2 tablespoons nonfat or reduced-fat mayonnaise

¼ cup orange juice

2 tablespoons spicy mustard

1 tablespoon finely chopped fresh tarragon, or 1 teaspoon dried

¼ teaspoon ground black pepper

1. Cook the pasta until barely al dente according to package directions. Add the asparagus, snow peas, and carrots, and cook for another 30 seconds, or just until the asparagus and snow peas turn bright green. Drain, rinse with cold water, and drain again. Transfer the mixture to a large bowl.

2. In a small bowl, stir together the dressing ingredients. Pour the dressing over the pasta and vegetables, and toss gently to mix well. Cover the salad and chill for at least 2 hours before serving.

NUTRITIONAL FACTS (PER 1-CUP SERVING)		
Calories: 141	Fat: 0.8 g	Protein: 6 g
Cholesterol: 0 mg	Fiber: 3.5 g	Sodium: 130 mg

Blueberry-Orange Muffins

1. To make the topping, combine the topping ingredients in a small bowl until moist and crumbly. Set aside.

2. In a large bowl, combine the flour, oat bran, sugar, baking powder, baking soda, and orange rind, and stir to mix well. Add the orange juice and egg whites, and stir just until the dry ingredients are moistened. Fold in the blueberries.

3. Coat muffin cups with nonstick cooking spray, and fill $\frac{3}{4}$ full with the batter. Sprinkle the topping over the batter. Bake at 350°F for 16 to 18 minutes, or just until a wooden toothpick inserted in the center of a muffin comes out clean.

4. Remove the muffin tin from the oven, and allow it to sit for 5 minutes before removing the muffins. Serve warm or at room temperature.

Yield: 14 muffins

2 cups whole wheat flour

$\frac{3}{4}$ cup plus 2 tablespoons oat bran

$\frac{1}{2}$ cup sugar

1 teaspoon baking powder

1 teaspoon baking soda

1 teaspoon dried grated orange rind, or 1 tablespoon fresh

1$\frac{1}{4}$ cups orange juice

2 egg whites

1 cup fresh or frozen blueberries

TOPPING

3 tablespoons quick-cooking oats

1 tablespoon plus 1$\frac{1}{2}$ teaspoons oat bran

2 tablespoons sugar

2 teaspoons frozen orange juice concentrate, thawed

NUTRITIONAL FACTS (PER MUFFIN)		
Calories: 132	Fat: 0.8 g	Protein: 4.4 g
Cholesterol: 0 mg	Fiber: 3.7 g	Sodium: 92 mg

Cappuccino Cheesecake

Yield: 10 servings

CRUST

6½ large (2½-x-5-inch) fat-free
  graham crackers

2 tablespoons chocolate syrup

FILLING

15 ounces nonfat ricotta cheese

1 cup nonfat or reduced-fat cream
  cheese

¼ cup plus 1 tablespoon
  unbleached flour

¾ cup sugar

½ cup fat-free egg substitute

3 tablespoons coffee liqueur

1 teaspoon vanilla extract

TOPPING

1½ cups fresh strawberry slices
  (optional)

If you are unable to find fat-free graham crackers, feel free to substitute regular graham crackers. All graham crackers are low in fat.

1. To make the crust, break the crackers into pieces, and place in the bowl of a food processor or in a blender. Process into fine crumbs. Measure the crumbs. There should be 1 cup. (Adjust the amount if necessary.)

2. Return the crumbs to the food processor, and add the chocolate syrup. Process until moist and crumbly. Coat a 9-inch springform pan with nonstick cooking spray, and use a spoon to pat the crust mixture over the bottom of the pan and ¼ inch up the sides. (Dip the spoon in sugar periodically, if necessary, to prevent sticking.) Bake at 350°F for 8 minutes, or until the edges feel firm and dry. Set aside to cool.

3. Place all of the filling ingredients in a food processor, and process until smooth. Pour the filling into the crust, and bake at 350°F for 40 minutes, or until the center feels firm when lightly touched.

4. Turn the oven off, and let the cake cool in the oven with the door ajar for 1 hour. Refrigerate for at least 8 hours. Release the sides of the pan, and, if desired, arrange the strawberry slices around the border of the top of the cake, with the pointed sides facing outward. Cut into wedges and serve.

NUTRITIONAL FACTS (PER SERVING)		
Calories: 208	Fat: 0.3 g	Protein: 13 g
Cholesterol: 4 mg	Fiber: 0.5 g	Sodium: 268 mg

Easter Dinner

SERVES 8 TO 10

Creamy Cucumber Dip (page 44)
With Fresh Vegetables and Crackers

Rosemary Roasted Tenderloin (page 132)

Creamy Corn Pudding (page 133)

Company Carrot-Raisin Salad (page 133)

Fresh-Steamed Asparagus
With Honey Mustard Sauce (page 134)

Chocolate Raspberry Torte (page 135)

Rosemary Roasted Tenderloin

Yield: 12 servings

3 pork tenderloins, 1 pound each

MARINADE

¼ cup plus 1 tablespoon frozen apple juice concentrate, thawed

2 tablespoons plus 1½ teaspoons Dijon mustard

2 tablespoons plus 1½ teaspoons fresh rosemary leaves, or 2½ teaspoons dried

5 cloves garlic, crushed

½ teaspoon coarsely ground black pepper

1. Trim the tenderloins of any visible fat and membranes. Rinse with cool water, and pat dry with paper towels. Place the tenderloins in a shallow nonmetal dish.

2. In a small bowl, combine the marinade ingredients. Pour the marinade over the meat, turning the tenderloins to coat all sides. Cover and refrigerate for several hours or overnight.

3. When ready to bake, coat a 13-x-16-inch roasting pan with nonstick cooking spray and place the tenderloins in the pan, spacing them at least 2 inches apart. Pour any remaining marinade over the tenderloins, and bake at 350°F for about 45 minutes, or until an instant-read thermometer inserted in the center of a tenderloin registers 160°F and the meat is no longer pink inside.

4. Remove the pan from the oven, cover loosely with aluminum foil, and let sit for 5 minutes before slicing thinly at an angle. Serve immediately.

NUTRITIONAL FACTS (PER 3-OUNCE SERVING)

Calories: 144	Fat: 4.2 g	Protein: 24.6 g
Cholesterol: 79 mg	Fiber: 0 g	Sodium: 76 mg

Creamy Corn Pudding

1. Place 1½ cups of the corn and all of the remaining ingredients in a blender or food processor. Process for 1 minute, or until the mixture is smooth. Place the processed mixture in a large bowl, add the remaining corn kernels, and stir to mix well.

2. Coat a 2½-quart casserole dish with nonstick cooking spray, and pour the corn mixture into the dish. Bake at 350°F for 1 hour and 15 minutes, or until a sharp knife inserted midway between the center of the dish and the rim comes out clean. Remove the dish from the oven, and let sit for 10 minutes before serving.

Yield: 10 servings

4½ cups fresh or frozen (thawed) whole kernel corn

½ cup chopped onion

1½ cups skim milk

¾ cup fat-free egg substitute

3 tablespoons unbleached flour

¼ teaspoon ground white pepper

¼ teaspoon ground nutmeg

½ teaspoon salt

NUTRITIONAL FACTS (PER ½-CUP SERVING)

Calories: 84	Fat: 0.8 g	Protein: 3.9 g
Cholesterol: 0 mg	Fiber: 2.1 g	Sodium: 136 mg

Company Carrot-Raisin Salad

1. Combine the carrots, celery, and raisins in a large bowl, and toss to mix well. Combine the dressing ingredients in a small bowl, and pour over the carrot mixture. Toss to mix well.

2. Cover the salad and chill for several hours or overnight before serving.

Yield: 10 servings

5 cups grated carrots (about 2 pounds)

¾ cup thinly sliced celery

⅔ cup dark raisins

DRESSING

⅓ cup nonfat or reduced-fat mayonnaise

¼ cup frozen apple juice concentrate, thawed

NUTRITIONAL FACTS (PER ½-CUP SERVING)

Calories: 83	Fat: 0.2 g	Protein: 1.2 g
Cholesterol: 0 mg	Fiber: 2.4 g	Sodium: 126 mg

Fresh-Steamed Asparagus With Honey Mustard Sauce

Yield: 10 servings

2½ pounds fresh asparagus spears

HONEY MUSTARD SAUCE

2 tablespoons honey

2 tablespoons Dijon mustard

2 tablespoons lemon juice

¼ cup nonfat or reduced-fat mayonnaise

1. Combine the sauce ingredients in a small saucepan, and stir until smooth. Set aside.

2. Rinse the asparagus with cool running water, and snap off the tough stem ends. Arrange the asparagus spears in a microwave or conventional steamer. Cover and cook at high power or over medium-high heat for 4 to 6 minutes, or just until the spears are crisp-tender. Transfer the asparagus to a serving dish.

3. While the asparagus are cooking, place the sauce over medium heat, and cook, stirring constantly, just until the sauce is heated through. Drizzle the sauce over the asparagus, and serve immediately.

NUTRITIONAL FACTS (PER SERVING)

Calories: 44	Fat: 0.3 g	Protein: 2.5 g
Cholesterol: 0 mg	Fiber: 2.3 g	Sodium: 109 mg

Chocolate Raspberry Torte

1. In a large bowl, combine the flours, sugar, cocoa, and baking soda, and stir to mix well. Add the coffee or water and the milk and vanilla extract, and mix with a wire whisk until the batter is smooth. (The batter will be thin.)

2. Coat four 8-inch round pans with nonstick cooking spray. Divide the batter among the pans, and bake at 350°F for 18 to 20 minutes, or just until the top springs back when lightly touched and a wooden toothpick inserted in the center comes out clean. Be careful not to overbake. Let the cakes cool to room temperature in the pans.

3. Invert 1 cake onto a serving platter, and spread with ¼ cup of the jam. Add the next two layers, spreading each with jam. Top with the final layer.

4. Place the whipped topping in a small bowl, and gently fold the yogurt into the topping. Spread the frosting over the sides and top of the cake. Chill the cake for several hours, cut into wedges, and serve.

Yield: 16 servings

1½ cups unbleached flour

1 cup oat flour

1½ cups sugar

½ cup cocoa powder

2 teaspoons baking soda

1 cup coffee, cooled to room temperature, or 1 cup water

1½ cups skim milk

2 teaspoons vanilla extract

¾ cup raspberry jam or fruit spread

FROSTING

1¼ cups light whipped topping

⅓ cup nonfat raspberry yogurt

NUTRITIONAL FACTS (PER SERVING)

Calories: 210	Fat: 1.8 g	Protein: 3.7 g
Cholesterol: 0 mg	Fiber: 2 g	Sodium: 136 mg

Part Three

Celebrations and Parties

Each calendar year is studded with special days that invite us to share in celebrations ranging from a Halloween costume party to a Fourth of July fireworks display to the Saint Patrick's Day wearing of the green. For most of us, each of these days provides a welcome time of relaxation and festive events. Perhaps most important, each is a wonderful reason to get together with family and friends.

Over the years, the uniqueness of each holiday has come to be reflected by certain types of food and gatherings. The Fourth of July, for instance, almost always means a cookout or picnic, while Saint Patty's Day wouldn't seem right without corned beef and a liberal sprinkling of green. With today's emphasis on healthy, low-fat eating, though, many people are now looking for new menu ideas that provide good nutrition without sacrificing good taste. The remainder of Part Three will fill the bill by presenting festive menus that will delight your guests with great-tasting, satisfying fare that is also high in nutrition.

The calendar year begins with a New Year's Day menu featuring Hoppin' John—a traditional good-luck dish that's served over brown rice for hearty eating. For those who prefer a meat entrée, Braised Beef Round With Potatoes and Car-

rots is a delicious alternative. Rounding out the meal is Country-Style Cabbage, spicy Cinnamon Apples, savory Cornmeal Muffins, and a super-moist Fat-Free Carrot Cake With Creamy Cheese Frosting.

Valentine's Day brings a romantic and elegant dinner for two. After an appetizer of Spiced Artichoke Spread, treat your special someone to a light Spinach and Mushroom Salad followed by either Lemon Scallops Linguine or Glazed Turkey Cutlets With Rice. Dilled Carrots are the perfect accompaniment to either entrée. For dessert, choose between Poached Pears, turned an appropriate red with Warm Raspberry Sauce, and creamy Tiramisu for Two.

Next comes Saint Patrick's Day, where green abounds in a meal that includes Green Garden Salad, Chunky Split Pea Soup, Spinach and Cheese Pie, Mint Brownie Pie à la Mode with minty green glaze, and Saint Paddy's Fruit Platter. Even traditionalists will love this menu, which features corned beef in the guise of piping hot Mini Reuben Melts, as well as an easy-to-make Irish Soda Bread.

As winter gives way to spring, celebrate with a Memorial Day buffet of Flaky Spinach Pies, chilled Gazpacho, and Mediterranean-inspired salads. Lemon Blitz Cake—made easy with store-bought angel food cake—is the knock-out dessert.

The Fourth of July brings a cookout, where blackened Grilled Grouper or spicy Salsa Burgers take center stage. Accompanying the entrée is a trio of fresh salads, made fat-free and delicious. Old-Fashioned Blueberry Cobbler, cooled off with nonfat vanilla ice cream, adds a patriotic climax to this midsummer feast. Or make no-bake Berries and Cream Cake for an appropriately red, white, and blue finale.

Labor Day—often the last hurrah of the barbecue season—becomes a Caribbean festival with a meal that features either Grenadian-Style Grilled Chicken or Caribbean Shrimp on a Stick as the star attraction. Continuing the spicy theme are Jamaican Red Beans and Rice, Cuban Black Bean Salad, Baked Plantain, and Zesty Coleslaw. Chilled Key Lime Pie is the refreshingly cool finish to this low-fat taste of the islands.

Finally, there's a hearty Halloween buffet that's sure to delight trick-or-treaters and parents alike. Hot Apple Cider provides much-needed warmth on a chilly fall evening, while Fiesta Quesadillas, Two-Bean Chili, and Mini Mexican Corn Muffins satisfy even the hungriest ghosts and goblins. What's for dessert? Black Magic Cake, of course.

As you use one of the following menus to plan a party or get-together, feel free to borrow recipes from other menus or from other sections of the book. For instance, if the menu you've chosen includes an appetizer that you feel wouldn't appeal to your family, just look in Part One, which gives recipes for dozens of delightful appetizers. Or perhaps the menu includes a dessert that requires last-minute attention, but you are planning a no-fuss picnic lunch. Turn to Part Four, where you'll be sure to find a dessert that's both delicious and portable.

So fire up the grill—or build a fire in the fireplace—and invite your friends over for a special-occasion meal that's low on fat and high on taste. With these easy-to-follow recipes and easy-serving menus, your next get-together is sure to be one that will not only please your guests, but will leave you time to enjoy the festivities, too.

New Year's Day

Resolving to eat more healthfully is probably *the* most common New Year's resolution. Fortunately, this hearty winter's meal is just what the doctor ordered.

While dinner finishes cooking, stave off hunger with Broccoli Cheese Dip. For an attractive presentation, remove three or four large outer leaves from a head of cabbage, and use them to form a bowl for the dip. Then place the dip in the center of a platter, and surround it with raw vegetables and whole grain crackers.

The traditional New Year's Day meal of Hoppin' John—minus the ham hocks—takes center stage as a high-nutrient, low-fat entrée. Rich in protein, vitamins, and minerals, beans are the perfect fat-free alternative to meat. As a bonus, beans are loaded with complex carbohydrates and cholesterol-lowering soluble fiber.

If Hoppin' John is not your pleasure, try Braised Beef Round With Potatoes and Carrots. Made with the leanest beef available, this stick-to-your-ribs dish is sure to delight your family's meat-and-potato lovers.

Country-Style Cabbage, Cinnamon Apples, and Moist Cornmeal Muffins round out this simple yet satisfying meal. Last but not least is luscious Fat-Free Carrot Cake. Moistened with fruit juice instead of the usual oil and topped with a creamy fat-free frosting, this is certain to become a family favorite.

A little advance planning makes this meal a breeze. The day before the party, make the Broccoli Cheese Dip and cut up the raw vegetables. Then keep the vegetables crisp by storing them in airtight plastic containers.

Hoppin' John, too, can be prepared the day before the party, and then reheated just before serving. If you've chosen to make the Braised Beef, start preparing it about two and a half hours before serving. This delicious dish requires little attention as it bakes.

Moist Cornmeal Muffins and Fat-Free Carrot Cake can also be baked a day in advance. Just before serving, reheat the muffins in a microwave or conventional oven to bring out that fresh-baked flavor. The carrot cake, of course, must be refrigerated until you're ready to bring it out to rave reviews.

New Year's Dinner

SERVES 6 TO 8

Broccoli Cheese Dip (page 51)
With Raw Vegetables and Crackers

Hoppin' John (page 141) *with Brown Rice* (page 141)
or Braised Beef Round With Potatoes and Carrots (page 143)

Country-Style Cabbage (page 144)

Cinnamon Apples (page 144)

Moist Cornmeal Muffins (page 145)

Fat-Free Carrot Cake
With Creamy Cheese Frosting (page 146)

Hoppin' John

This hearty dish is a New Year's tradition in the South, where it is believed to bring good luck when eaten on New Year's Day.

1. Place the black-eyed peas in a 4-quart pot, and add 2½ quarts of water. Cover and soak for 4 hours or overnight. (Place the pot in the refrigerator if soaking for more than 4 hours.) When you are ready to cook, drain off the soaking water and return the peas to the pot.

2. Add all of the remaining ingredients, except for the toppings, to the pot, and bring the mixture to a boil over high heat. Lower the heat, and cover and simmer for 45 minutes to an hour, or until the beans are tender and the liquid has thickened. Stir occasionally, and add more water if needed. (The liquid should barely cover the peas.)

3. Serve hot over brown rice, garnishing each serving with 1 tablespoon each of tomatoes and scallions, if desired. Pass the Tabasco sauce if your family and friends like it hot!

Yield: 9 servings

3 cups dried black-eyed peas, sorted

4 cups water or unsalted chicken stock

1 medium yellow onion, chopped

1½ teaspoons crushed fresh garlic

1½ teaspoons dried sage

2 teaspoons chicken or vegetable bouillon granules, or 8 ounces lean ham, diced

¼ teaspoon ground black pepper

¼ teaspoon ground cayenne pepper

TOPPINGS

1 cup finely chopped tomatoes (optional)

1 cup finely chopped scallions (optional)

Tabasco pepper sauce (optional)

NUTRITIONAL FACTS (PER 1-CUP SERVING)

Calories: 195	Fat: 0.7 g	Protein: 13 g
Cholesterol: 0 mg	Fiber: 4.6 g	Sodium: 187 mg

Brown Rice

Rinsing the rice before cooking is not absolutely necessary, but does make the rice fluffier. This recipe will guide you in making delicious brown rice on your stove top. For instructions on making the fluffiest rice imaginable in a rice cooker, see the inset on page 142.

1. Place the rice in a strainer, and rinse under running water.

2. Place the rice and the vegetable stock or water in a 2½-quart pot, and bring to a boil over high heat. Reduce the heat to low, stir the rice, and cover.

Yield: 8 servings

2 cups uncooked long grain brown rice

4½ cups unsalted vegetable stock or water

3. Allow the rice to simmer, covered, for 50 minutes, or until the rice is tender and the liquid has been absorbed. Do not stir the rice while it is cooking, as this can result in sticky rice.

4. Remove the rice from the heat, and let sit, covered, for 5 minutes. Fluff with a fork, and serve hot.

NUTRITIONAL FACTS (PER ¾-CUP SERVING)

Calories: 162	Fat: 1.2 g	Protein: 3.7 g
Cholesterol: 0 mg	Fiber: 2.6 g	Sodium: 7 mg

Using a Rice Cooker

A rice cooker, which is available in most department stores, makes it a snap to cook dry, fluffy rice—even when brown rice is on the menu. As a bonus, most rice cookers act as warmers to keep the prepared rice at the right temperature until serving time. The following simple directions will give you perfect brown rice each and every time you make it.

Perfect Brown Rice

Yield: 12 servings

2 cups uncooked long grain brown rice

5 cups unsalted vegetable stock or water

1. Place the rice in a strainer, and rinse under running water.

2. Place the rice and the vegetable stock or water in a 2-quart or larger rice cooker. Turn the cooker on, and leave undisturbed until the cooking cycle is complete.

3. Leave the rice in the cooker on the warming cycle to keep hot, and serve.

Braised Beef Round With Potatoes and Carrots

Top round is one of the leanest beef cuts available. For this recipe, select a top round roast, which may be sold as London broil.

1. Trim any visible fat from the meat. Rinse the meat, and pat it dry with paper towels. Spread the garlic over both sides of the meat, and sprinkle both sides with pepper.

2. Coat a large cast iron skillet or Dutch oven with nonstick cooking spray, and preheat over medium-high heat. Place the meat in the skillet, and brown it for 2 minutes on each side. Remove the skillet from the heat, and spread the onions over the meat. Place the bay leaves and tomato juice in the bottom of the skillet, cover the skillet tightly, and bake at 325°F for 1 hour and 45 minutes.

3. Remove the skillet from the oven, and carefully remove the cover. (Steam will escape.) Place the potatoes and carrots around the meat, cover the skillet tightly, and return it to the oven for another 45 minutes, or until the meat and vegetables are tender. Transfer the meat and vegetables to a serving platter, and keep warm.

4. To make the gravy, discard the bay leaves and pour the meat drippings into a fat separator cup. (If you don't have a separator cup, pour the drippings into a bowl, add a few ice cubes, and skim off the fat once it rises and hardens.) Pour the fat-free drippings into a 2-cup measure, and add enough water to bring the volume up to 1½ cups. Pour the mixture into a 1-quart saucepan, add the bouillon granules, and bring the mixture to a boil over medium heat.

5. Combine the flour and water in a jar with a tight-fitting lid, and shake until smooth. Slowly pour the flour mixture into the boiling gravy. Cook and stir until the gravy is thickened and bubbly.

6. Transfer the gravy to a warmed gravy boat or pitcher, and serve hot with the meat and vegetables.

Yield: 8 servings

2½-pound top round roast or London broil

2 teaspoons crushed fresh garlic

¼ teaspoon coarsely ground black pepper

1 medium yellow onion, thinly sliced

2 bay leaves

½ cup tomato juice

1½ pounds potatoes (about 5 medium), scrubbed and quartered

1¼ pounds carrots (about 6 large), peeled and cut into 2-inch pieces

GRAVY

1½ teaspoons beef bouillon granules

¼ cup unbleached flour

½ cup water

NUTRITIONAL FACTS (PER SERVING)

Calories: 295	Fiber: 5.1 g
Chol.: 59 mg	Protein: 28 g
Fat: 4.6 g	Sod.: 344 mg

Country-Style Cabbage

Yield: 8 servings

1 large head cabbage (about 2 pounds)

2 tablespoons water

¾ teaspoon chicken bouillon granules

⅛ teaspoon ground black pepper

2 tablespoons cider vinegar

1. Clean and trim the cabbage. Cut the cabbage into quarters, remove the core, and cut each quarter crosswise into 1-inch pieces.

2. Place the water in the bottom of a large skillet or a Dutch oven, and add the cabbage, bouillon granules, and pepper. Cover and cook over medium-low heat, stirring occasionally, for about 15 minutes, or until the cabbage is wilted and tender.

3. Stir in the vinegar, and serve hot.

NUTRITIONAL FACTS (PER ⅔-CUP SERVING)

Calories: 28	Fat: 0.2 g	Protein: 1.5 g
Cholesterol: 0 mg	Fiber: 2.7 g	Sodium: 115 mg

Cinnamon Apples

Yield: 8 servings

½ cup frozen apple juice concentrate, thawed

4 teaspoons cornstarch

8 cups apple slices (about 10 medium)

1 teaspoon ground cinnamon

1. In a small bowl, combine 2 tablespoons of the apple juice concentrate with the cornstarch. Stir to mix, and set aside.

2. Place the apple slices, the remaining apple juice concentrate, and the cinnamon in a 2½-quart pot, and bring the mixture to a boil over high heat. Reduce the heat to low, cover, and simmer, stirring occasionally, for 15 to 20 minutes, or just until the apples are tender.

3. Stir the cornstarch mixture and add to the apple mixture. Cook and stir until the sauce is thickened and clear. Remove from the heat, cool slightly, and serve warm.

NUTRITIONAL FACTS (PER ½-CUP SERVING)

Calories: 97	Fat: 0.4 g	Protein: 0.3 g
Cholesterol: 0 mg	Fiber: 2.2 g	Sodium: 4 mg

Moist Cornmeal Muffins

1. In a large bowl, combine the cornmeal, baking powder, and baking soda, and stir to mix well. Add the egg whites, honey, and buttermilk, and stir just until the dry ingredients are moistened.

2. Coat muffin cups with nonstick cooking spray, and fill $\frac{2}{3}$ full with the batter. Bake at 350°F for 15 to 18 minutes, or just until a wooden toothpick inserted in the center of a muffin comes out clean. Be careful not to overbake.

3. Remove the muffin tin from the oven, and allow it to sit for 5 minutes before removing the muffins. Serve warm or at room temperature.

Yield: 12 muffins

2 cups whole grain cornmeal

2 teaspoons baking powder

$\frac{1}{2}$ teaspoon baking soda

3 egg whites

2 tablespoons honey

$1\frac{3}{4}$ cups nonfat buttermilk

NUTRITIONAL FACTS (PER MUFFIN)		
Calories: 103	Fat: 0.9 g	Protein: 3.7 g
Cholesterol: 0 mg	Fiber: 2 g	Sodium: 148 mg

Fat-Free Carrot Cake With Creamy Cheese Frosting

Yield: 16 servings

3 cups unbleached flour

1½ cups sugar

2½ teaspoons baking soda

2 teaspoons ground cinnamon

1⅓ cups orange juice

¾ cup fat-free egg substitute

2 teaspoons vanilla extract

4 cups grated carrots (about 8 medium)

½ cup golden raisins or chopped walnuts (optional)

CREAMY CHEESE FROSTING

1 cup nonfat or reduced-fat cream cheese

1½ cups nonfat ricotta cheese

½ cup sugar

1 tablespoon lemon juice

1½ teaspoons vanilla extract

2 tablespoons instant vanilla pudding mix

Far from being junk food, this cake provides almost a whole day's supply of vitamin A in each serving.

1. In a large bowl, combine the flour, sugar, baking soda, and cinnamon, and stir to mix well. Stir in the orange juice, egg substitute, and vanilla extract. Fold in the carrots and the raisins or walnuts if desired.

2. Coat a 9-x-13-inch pan with nonstick cooking spray. Spread the batter evenly in the pan, and bake at 300°F for 50 to 55 minutes, or just until a wooden toothpick inserted in the center of the cake comes out clean. Cool to room temperature.

3. To make the frosting, place all of the frosting ingredients except the pudding mix in the bowl of a food processor, and process until smooth. Add the pudding mix, and process just until the frosting is well mixed.

4. Spread the frosting over the cooled cake. Cut into squares and serve immediately or refrigerate.

NUTRITIONAL FACTS (PER SERVING)

Calories: 248	Fat: 0.3 g	Protein: 10 g
Cholesterol: 2 mg	Fiber: 1.5 g	Sodium: 261 mg

Valentine's Day

Want that special someone all to yourself? Set the mood with lovely dishes, linens, flowers, and candlelight, and whip up this simple but elegant Valentine's Day dinner. Then settle in for a romantic evening for two.

Get things started with Spiced Artichoke Spread served with warm French bread and a glass of dry white wine. Next comes a simple Spinach and Mushroom Salad with homemade Sweet and Spicy French Dressing. For the main course, choose from Lemon Scallops Linguine and Glazed Turkey Cutlets With Rice. Paired with Dilled Carrots, either entrée will fill you up without weighing you down. For dessert, this menu offers two delightful options—Poached Pears With Warm Raspberry Sauce and Tiramisu for Two.

With a little planning, this dinner requires minimal last-minute attention. The day before the dinner, prepare Spiced Artichoke Spread just to the point of baking so that you'll be able to pop it into the oven before serving. Rinse the salad greens with cool water, and shake off any excess liquid. Then wrap the greens in paper towels and store them in a covered container or plastic bag in the refrigerator. By making the accompanying dressing at the same time you wash the greens, you'll allow the flavors of the dressing ingredients to mingle.

Both entrées must be prepared directly before serving. Fortunately, both the linguine and the glazed turkey cutlets—as well as the accompanying Dilled Carrots—are a snap to make, and will require little of your time.

If you've chosen to treat your guest of honor to poached pears, poach the fruit a day ahead of time, and refrigerate it so that it will be well chilled by serving time. The raspberry sauce can also be made a day in advance, and then reheated just before serving. If you prefer the Tiramisu, make the dessert several hours before dinner, omitting the whipped topping, and chill the layered confection in its goblets. Before serving, just add a dollop of topping and a sprinkling of cocoa for an impressive dessert that's sure to please.

Valentine's Day Dinner

SERVES 2

Spiced Artichoke Spread (page 37) with French Bread

Spinach and Mushroom Salad (page 149) with Sweet and Spicy French Dressing (page 149)

Lemon Scallops Linguine (page 150) or Glazed Turkey Cutlets With Rice (page 151)

Dilled Carrots (page 152)

Poached Pears With Warm Raspberry Sauce (page 153) or Tiramisu for Two (page 154)

Spinach and Mushroom Salad

1. Divide the spinach between 2 individual salad bowls or plates. Arrange the mushrooms, pepper rings, and garbanzo beans over the lettuce.

2. Serve with Sweet and Spicy French Dressing.

Yield: 2 servings

3½ cups torn spinach leaves

⅓ cup mushroom slices

4 thin rings of red bell pepper

¼ cup drained canned garbanzo beans

NUTRITIONAL FACTS (PER 2-CUP SERVING, SALAD ONLY)

Calories: 60	Fat: 0.8 g	Protein: 5 g
Cholesterol: 0 mg	Fiber: 5 mg	Sodium: 79 mg

Sweet and Spicy French Dressing

1. Place all the ingredients in a blender, and process for 1 minute.

2. Transfer the dressing to a small bowl, cover, and chill before serving.

Yield: ¾ cup

2 tablespoons chopped onion

½ cup apple juice

3 tablespoons white wine vinegar

2 tablespoons tomato paste

1 clove garlic

½ teaspoon paprika

¼ teaspoon chili powder

¼ teaspoon salt

Dash cayenne pepper

NUTRITIONAL FACTS (PER TABLESPOON)

Calories: 8	Fat: 0 g	Protein: 0.1 g
Cholesterol: 0 mg	Fiber: 0.1 g	Sodium: 43 mg

Lemon Scallops Linguine

Yield: 2 servings

4 ounces linguine pasta

1 clove garlic, crushed

8 ounces large uncooked scallops, rinsed and patted dry

1½ cups fresh snow peas

1½ teaspoons minced fresh oregano, or ½ teaspoon dried

SAUCE

¼ cup water

2 tablespoons lemon juice

½ teaspoon chicken bouillon granules

1 teaspoon cornstarch

This delightful dish is equally delicious when made with shrimp.

1. Combine the sauce ingredients in a small bowl, and stir until the cornstarch is dissolved. Set aside.

2. Cook the linguine al dente according to package directions. Drain and set aside.

3. Coat a large nonstick skillet with olive oil cooking spray. Place over medium-high heat, add the garlic and scallops, and stir-fry for a few minutes, until the scallops are nearly opaque. Add the snow peas and oregano, and stir-fry for another couple of minutes, or until the snow peas are crisp-tender and the scallops are done. (Add a tablespoon of water if the skillet becomes too dry.)

4. Reduce the heat to low, add the linguine to the scallop mixture, and toss gently to mix. Stir the sauce ingredients and pour over the linguine. Toss gently until the sauce is thickened and clear. Serve immediately.

NUTRITIONAL FACTS (PER SERVING)		
Calories: 345	Fat: 2.1 g	Protein: 28 g
Cholesterol: 37 mg	Fiber: 4.7 g	Sodium: 442 mg

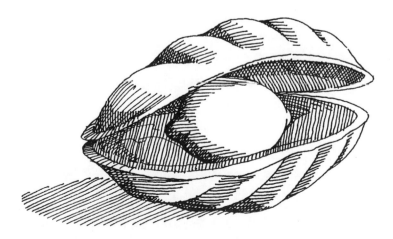

Glazed Turkey Cutlets With Rice

For variety, substitute pork tenderloin medallions for the turkey.

1. Combine the glaze ingredients in a small bowl, and stir until the cornstarch is dissolved. Set aside.

2. Coat a large nonstick skillet with cooking spray, and preheat the skillet over medium-high heat. Place the garlic and the turkey cutlets in the skillet, and brown for 2 minutes on each side, or until the meat is no longer pink inside. Transfer the cutlets to a plate and keep warm.

3. Place the skillet over low heat. Stir the glaze mixture, and pour it into the skillet. Cook, stirring constantly, for 30 to 60 seconds, or until the glaze is thickened and bubbly. Add the turkey cutlets to the skillet, and turn them in the glaze until completely coated. Remove the skillet from the heat.

4. Place 1¼ cups of Broccoli-Rice Pilaf on each of 2 dinner plates. Arrange half of the turkey cutlets over each mound of pilaf, and serve immediately.

Yield: 2 servings

½ teaspoon crushed fresh garlic

4 turkey breast cutlets, 2 ounces each

1 recipe Broccoli-Rice Pilaf, prepared (below)

GLAZE

2 tablespoons apricot preserves or fruit spread

2 tablespoons orange juice

1½ tablespoons seasoned rice vinegar

1 teaspoon cornstarch

¾ teaspoon fresh rosemary, or ¼ teaspoon dried

NUTRITIONAL FACTS (PER SERVING, TURKEY ONLY)

Calories: 194	Fat: 1 g	Protein: 26 g
Cholesterol: 73 mg	Fiber: 0.3 g	Sodium: 273 mg

Broccoli-Rice Pilaf

1. Place the rice in a strainer, and rinse under cold running water.

2. Place the rice and the water or chicken stock in a 1-quart pot, and bring to a boil over high heat. Reduce the heat to low, stir the rice, and cover.

3. Allow the rice to simmer, covered, for about 50 minutes, or until the rice is cooked and the liquid has been absorbed. Do not stir the rice while it is cooking, as this can result in sticky rice.

Yield: 2 servings

½ cup uncooked brown rice

1 cup plus 2 tablespoons water or unsalted chicken stock

1 cup fresh broccoli florets

4. Remove the rice from the heat, and let sit, covered, for 5 minutes. Meanwhile, bring a 1-quart pot of water to a boil. Add the broccoli, and boil for about 30 seconds, or just until the broccoli is crisp-tender. Drain the broccoli, stir it into the cooked rice, and serve.

NUTRITIONAL FACTS (PER 1$\frac{1}{4}$-CUP SERVING)

Calories: 183	Fat: 1.5 g	Protein: 5 g
Cholesterol: 0 mg	Fiber: 2.8 g	Sodium: 15 mg

Dilled Carrots

Yield: 2 servings

2 medium-large carrots, diagonally sliced $\frac{1}{4}$-inch thick

$\frac{1}{4}$ teaspoon sugar

1 tablespoon plus 1$\frac{1}{2}$ teaspoons water

1 teaspoon lemon juice

1 teaspoon butter-flavored sprinkles

1$\frac{1}{2}$ teaspoons minced fresh dill

1. Place the carrots in a 1-quart pot. In a small bowl, combine the sugar, water, lemon juice, and sprinkles, and pour over the carrots. Cover and place over low heat for 4 to 5 minutes, or until the carrots are tender.

2. Uncover the pot, and cook and stir for 2 minutes, or until most of the water has evaporated.

3. Add the dill and toss to mix well. Serve immediately.

NUTRITIONAL FACTS (PER $\frac{2}{3}$-CUP SERVING)

Calories: 29	Fat: 0 g	Protein: 1 g
Cholesterol: 0 mg	Fiber: 2 g	Sodium: 58 mg

Poached Pears
With Warm Raspberry Sauce

1. Peel the pears, leaving the stems intact.

2. Place the pear nectar in the bottom of a microwave or conventional stove-top steamer, and transfer the pears to the steamer. Cover and cook at high power or over medium-high heat for 4 to 5 minutes, or until tender.

3. Drain the pears, reserving the nectar. Cover the pears and chill for several hours or overnight.

4. To make the sauce, place the cornstarch and sugar in a small saucepan, and stir to mix well. Stir in $\frac{1}{3}$ cup of the reserved nectar, and cook and stir over medium-low heat until the mixture is thick and bubbly. Stir in the raspberries, and cook and stir for another minute or 2, or until thick and bubbly.

5. Place the chilled pears in individual serving dishes, and pour the warm sauce over the fruit. Serve immediately.

Yield: 2 servings

2 pears

$\frac{1}{3}$ cup pear nectar

2 teaspoons cornstarch

1 tablespoon plus 1 teaspoon sugar

$\frac{1}{2}$ cup fresh or frozen raspberries

NUTRITIONAL FACTS (PER SERVING)		
Calories: 180	Fat: 0.8 g	Protein: 1 g
Cholesterol: 0 mg	Fiber: 6.6 g	Sodium: 2 mg

Tiramisu for Two

Yield: 2 servings

¾ cup nonfat ricotta cheese

2 tablespoons confectioners' sugar

¼ teaspoon vanilla extract

1 cup fresh or frozen (thawed) strawberries

1½ teaspoons sugar

2 slices (½-inch each) fat-free pound cake

2 tablespoons plus 2 teaspoons coffee liqueur

¼ cup light whipped topping

¼ teaspoon cocoa powder

1. Combine the ricotta cheese, confectioners' sugar, and vanilla extract in the bowl of a food processor, and process until smooth. Set aside.

2. Combine the strawberries and sugar in a small bowl, and mash them together. Set aside.

3. Crumble 1 piece of the pound cake, and divide it between two 10-ounce balloon wine glasses. In each glass, top the cake with 2 tablespoons of the strawberry mixture, 2 teaspoons of the coffee liqueur, and 3 tablespoons of the ricotta mixture. Repeat the layers. Top each dessert with 2 tablespoons of the light whipped topping, and sprinkle with ⅛ teaspoon of cocoa. Serve immediately.

NUTRITIONAL FACTS (PER SERVING)

Calories: 285	Fat: 1.4 g	Protein: 14 g
Cholesterol: 0 mg	Fiber: 2.1 g	Sodium: 169 mg

Saint Patrick's Day

Green is the theme of this light-hearted Irish holiday. In keeping with tradition, this hearty home-style dinner features green aplenty.

Corned beef, often featured on Saint Paddy's Day, appears—in a dramatically slimmed-down version, of course—in the Mini Reuben Melt appetizers. For the next course, what could be greener than a steaming bowl of Chunky Split Pea Soup? Following the soup, savory Spinach and Cheese Pie is accompanied by a fresh Green Garden Salad and traditional Irish Soda Bread for a filling but not fattening main course. And what's for dessert? Fudgy Mint Brownie Pie à la Mode with a minty green glaze. Top with your choice of fat-free vanilla or mint ice cream, and add a fruit platter—of green fruit, of course—for those guests who prefer something light.

Eating green brings more than the luck of the Irish. Green fruits, vegetables, and legumes are loaded with fiber, vitamins, and minerals, and are free of fat. This meal is also relatively effortless.

Everything but the Mini Reuben Melts can be prepared well in advance.

On the day before your party, rinse the salad greens with cool water, and shake off any excess liquid. Then wrap the greens in paper towels, place them in an airtight container, and chill until you're ready to assemble the salad.

Also feel free to fully prepare both the soup and the spinach pies a day in advance. Reheat the soup on the stove top, and the pies in a microwave or conventional oven.

The brownies, too, can be baked the day before your party. Just cover them, and they'll keep beautifully. The fruit platter, of course, cannot be made too far in advance, but can easily be arranged several hours before the meal. Cover the platter and chill until serving time.

Bake the Irish Soda Bread in the morning for the best flavor, and reheat it just before serving. What about the rest of the meal? It can easily be made during the hour before your guests arrive.

Saint Patrick's Day Dinner

SERVES 8 TO 10

Mini Reuben Melts (page 34)

Chunky Split Pea Soup (page 157)

Irish Soda Bread (page 157)

Spinach and Cheese Pie (page 158)

Green Garden Salad (page 159) *with*
Creamy Cucumber Dressing (page 159)

Mint Brownie Pie à la Mode (page 160)

Saint Paddy's Fruit Platter (page 161)

Chunky Split Pea Soup

1. Place all of the ingredients in a 6-quart pot, and bring to a boil over high heat. Reduce the heat to low, cover, and simmer for $1\frac{1}{4}$ to $1\frac{1}{2}$ hours, or until the peas are soft and the soup is thick.

2. Ladle the soup into individual serving bowls, and serve hot.

Yield: 10 servings

$2\frac{1}{2}$ cups dried split green peas

10 cups water or vegetable stock

8 ounces diced smoked turkey sausage

1 large Spanish onion, diced

2 cups diced potatoes

$1\frac{1}{2}$ cups diced carrots

1 cup sliced celery

3 cloves garlic, crushed

2 teaspoons chicken bouillon granules

$2\frac{1}{4}$ teaspoons dried sage

$1\frac{1}{4}$ teaspoons dried thyme

$\frac{1}{4}$ teaspoon ground black pepper

NUTRITIONAL FACTS (PER $1\frac{1}{3}$-CUP SERVING)

| Calories: 257 | Fat: 1.6 g | Protein: 17.7 g |
| Cholesterol: 12 mg | Fiber: 8.1 g | Sodium: 463 mg |

Irish Soda Bread

1. Combine the flours, brown sugar, baking soda, and baking powder in a large bowl, and stir to mix well, pressing out any lumps with the back of a spoon. Stir in the raisins or currants. Add the egg whites and just enough of the buttermilk to form a stiff dough, and stir just until the dry ingredients are moistened.

2. Turn the dough onto a floured surface, and shape into a 7-inch circle. Coat a 9-inch round pan with cooking spray, and place the dough in the center of the pan. Brush the top lightly with milk, and use a sharp knife to cut a $\frac{1}{2}$-inch-deep X in the top.

3. Bake at 350°F for 35 to 40 minutes, or just until a wooden toothpick inserted in the center of the loaf comes out clean. Cut into wedges and serve warm.

Yield: 16 slices

2 cups whole wheat flour

2 cups unbleached flour

$\frac{1}{3}$ cup light brown sugar

2 teaspoons baking soda

2 teaspoons baking powder

1 cup dark raisins or currants

2 egg whites

$1\frac{1}{3}$ cups nonfat buttermilk

Skim milk

NUTRITIONAL FACTS (PER SERVING)

| Calories: 161 | Fat: 0.6 g | Protein: 5.1 g |
| Cholesterol: 0 mg | Fiber: 2.7 g | Sodium: 234 mg |

Spinach and Cheese Pie

Yield: 10 servings

CRUST

4 cups cooked brown rice, barley, or bulgur wheat

¼ cup fat-free egg substitute, or 2 egg whites

FILLING

2 cups sliced fresh mushrooms

2 tablespoons dry white wine or water

2 packages (10 ounces each) frozen chopped spinach, thawed and squeezed dry

2 cups evaporated skim milk

2 cups fat-free egg substitute

2 cups shredded nonfat or reduced-fat mozzarella cheese

¼ cup minced fresh parsley

1 teaspoon crushed fresh garlic

1 teaspoon dried thyme

¼ teaspoon ground black pepper

¼ cup grated nonfat or reduced-fat Parmesan cheese

This recipe makes 2 pies, each of which provides 5 generous servings.

1. To make the crust, combine the rice and egg substitute in a medium-sized bowl, and stir to mix well. Coat two 9-inch deep dish pie pans with nonstick cooking spray. Divide the crust mixture evenly between the two pans, and use the back of a spoon to pat the mixture over the bottom and sides of each pan. Set aside.

2. Place the mushrooms and the wine or water in a 3-quart pot. Cook and stir over medium heat until the mushrooms are tender and the liquid has evaporated. Remove the pot from the heat, and stir in first the spinach; then the evaporated milk; and then the egg substitute, mozzarella cheese, parsley, garlic, thyme, and pepper.

3. Divide the pie filling evenly between the two pie crusts, and top each of the filled pies with half of the Parmesan cheese. Bake at 375°F for 45 minutes, or until a sharp knife inserted in the center of each pie comes out clean. Remove the pies from the oven, and let sit for 5 minutes before cutting into wedges and serving.

NUTRITIONAL FACTS (PER SERVING)

Calories: 198	Fat: 0.8 g	Protein: 20.5 g
Cholesterol: 7 mg	Fiber: 2.5 g	Sodium: 340 mg

A Hearty New Year's Day Dinner
Top: Moist Cornmeal Muffins (page 145)
Center Left: Country-Style Cabbage (page 144)
Center Right: Cinnamon Apples (page 144)
Bottom: Braised Beef Round With Potatoes and Carrots (page 143)

A Romantic Valentine's Day Dinner
Top: Spinach and Mushroom Salad (page 149)
Bottom Left: Lemon Scallops Linguine (page 150)
Bottom Right: Dilled Carrots (page 152)

A Saint Paddy's Day Feast
Top: Irish Soda Bread (page 157)
Center Left: Mini Reuben Melts (page 34)
Center Right: Green Garden Salad (page 159)
With Creamy Cucumber Dressing (page 159)
Bottom: Spinach and Cheese Pie (page 158)

A Refreshingly Light Memorial Day Buffet
Top Left: Garlic and Herb Croutons (page 165)
Top Right: Florentine Pasta Salad (page 166)
Center Left: Mediterranean White Bean Salad (page 168)
Bottom: Spicy Gazpacho (page 165)

Green Garden Salad

1. Place the lettuce in a large salad bowl. Add the cucumbers, cabbage, carrot, onion, raisins, and sunflower seeds, if desired, and toss to mix.

2. Serve with Creamy Cucumber Dressing.

Yield: 10 servings

11 cups torn romaine lettuce

1½ cups sliced cucumbers

1¼ cups coarsely shredded purple cabbage

1 cup coarsely shredded carrot

4–5 thin slices sweet onion, separated into rings

⅓ cup dark raisins

⅓ cup hulled sunflower seeds (optional)

NUTRITIONAL FACTS
(PER 1½-CUP SERVING, SALAD ONLY)

Calories: 41	Fat: 0.3 g	Protein: 1.5 g
Cholesterol: 0 mg	Fiber: 1.8 g	Sodium: 12 mg

Creamy Cucumber Dressing

1. Place all of the ingredients except for the cucumber in a food processor or blender, and process until smooth. Add the cucumber, and process for a few seconds, just until the cucumbers are finely chopped.

2. Transfer the dressing to a small bowl, cover, and chill before serving.

Yield: 1¾ cups

¾ cup dry curd or nonfat cottage cheese

¼ cup nonfat or reduced-fat mayonnaise

¼ cup white wine vinegar

2 tablespoons minced fresh parsley

2 tablespoons chopped scallions

2 cloves garlic

¼ teaspoon ground white pepper

¼ teaspoon salt

1 cup coarsely chopped peeled and seeded cucumber

NUTRITIONAL FACTS (PER TABLESPOON)

Calories: 6	Fat: 0 g	Protein: 0.7 g
Cholesterol: 0 mg	Fiber: 0.1 g	Sodium: 38 mg

Mint Brownie Pie à la Mode

Yield: 10 servings

½ cup plus 2 tablespoons
   unbleached flour

½ cup quick-cooking oats

1 cup sugar

½ cup cocoa powder

⅛ teaspoon baking powder

¼ cup plus 2 tablespoons plain
   nonfat yogurt

2 tablespoons water

4 egg whites

1 teaspoon vanilla extract

⅓ cup chopped walnuts (optional)

5 cups nonfat vanilla or mint ice
   cream

GLAZE

½ cup confectioners' sugar

2 drops peppermint extract

1 drop green food coloring

2 teaspoons skim milk

1. In a medium-sized bowl, combine the flour, oats, sugar, cocoa, and baking powder, and stir to mix well. Stir in the yogurt, water, egg whites, and vanilla extract. Fold in the nuts if desired.

2. Coat a 9-inch round pan with nonstick cooking spray. Spread the batter evenly in the pan, and bake at 325°F for about 25 minutes, or just until the edges are firm and the center is almost set. Be careful not to overbake. Cool to room temperature.

3. To make the glaze, combine the confectioners' sugar, peppermint extract, and food coloring in a small bowl. Stir in the milk. If using a microwave oven, place the glaze in a microwave-safe dish, and microwave uncovered on high power for 15 seconds, or until runny. If using a conventional stove top, transfer the glaze to a small saucepan and place over low heat until runny.

4. Drizzle the glaze back and forth over the cooled pie, and set aside for a few minutes to allow the glaze to set. Cut the pie into wedges. Transfer the wedges to individual serving dishes, top each piece with ½ cup of nonfat ice cream, and serve immediately.

NUTRITIONAL FACTS (PER SERVING)

Calories: 247	Fat: 0.8 g	Protein: 9.4 g
Cholesterol: 0 mg	Fiber: 1.6 g	Sodium: 132 mg

Saint Paddy's Fruit Platter

1. Peel the kiwis, and slice them into ¼-inch slices. Remove the seeds from the honeydew melon half, and cut the half into 2 pieces. Peel each piece, and slice it into wedges.

2. Arrange the kiwi slices around the outer edges of a round 12-inch platter. Arrange the melon wedges, slightly overlapping, in a circle within the larger circle created by the kiwis. Arrange the grapes in the center of the platter, and serve.

Yield: 10 servings

5 kiwi fruits

½ large honeydew melon

1-pound bunch green seedless grapes

NUTRITIONAL FACTS (PER SERVING)

Calories: 79	Fat: 0.4 g	Protein: 1 g
Cholesterol: 0 mg	Fiber: 2.3 g	Sodium: 9 mg

Memorial Day

If you really want to go fat-free, think beans and pasta. That's just what you'll find an abundance of in this Mediterranean-inspired menu. Served buffet-style on the deck or patio, this menu is perfect on a warm May afternoon. Or substitute a cold appetizer for the spinach pies and pack the meal as a picnic.

For starters, bring out some piping hot Flaky Spinach Pies. Then serve chilled Spicy Gazpacho and some Italian Eggplant Spread along with plenty of crusty Italian bread or homemade toasted Pita Chips.

Choose two main-dish salads from the four savory possibilities: Florentine Pasta Salad, Neptune Pasta Salad, Mediterranean White Bean Salad, and Italian Ham and Cheese Salad. Complemented with a platter of seasonal fresh fruit, these salads offer a variety of palate-pleasing flavors.

For dessert, wow family and friends with Lemon Blitz Cake. Light, luscious, and lemony, this simple-to-make but spectacular cake is a sure-fire hit.

Avoid a time crunch by preparing the spinach pies in advance just to the point of baking. Then freeze them and pop them into the oven when needed. The main-dish salads, the Spicy Gazpacho, and the Italian Eggplant Spread are best prepared several hours before serving—or even the day before the party—to allow the flavors to develop. The filling for Lemon Blitz Cake is best prepared the day before, too. Then assemble the cake right before the party begins and wait for rave reviews.

Memorial Day Dinner

SERVES 10 TO 12

Flaky Spinach Pies (page 25)

Spicy Gazpacho (page 165) *with*
Garlic and Herb Croutons (page 165)

Italian Eggplant Spread (page 46)

Florentine Pasta Salad (page 166)
or Neptune Pasta Salad (page 167)

Italian Ham and Cheese Salad (page 167)
or Mediterranean White Bean Salad (page 168)

Seasonal Fresh Fruit Platter

Lemon Blitz Cake (page 169)

Spicy Gazpacho

1. Combine the vegetables in a large bowl. Combine the remaining ingredients, except for the sour cream and croutons, in a medium-sized bowl, and pour over the vegetables. Toss to mix well. Cover the soup and chill for several hours or overnight.

2. Ladle the soup into individual serving bowls, and garnish each serving with a tablespoonful of sour cream, if desired, and the Garlic and Herb Croutons. Serve cold.

Yield: 12 servings

5 cups diced ripe tomatoes

1½ cups peeled, diced cucumber

1 medium green bell pepper, chopped

1 medium red bell pepper, chopped

⅔ cup sliced scallions

½ cup red wine vinegar

1½ cups tomato juice

1 tablespoon plus 1½ teaspoons minced fresh oregano

1½ teaspoons chili powder

3 cloves garlic, crushed

1½ teaspoons sugar

¼ teaspoon ground black pepper

½ teaspoon salt

¾ cup nonfat sour cream or plain nonfat yogurt (optional)

Garlic and Herb Croutons (below)

NUTRITIONAL FACTS (PER ¾-CUP SERVING, SOUP ONLY)

Calories: 34	Fat: 0.3 g	Protein: 1.3 g
Cholesterol: 0 mg	Fiber: 1.9 g	Sodium: 100 mg

Garlic and Herb Croutons

1. Rub the inside of a large bowl with the garlic, and sprinkle with the oregano. Place the bread cubes in the bowl, and spray lightly with the cooking spray. Toss gently, and spray again. Sprinkle with the Parmesan, and toss to coat.

2. Coat a large baking sheet with nonstick cooking spray. Arrange the bread cubes in a single layer on the sheet, and bake at 350°F for about 10 minutes, or until the croutons are lightly browned and crisp.

Yield: 4 cups

1½ teaspoons crushed fresh garlic

½ teaspoon dried oregano

6 cups French bread cubes

Olive oil cooking spray

2 tablespoons grated nonfat Parmesan cheese

3. Cool the croutons to room temperature, and store in an airtight container until ready to use.

NUTRITIONAL FACTS (PER 3-TABLESPOON SERVING)

Calories: 32	Fat: 0.3 g	Protein: 1 g
Cholesterol: 0 mg	Fiber: 0.2 g	Sodium: 67 mg

Florentine Pasta Salad

Yield: 12 servings

1 cup chopped sun-dried tomatoes (not packed in oil)

1 cup water

1 pound bow tie pasta

8 cups chopped fresh spinach

1 can (1 pound) cannellini or kidney beans, drained and rinsed

2/3 cup fat-free Italian dressing

3–4 cloves garlic, crushed

1. If using a microwave oven, place the sun-dried tomatoes and water in a glass bowl, and microwave uncovered at high power for 2 minutes. If using a conventional stove top, place the tomatoes and water in a small saucepan, bring to a boil, and boil for 20 seconds. Set the cooked tomatoes aside for about 20 minutes, or until they have absorbed the water and cooled.

2. Cook the pasta al dente according to package directions. Drain, rinse with cold water, and drain again.

3. Place the pasta in a large bowl. Add the remaining ingredients, including the cooled tomatoes, and mix well.

4. Cover the salad and chill for at least 2 hours before serving.

NUTRITIONAL FACTS (PER 1 1/3-CUP SERVING)

Calories: 200	Fat: 0.9 g	Protein: 8.8 g
Cholesterol: 0 mg	Fiber: 5.7 g	Sodium: 269 mg

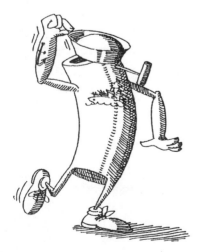

Neptune Pasta Salad

For variety, substitute fresh asparagus pieces for the broccoli.

Yield: 12 servings

1. Cook the pasta until barely al dente according to package directions. Add the broccoli, and cook for another 30 seconds, or just until the broccoli is bright green and crisp-tender. Drain, rinse with cold water, and drain again.

2. Place the pasta mixture in a large bowl. Add the crab meat or shrimp, pepper, and scallions, and toss to mix.

3. In a small bowl, combine the dressing ingredients, and stir to mix. Pour the dressing over the pasta, and toss to mix.

4. Cover the salad and chill for at least 2 hours before serving.

12 ounces tricolor rotini pasta

2 cups fresh broccoli florets (about 1/2 pound)

3 cups cooked crab meat or shrimp (about 1 1/4 pounds)

1 red bell pepper, cut into thin strips

4 scallions, thinly sliced

DRESSING

1/2 cup plus 2 tablespoons nonfat or reduced-fat mayonnaise

1/2 cup fat-free Italian dressing

1 1/2 tablespoons finely chopped fresh oregano, or 1 1/2 teaspoons dried

NUTRITIONAL FACTS (PER 1-CUP SERVING)

Calories: 175	Fat: 1.2 g	Protein: 13 g
Cholesterol: 30 mg	Fiber: 1.8 g	Sodium: 316 mg

Italian Ham and Cheese Salad

Yield: 12 servings

1. Cook the pasta al dente according to package directions. Drain, rinse with cold water, and drain again.

2. Place the pasta in a large bowl. Add the ham, mozzarella, peppers, and scallions, and toss to mix.

3. In a small bowl, combine the dressing ingredients, and stir to mix well. Pour the dressing over the pasta mixture, and toss to mix.

4. Cover the salad and chill for at least 2 hours before serving.

12 ounces penne pasta

1 1/2 cups diced lean ham

1 1/2 cups diced nonfat or reduced-fat mozzarella cheese

1 green bell pepper, cut into thin strips

1 red bell pepper, cut into thin strips

4 scallions, thinly sliced

DRESSING

1/2 cup plain nonfat yogurt

1/4 cup plus 2 tablespoons nonfat or reduced-fat mayonnaise

3 tablespoons Dijon mustard

1 1/2 tsp. dried Italian seasoning

NUTRITIONAL FACTS (PER 1-CUP SERVING)

Calories: 171	Fat: 1 g	Protein: 15 g
Cholesterol: 13 mg	Fiber: 1.5 g	Sodium: 435 mg

Mediterranean White Bean Salad

Yield: 12 servings

2 cups bulgur wheat

4 cups boiling water

3 cans (1 pound each) white beans, drained and rinsed

1½ cups thinly sliced celery

1½ cups chopped red onion

¾ cup minced fresh parsley

DRESSING

½ cup plus 1 tablespoon white wine vinegar or lemon juice

2 tablespoons olive oil (optional)

3 tablespoons Dijon mustard

1 tablespoon sugar

1 tablespoon crushed fresh garlic

¾ teaspoon ground cumin

¼ teaspoon ground black pepper

1. Place the bulgur wheat in a large heat-proof bowl. Add the boiling water, stir, and set aside for 30 minutes.

2. Combine the beans, celery, onion, and parsley in a large bowl, and stir to mix.

3. Combine the dressing ingredients in a jar with a tight-fitting lid, and shake to mix well. Pour the dressing over the bean mixture, and toss to mix. Drain the bulgur of any excess water, and add the bulgur to the bean mixture. Toss well.

4. Cover the salad and chill for at least 2 hours before serving.

NUTRITIONAL FACTS (PER 1-CUP SERVING)		
Calories: 196	Fat: 0.9 g	Protein: 9 g
Cholesterol: 0 mg	Fiber: 11 g	Sodium: 115 mg

Lemon Blitz Cake

1. To make the filling, combine the cornstarch and sugar in a medium-sized saucepan, and stir to mix well. Use a wire whisk to slowly whisk in the milk. Place over medium heat, and bring to a boil, stirring constantly. Continue to cook and stir for 1 minute, or until the mixture is thickened and bubbly.

2. Remove the milk mixture from the heat, and whisk in the lemon juice and rind. Cover and chill for several hours or overnight to thicken.

3. Just before assembling the cake, make the topping by gently folding the yogurt into the whipped topping. Set aside.

4. To assemble the cake, use a bread knife to cut the cake lengthwise into 3 layers. Stir the filling. Place the bottom cake layer on a serving platter, and spread with half of the filling. Repeat with the second layer. Top with the third cake layer, and spread the topping over the top and sides of cake.

5. Chill the cake for 1 to 2 hours, slice, and serve.

Yield: 12 servings

1 angel food cake (1 pound)

FILLING

$\frac{1}{4}$ cup cornstarch

$\frac{2}{3}$ cup sugar

1$\frac{2}{3}$ cups skim milk

$\frac{1}{2}$ cup lemon juice

1 tablespoon freshly grated lemon rind

TOPPING

$\frac{3}{4}$ cup nonfat lemon yogurt

1$\frac{1}{2}$ cups light whipped topping

NUTRITIONAL FACTS (PER SERVING)		
Calories: 174	Fat: 1.3 g	Protein: 4.9 g
Cholesterol: 0 mg	Fiber: 0.8 g	Sodium: 238 mg

Time-Saving Tip

Instead of making the lemon filling from scratch, use 2$\frac{1}{4}$ cups of canned lemon pie filling for a truly fuss-free dessert!

The Fourth of July

This midsummer holiday is a great excuse to fire up the grill and invite friends and family to share in the bounty. Celebrate your independence from fat with this light and refreshing menu.

First, munch on some cool, fresh melon while you wait for dinner. Cantaloupes, honeydew melons, and watermelons are all plentiful at this time of year.

The catch of the day is Blackened Grilled Grouper. This version, made with fresh onions and garlic, needs no oil to remain moist. Or, if you prefer, grill up some spicy Salsa Burgers instead. Made from the leanest ground beef available, these burgers are a sure-fire hit.

A trio of fresh, cool salads are served on the side, including a traditional potato salad, made untraditionally low in fat. The crowning touch is Old-Fashioned Blueberry Cobbler—a dish that's almost as American as apple pie. Bursting with fresh berry flavor and topped by a cooling scoop of nonfat ice cream, this dessert is fat-free and has far less sugar than most cobblers. Don't feel like cooking? Try Berries and Cream Cake, instead. This elegant dessert is a snap to assemble, and is appropriately decorated with fresh berries in the colors of Old Glory.

To avoid hectic party preparations in the summer heat, get a head start the day before the fourth. If fish is your choice of entrée, prepare the coating and refrigerate it a day ahead of time. Then rub the coating on the fish right before grilling. If you plan to make burgers instead, the Salsa Burger mixture, too, can be prepared and chilled a day in advance.

Both the All-American Potato Salad and the Two-Bean Salad can also be made the day before your party and chilled until guests arrive. Make the Fresh Tomato Salad several hours before the meal to let the flavors mingle, but don't make this salad the day before, as the tomatoes will lose their firmness and brightness if left in the dressing overnight.

If you've chosen to serve the cobbler, mix up the filling several hours in advance. This dish is quickly assembled and popped into the oven an hour before serving time. If Berries and Cream Cake is on the menu, fill your store-bought angel food cake with ice cream the day before the gathering, wrap the cake, and freeze it. Then top the cake with fruit just before serving, and get ready to enjoy the fireworks—and an all-American feast—along with your guests.

Fourth of July Cookout

SERVES 6 TO 8

Fresh Melon Platter

Blackened Grilled Grouper (page 173)
or Salsa Burgers (page 173)

All-American Potato Salad (page 175)

Fresh Tomato Salad (page 175)

Two-Bean Salad (page 176)

Old-Fashioned Blueberry Cobbler (page 177)
or Berries and Cream Cake (page 178)

Blackened Grilled Grouper

This dish is equally delicious when made with swordfish, fresh tuna, mahi mahi, amberjack, orange roughy, or any other firm-fleshed fish.

1. Place all of the coating ingredients in a food processor or blender, and process until finely ground. Set aside.

2. Rinse the fish steaks and pat dry. Rub 2 teaspoons of the coating on each side of each steak. Set aside for 10 minutes.

3. Grill the steaks over medium heat, covered, for about 5 minutes on each side, or until the meat is easily flaked with a fork. Garnish with the lemon wedges, and serve.

Yield: 9 servings

9 grouper steaks, 5 ounces each
Lemon wedges (garnish)

COATING

1 medium yellow onion, cut in pieces
5 cloves garlic, peeled
1 tablespoon plus 1½ teaspoons paprika
¾ teaspoon ground dried thyme
¾ teaspoon ground dried oregano
¼ teaspoon ground cayenne pepper
¼ teaspoon ground black pepper
¼ teaspoon salt

NUTRITIONAL FACTS (PER SERVING)

Calories: 142	Fat: 1.8 g	Protein: 27 g
Cholesterol: 68 mg	Fiber: 0.6 g	Sodium: 175 mg

Salsa Burgers

1. Combine the ground beef, bread crumbs, onion, salsa, and chili powder in a large bowl. Use a potato masher or fork to mix the ingredients thoroughly. Gently shape the mixture into 10 (4-inch) patties.

2. Grill the burgers over medium heat for 7 to 9 minutes on each side, or until the meat is thoroughly cooked. (There should be no traces of pink inside.) Serve each burger on a multigrain bun with your choice of toppings.

Yield: 10 servings

2 pounds 96% lean ground beef
1 cup soft bread crumbs
⅔ cup finely chopped onion
½ cup prepared salsa
2 teaspoons chili powder
8 multigrain burger buns

TOPPINGS

¼ cup nonfat sour cream (optional)
½ cup prepared salsa (optional)
2 tomatoes, thinly sliced (optional)
1 onion, thinly sliced (optional)
8 lettuce leaves (optional)
1 cup nonfat or reduced-fat shredded Cheddar cheese (optional)

NUTRITIONAL FACTS (PER BURGER WITH BUN)

Calories: 243	Fat: 4.6 g	Protein: 19 g
Cholesterol: 33 mg	Fiber: 2.7 g	Sodium: 514 mg

Cooking With Charcoal

When using a gas or electric grill, it is usually a simple matter to determine whether the heat is low, medium, or high. When using charcoal, however, judging the temperature is a bit more difficult. For the best results when cooking with charcoal, use the following steps as a guide to building your fire and adjusting it for proper cooking.

1. Position a pyramid of coals in the center of your barbecue, and light it about 45 minutes before cooking.

2. When the coals are covered with a light gray ash, the fire is ready. Spread the charcoal out to cover the grill.

3. To judge the temperature of the fire, *cautiously* hold your hand, palm side down, 4 to 6 inches above the coals. Count the number of seconds you can hold your hand in that position, and use the following key to approximate the temperature:

Low	=	5 seconds
Medium	=	4 seconds
Medium-high	=	3 seconds
High	=	2 seconds

4. If the temperature is too hot for your needs, raise the grill rack and spread the coals farther apart. Close the air vents or carefully remove some of the coals if necessary. If the temperature is too cool, lower the grill rack; move the coals closer together, towards the center of the grill; tap off the ashes; open more air vents; or, if desired, add more coals.

5. If the fire needs to be remade during cooking, place new coals around the outside of the burning charcoal. Move the new coals towards the center once they become lit.

Barbecuing is a great way to enjoy the warm weather and to create delicious meals for family and friends. By taking the time to use your barbecue as effectively as possible, you'll make this popular activity all the more pleasurable and insure your reputation as a skilled outdoor chef.

All-American Potato Salad

1. Cut the potatoes into $\frac{3}{4}$-inch pieces, and place in a microwave or stove-top steamer. Cover and cook at high power or over medium-high heat for 8 to 10 minutes, or until tender. Rinse with cool water and drain.

2. Place the potatoes in a large bowl. Add the celery, onion, carrot, and relish, and toss gently to mix.

3. Combine the dressing ingredients in a small bowl, and stir to mix well. Add the dressing to the potato mixture, and toss gently to mix.

4. Cover the salad and chill for at least 2 hours before serving.

Yield: 8 servings

2 pounds medium-sized red potatoes, unpeeled

$\frac{1}{3}$ cup thinly sliced celery

$\frac{1}{3}$ cup finely chopped onion

$\frac{1}{3}$ cup grated carrot

1 tablespoon plus 1 $\frac{1}{2}$ teaspoons sweet pickle relish

DRESSING

$\frac{1}{3}$ cup nonfat or reduced-fat mayonnaise

$\frac{1}{3}$ cup nonfat sour cream

2 tablespoons spicy mustard

$\frac{1}{4}$ teaspoon ground black pepper

NUTRITIONAL FACTS (PER $\frac{3}{4}$-CUP SERVING)		
Calories: 139	Fat: 0.2 g	Protein: 3.5 g
Cholesterol: 0 mg	Fiber: 2.9 g	Sodium: 185 mg

Fresh Tomato Salad

To keep the tomatoes bright and firm, make this salad no more than 2 to 4 hours before serving.

1. Place the vegetables in a shallow dish. Combine the dressing ingredients in a small bowl, and pour over the vegetables. Toss to mix well.

2. Cover the salad and chill for several hours, stirring occasionally, before serving.

Yield: 9 servings

4 large ripe tomatoes, cut into wedges

1 medium sweet onion, cut into thin wedges

1 medium green bell pepper, cut into thin strips

DRESSING

3 tablespoons red wine vinegar

1 tablespoon sugar

1 tablespoon finely chopped fresh basil

NUTRITIONAL FACTS (PER $\frac{1}{2}$-CUP SERVING)		
Calories: 29	Fat: 0.3 g	Protein: 0.9 g
Cholesterol: 0 mg	Fiber: 1.3 g	Sodium: 7 mg

Two-Bean Salad

Yield: 8 servings

1½ pounds fresh green beans

1 can (1 pound) red kidney beans, drained and rinsed

¾ cup chopped onion

¾ cup chopped green bell pepper

DRESSING

¼ cup plus 2 tablespoons red wine vinegar

2 tablespoons sugar

¼ teaspoon ground black pepper

¼ teaspoon salt

1. Cut the green beans into 1-inch pieces, and place in a microwave or stove-top steamer. Cover and cook at high power or over medium-high heat for 6 to 8 minutes, or until tender. Rinse with cool water and drain.

2. Place the green beans in a large bowl. Add the kidney beans, onion, and green pepper, and toss to mix.

3. Combine the dressing ingredients in a small bowl, and stir to mix well. Pour the dressing over the bean mixture, and toss to mix.

4. Cover the salad and chill for several hours or overnight, stirring occasionally, before serving.

NUTRITIONAL FACTS (PER ¾-CUP SERVING)

Calories: 81	Fat: 0.3 g	Protein: 4.6 g
Cholesterol: 0 mg	Fiber: 5 g	Sodium: 38 mg

Old-Fashioned Blueberry Cobbler

1. Coat a 2½-quart casserole dish with nonstick cooking spray. Combine the filling ingredients in a medium-sized bowl, and set aside for 15 minutes to allow the juices to develop. Then stir gently to mix well, and transfer to the prepared dish.

2. Combine all of the topping ingredients except for the buttermilk in a medium-sized bowl, and stir to mix well. Add the buttermilk, and stir just until the dry ingredients are moistened. Drop heaping tablespoonfuls of the batter onto the blueberry mixture to make 8 biscuits.

3. Bake at 375°F for about 45 minutes, or until the filling is bubbly and the topping is golden brown. If the topping starts to brown too quickly, cover the dish loosely with aluminum foil during the last 10 minutes of baking. Remove the cobbler from the oven, and let it sit for 10 minutes. Serve warm, topping each serving with a scoop of the nonfat ice cream.

Yield: 8 servings

FRUIT FILLING

6 cups fresh or frozen (thawed) blueberries

3 tablespoons cornstarch

⅓ cup sugar

1 tablespoon frozen orange juice concentrate, thawed

TOPPING

⅓ cup oat bran

⅔ cup unbleached flour

¼ cup sugar

1½ teaspoons baking powder

½ cup nonfat buttermilk

1 quart nonfat vanilla ice cream

NUTRITIONAL FACTS (PER SERVING, WITH ICE CREAM)

Calories: 248	Fat: 0.9 g	Protein: 5.6 g
Cholesterol: 2 mg	Fiber: 3.9 g	Sodium: 137 mg

Berries and Cream Cake

Yield: 10 servings

1 angel food cake (1 pound)

3 cups nonfat vanilla, strawberry, or blueberry ice cream, slightly softened

3 cups fresh strawberry slices

1½ cups fresh blueberries

1. With a serrated knife, cut a 2-inch-deep channel in the top of the angel food cake, leaving $\frac{3}{8}$ inch of cake intact on either side of the channel. Spoon the ice cream evenly into the hollowed-out channel. Wrap the cake tightly with aluminum foil or plastic wrap, and freeze for at least 12 hours.

2. Up to 2 hours before assembling the dessert, combine the strawberries and blueberries in a large bowl. Cover and chill until ready to serve.

3. Place the frozen cake in the center of a 12-inch round platter. Arrange 2 cups of the fruit mixture over the top of the cake to cover the ice cream. Arrange the remaining fruit around the base of the cake. Let the cake sit for 5 minutes before slicing and serving, accompanying each piece of cake with some of the mixed fruit.

NUTRITIONAL FACTS (PER SERVING)		
Calories: 188	Fat: 0.4 g	Protein: 5.1 g
Cholesterol: 1 mg	Fiber: 2 g	Sodium: 160 mg

Labor Day

As summer turns to fall, and thoughts of the new school year begin, celebrate one of the last great cookout days of the year with this Caribbean-style feast. Piquant island seasonings are the perfect complement to grilled chicken and shrimp, as well as to a variety of side dishes, making this meal flavorful and satisfying without added fat.

A cool platter of fruit dip surrounded with tropical fruits makes for a great start. Try sliced fresh mango and pineapple along with whole strawberries.

The main course, Grenadian-Style Grilled Chicken, offers a low-fat taste of the islands. The spicy coating keeps the meat moist so that there is no need to baste with an oily sauce. Or, if you prefer, grill up some Caribbean Shrimp on a Stick. Made with a delightful citrus-and-mango marinade, this dish is sure to win raves.

Beans are filling without being fattening, and this menu offers a choice of two savory bean dishes: Jamaican Red Beans and Rice, and Cuban Black Bean Salad. Zesty Coleslaw and island-inspired Baked Plantain round out the accompaniments, adding just the right touch to this light summer meal.

Last but not least, is *real* Key Lime Pie. Enjoy—this version is absolutely fat-free and has about half the calories of the traditionally made dessert.

Give yourself more time to chat with your guests—and to enjoy your own party—by using some plan-ahead strategies. The Fresh Fruit Dip, for instance, can be quickly made the day before your party. Cut the accompanying fruit up on the morning of the cookout, and chill it in covered containers until you're ready to assemble your platter.

If chicken is on the menu, coat the pieces a day ahead of time, and refrigerate them until you're ready to complete your preparations. If you plan to make shrimp, marinate the seafood overnight. It should take only minutes to make up the skewers and grill these delicacies once guests arrive.

Both Cuban Black Bean Salad and Zesty Coleslaw are perfect make-ahead dishes, as they can be fully prepared the day before your party, allowing the pungent flavors of each dish to mingle. Prepare the plaintain to the point of baking a day in advance. Then pop it into the oven 20 minutes before serving time. And the Jamaican Red Beans and Rice? This satisfying dish can be quickly put on to cook an hour before serving.

Our menu's cooling dessert—light and refreshing Key Lime Pie—is quite impressive, yet fairly simple to make. Whip it up the day before your cookout, keep it chilled until serving time, and bask in the praise of family and friends.

Labor Day Cookout

SERVES 6 TO 8

Tropical Fruit Platter (page 181)

Grenadian-Style Grilled Chicken (page 182)
or Caribbean Shrimp on a Stick (page 183)

Jamaican Red Beans and Rice (page 184)
or Cuban Black Bean Salad (page 185)

Baked Plantain (page 186)

Zesty Coleslaw (page 186)

Key Lime Pie (page 187)

Tropical Fruit Platter

When you create the decorative pineapple bowl, crush some of the scooped-out pineapple and use it to make your Fresh Fruit Dip.

1. To make the pineapple bowl for the dip, cut the pineapple in half crosswise. Using a sharp knife, cut around the fruit in the lower half of the pineapple, separating the flesh from the shell. Use a spoon to remove the flesh. Trim away any ragged edges of fruit, and use this fruit to make the dip. Slice any remaining fruit, including the fruit in the upper half of the pineapple. Set the pineapple bowl and slices aside.

2. Peel the mangoes and cut the flesh into strips. Rinse the strawberries and pat dry. Set aside.

3. To assemble the platter, place the pineapple bowl in the center of a 12-inch serving plate. (Trim the bottom with a sharp knife, if necessary, to allow it to stand firmly.) Fill the bowl with the Fresh Fruit Dip.

4. Arrange half of the pineapple slices on one side of the bowl, and half on the opposite side of the bowl. Similarly arrange the mango strips in 2 sections on opposite sides of the bowl. Fill in the spaces between the pineapple and mango with the strawberries. Garnish the platter with the mint leaves, if desired, and serve.

Yield: 10 servings

1 large pineapple

3 large mangoes

1 pint large strawberries

1 recipe Fresh Fruit Dip (page 56), made with pineapple

12–15 fresh mint leaves (garnish)

NUTRITIONAL FACTS (PER SERVING)		
Calories: 112	Fat: 0.5 g	Protein: 4 g
Cholesterol: 0 mg	Fiber: 3 g	Sodium: 68 mg

Grenadian-Style Grilled Chicken

Yield: 9 servings

9 boneless skinless chicken breast halves, 5 ounces each

COATING

2 medium yellow onions, chopped

2 tablespoons brown sugar

1½ teaspoons ground allspice

1½ teaspoons dried thyme

½ teaspoon ground cinnamon

½ teaspoon ground nutmeg

½ teaspoon crushed red pepper

1 teaspoon coarsely ground black pepper

¼ teaspoon salt

1. Place all of the coating ingredients in a food processor, and process until the mixture is finely chopped and well blended. Spread the mixture on both sides of the chicken breasts, cover, and chill for several hours or overnight.

2. When ready to cook, coat a disposable 9-x-13-inch aluminum pan with nonstick cooking spray. Arrange the chicken in a single layer in the pan, and pour any remaining juices over the chicken. Cover the pan tightly with aluminum foil.

3. Place the pan on the grill rack over low heat, and cook, with the grill covered, for 25 minutes, or until the juices run clear when the meat is pierced and the meat shows no trace of pink.

4. Carefully uncover the pan, and transfer the chicken to the grill rack. Continue cooking for 7 to 10 minutes, or just until the chicken is nicely browned, turning the chicken once and basting with any remaining pan juices. Serve hot.

NUTRITIONAL FACTS (PER SERVING)		
Calories: 170	Fat: 1.8 g	Protein: 33 g
Cholesterol: 82 mg	Fiber: 0.3 g	Sodium: 153 mg

Variation

If rain turns your cookout into a cook-in, it's simple to bake this chicken in the oven. Arrange the chicken in a coated 9-x-13-inch pan, as described above. Cover the pan with aluminum foil, and bake at 325°F for 25 minutes. Remove the chicken from the pan, and place under the broiler for 6 to 8 minutes, or just until brown, turning once, and basting with any remaining pan juices.

Caribbean Shrimp on a Stick

1. Place all of the marinade ingredients in a blender or food processor, and process until smooth. Place the shrimp in a shallow dish, and pour half of the marinade over the shrimp. (Refrigerate the other half of the marinade until you grill the shrimp.) Turn the shrimp to coat, cover, and refrigerate for several hours or overnight.

2. When ready to cook, thread 8 shrimp on each of 9 (12-inch) skewers, leaving a ¼-inch space between the shrimp. Grill over medium heat for 3 to 4 minutes on each side, or until the shrimp turn pink and are cooked through. Use the remaining marinade to baste the shrimp several times while cooking. Serve hot.

Yield: 9 servings

72 jumbo shrimp (about 3 pounds), peeled and deveined

MARINADE
½ cup orange juice

¼ cup lime juice

½ cup mango chutney

4 cloves garlic

½ teaspoon ground white pepper

1 teaspoon dried thyme

NUTRITIONAL FACTS (PER SERVING)

Calories: 160	Fat: 1.4 g	Protein: 24 g
Cholesterol: 221 mg	Fiber: 0.1 g	Sodium: 267 mg

Variation

If desired, you can cook Caribbean Shrimp on a Stick in the broiler of your oven. Broil for 3 to 4 minutes on each side, or until the shrimp turn pink and are thoroughly cooked.

Jamaican Red Beans and Rice

Yield: 8 servings

1⅓ cups uncooked brown rice

2¾ cups plus 2 tablespoons water

1 medium yellow onion, chopped

1 can (1 pound) red kidney beans, drained and rinsed

1¼ teaspoons chicken bouillon granules

¼ teaspoon ground black pepper

¼ teaspoon ground allspice

½ teaspoon coconut extract

1. Place the rice in a strainer, and rinse under cold running water. (Rinsing makes the rice fluffier.)

2. Place all of the ingredients, including the rice, in a 2½-quart pot, and bring to a boil over high heat. Reduce the heat to low, stir the rice, and cover.

3. Allow the rice to simmer, covered, for about 50 minutes, or until the rice is cooked and the liquid has been absorbed. Do not stir the rice while it is cooking, as this can result in sticky rice.

4. Remove the rice from the heat, and let sit, covered, for 5 minutes. Fluff with a fork, and serve hot.

NUTRITIONAL FACTS (PER ¾-CUP SERVING)

Calories: 165	Fat: 1 g	Protein: 5.4 g
Cholesterol: 0 mg	Fiber: 2 g	Sodium: 221 mg

Variation

For even fluffier rice, make this dish in a rice cooker, using 3¼ cups of water. (For information on using a rice cooker, see the inset on page 142.)

Cuban Black Bean Salad

1. Combine the beans, rice, tomato, celery, green pepper, onion, and cilantro in a large bowl, and toss to mix well.

2. Combine the dressing ingredients in a small bowl, and stir to mix well. Pour the dressing over the bean mixture, and toss to mix.

3. Cover the salad and chill for at least 2 hours before serving.

Yield: 8 servings

1 can (1 pound) black beans, drained and rinsed

2½ cups cooked brown rice, chilled

1 medium tomato, seeded and chopped

½ cup thinly sliced celery

½ cup chopped green bell pepper

½ cup chopped sweet onion

2 tablespoons minced fresh cilantro

DRESSING

3–4 tablespoons white wine vinegar

1 tablespoon olive oil (optional)

1 teaspoon dried oregano

1 teaspoon crushed fresh garlic

1 teaspoon sugar

¼ teaspoon salt

NUTRITIONAL FACTS (PER ¾-CUP SERVING)

Calories: 115	Fat: 0.7 g	Protein: 4.6 g
Cholesterol: 0 mg	Fiber: 4.3 g	Sodium: 153 mg

Baked Plantain

Yield: 8 servings

4 large ripe plantains

½ cup orange juice

Ground nutmeg

A member of the banana family, the plantain is widely used in Caribbean cooking. Ripe plantains have dark skins, an enticing banana fragrance, and a sweet flavor.

1. Coat a large baking sheet with butter-flavored nonstick cooking spray. Peel the plantains, and diagonally slice them ⅜ inch thick. Arrange the slices in a single layer on the pan.

2. Drizzle the orange juice over the plantain slices, and lightly sprinkle the slices with the nutmeg. Cover the pan with aluminum foil, and bake at 375°F for 10 minutes. Carefully remove the foil (steam will escape), and bake for an additional 10 minutes, or until the plantains are tender and lightly browned around the edges. Serve hot.

NUTRITIONAL FACTS (PER ½-CUP SERVING)

Calories: 104	Fat: 0.1 g	Protein: 0.7 g
Cholesterol: 0 mg	Fiber: 3.6 g	Sodium: 4 mg

Zesty Coleslaw

Yield: 8 servings

8 cups coarsely shredded cabbage (about 2 pounds)

1 cup grated carrot

DRESSING

½ cup nonfat or reduced-fat mayonnaise

2 tablespoons white wine vinegar

2 tablespoons pineapple juice

3 tablespoons spicy mustard

1½ tablespoons sugar

⅛ teaspoon ground black pepper

1. Combine the cabbage and carrot in a large bowl, and toss to mix well.

2. Combine the dressing ingredients in a small bowl, and stir to mix well. Pour the dressing over the cabbage mixture, and toss to mix.

3. Cover the salad and chill for several hours or overnight before serving.

NUTRITIONAL FACTS (PER ⅔-CUP SERVING)

Calories: 42	Fat: 0.4 g	Protein: 1 g
Cholesterol: 0 mg	Fiber: 1.7 g	Sodium: 213 mg

Key Lime Pie

1. To make the crust, break the crackers into pieces, and place in the bowl of a food processor or blender. Process into fine crumbs. Measure the crumbs. There should be 1¼ cups. (Adjust the amount if necessary.)

2. Return the crumbs to the food processor. Add the sugar, and process for a few seconds to mix. Add the egg substitute, and process until the mixture is moist and crumbly.

3. Coat a 9-inch deep dish pie pan with nonstick cooking spray, and use the back of a spoon to press the crumbs against the sides and bottom of the pan, forming an even crust. (Dip the spoon in sugar periodically, if necessary, to prevent sticking.) Bake at 350°F for 10 minutes, or until the edges feel firm and dry. Set aside to cool.

4. To make the filling, combine the cornstarch and sugar in a 2-quart saucepan. Slowly stir in the evaporated milk, and place over medium heat, stirring constantly with a wire whisk until the mixture is thickened and bubbly.

5. Reduce the heat to low. In a small bowl, blend ½ cup of the hot mixture into the egg substitute. Return the mixture to the saucepan, and cook, still stirring, for 2 to 3 minutes. Do not boil.

6. Remove the mixture from the heat, and stir in the lime juice. Pour the filling into the pie crust, and set aside.

7. To make the meringue, place the egg whites in the bowl of an electric mixer, and beat until foamy. Beat in the cream of tartar and salt, and continue beating until soft peaks form when the beaters are removed. Beat the sugar in slowly, adding 1 tablespoon at a time. Add the vanilla extract, and beat until the mixture is glossy and stiff peaks form when the beaters are removed.

8. Spread the meringue over the warm filling, swirling it with a knife or spoon. Make sure that the meringue touches all edges of the crust. Bake at 350°F for about 10 minutes, or just until the meringue is touched with brown. Chill for at least 8 hours or overnight.

9. Cut the pie into wedges, and serve. For easier serving, dip the knife in warm water before cutting each slice.

Yield: 8 servings

CRUST

8 large (2½-x-5-inch) fat-free or regular graham crackers

2 tablespoons sugar

2 tablespoons fat-free egg substitute

FILLING

¼ cup plus 2 tablespoons cornstarch

⅔ cup sugar

1 can (12 ounces) evaporated skim milk

½ cup fat-free egg substitute

½ cup key lime juice

MERINGUE TOPPING

3 egg whites, warmed to room temperature

¼ teaspoon cream of tartar

⅛ teaspoon salt

6 tablespoons sugar

1 teaspoon vanilla extract

NUTRITIONAL FACTS (PER SERVING)

Calories: 245	Fiber: 0.6 g
Cholesterol: 1 mg	Protein: 7.6 g
Fat: 0.4 g	Sodium: 214 mg

Variation

To save time and effort, omit the meringue topping, and simply chill the pie for 6 hours after filling. Then fold $\frac{1}{2}$ cup of nonfat vanilla yogurt into $1\frac{1}{2}$ cups of light whipped topping, and swirl the frosting over the chilled pie. Chill for at least 2 additional hours, and serve.

NUTRITIONAL FACTS (PER SERVING)

Calories: 241	Fat: 1.5 g	Protein: 7.5 g
Cholesterol: 2 mg	Fiber: 0.7 g	Sodium: 214 mg

Halloween

When the ghosts and goblins have finished making their rounds, lure them in from the chill of an October evening and warm them up with this hot and hearty buffet.

As your guests arrive, greet them with steaming mugs of Hot Apple Cider, kept warm and fragrant in a Crock Pot heated casserole or coffee maker. Then bring out warm Fiesta Quesadillas. Garnished with cool and creamy nonfat sour cream, these perfect pick-up meal starters are a favorite of small party-goers and parents alike.

The main course, Two-Bean Chili, is made low in fat with the leanest ground beef available. Or make the chili virtually fat-free by using TVP (texturized vegetable protein) instead of beef. Thick and hearty, the vegetarian version of this dish has been known to convert more than a few meat eaters.

Mini Mexican Corn Muffins complement the chili perfectly, and a fresh vegetable platter with Black Olive Dip rounds out the accompani-ments. Moist and fudgy Black Magic Cake with Fluffy Cocoa Frosting adds the finishing touch to this fuss-free menu.

With a little preparation, this buffet is a breeze. Fiesta Quesadillas are easily assembled ahead of time and baked at the last minute. Two-Bean Chili can be made the day before the party, reheated right before the party begins, and kept warm in a chafing dish. Mini Mexican Corn Muffins, too, can be made ahead, and then reheated as guests arrive. Black Olive Dip tastes even *better* when made in advance, as this allows the flavors to marry and blend, so whip this tempting dip up the day before your party, and chill until serving time. Also cut up the accompanying raw vegetables a day in advance, and keep them crisp and fresh in refrigerated plastic bags or airtight containers. Finally, bake the Black Magic Cake on the morning or afternoon of the party, and refrigerate the dessert until you present it as the crowning touch to a frighteningly good meal.

Halloween Buffet

SERVES 12 TO 14

Hot Apple Cider (page 63)

Fiesta Quesadillas (page 32)

Two-Bean Chili (page 191)

Mini Mexican Corn Muffins (page 192)

*Fresh Vegetable Platter
with Black Olive Dip* (page 52)

Black Magic Cake (page 193)

Two-Bean Chili

1. Place the ground beef in a 6-quart stock pot, and brown over medium-high heat, stirring constantly to crumble. Drain off any excess fat.

2. Add the tomatoes, tomato sauce, onion, green pepper, herbs and spices, and bouillon granules to the beef, and stir to mix well. Bring the mixture to a boil over high heat. Then reduce the heat to low, cover the pot, and simmer for 15 minutes.

3. Add the beans to the chili, and stir to mix well. Cover and simmer for 20 minutes. Stir in the vinegar.

4. Transfer the chili to a chafing dish or Crock-Pot heated casserole to keep warm, and serve, topping each serving with grated nonfat Cheddar cheese if desired.

Yield: 16 servings

2 pounds 96% lean ground beef

2 cans (1 pound each) unsalted crushed tomatoes

2 cans (1 pound each) unsalted tomato sauce

2 large onions, chopped

2 large green bell peppers, chopped

4–5 tablespoons chili powder

2 teaspoons dried oregano

1 teaspoon ground cumin

2 teaspoons beef bouillon granules

2 cans (1 pound each) kidney beans, drained and rinsed

2 cans (1 pound each) pinto beans, drained and rinsed

3 tablespoons red wine or cider vinegar

2 cups grated nonfat or reduced-fat Cheddar cheese (optional)

NUTRITIONAL FACTS (PER 1-CUP SERVING)

Calories: 191	Fat: 2.6 g	Protein: 15.5 g
Cholesterol: 23 mg	Fiber: 8.9 g	Sodium: 269 mg

Variation

To make Vegetarian Two-Bean Chili, use texturized vegetable protein (TVP)* instead of beef. Just heat $1\frac{3}{4}$ cups of water and 2 teaspoons of vegetable bouillon granules to the boiling point in a 6-quart stock pot, and stir in 2 cups of TVP. Remove the pot from the heat, and let the mixture sit for 5 minutes, or until all of the liquid has been absorbed. Then add the tomatoes and other ingredients—except the beef bouillon, which is no longer needed—according to the instructions provided above.

NUTRITIONAL FACTS (PER 1-CUP SERVING)

Calories: 171	Fat: 1.2 g	Protein: 13 g
Cholesterol: 0 mg	Fiber: 11.5 g	Sodium: 170 mg

*TVP is a protein-rich alternative to meat. Made from soy flour that has been formed into small nuggets, TVP is cholesterol-free and contains almost no fat. Look for TVP in health foods stores and many grocery stores.

Mini Mexican Corn Muffins

Yield: 24 muffins

1 cup whole wheat flour

1 cup whole grain yellow cornmeal

2 teaspoons baking powder

½ teaspoon baking soda

½ teaspoon whole cumin seeds

1½ cups nonfat buttermilk

2 egg whites

½ cup shredded nonfat or
   reduced-fat Cheddar cheese

1½ tablespoons finely chopped
   jalapeño peppers (optional)

1. Combine the flour, cornmeal, baking powder, baking soda, and cumin seeds in a large bowl, and stir to mix well. Add the buttermilk and egg whites, and stir just until the dry ingredients are moistened. Fold in the cheese and, if desired, the jalapeño peppers.

2. Coat mini-muffin tins with nonstick cooking spray, and fill each cup *completely full* with the batter. Bake at 350°F for about 10 minutes, or just until a wooden toothpick inserted in the center of a muffin comes out clean. Be careful not to overbake.

3. Remove the muffins tins from the oven, and allow them to sit for 5 minutes before removing the muffins. Serve warm.

NUTRITIONAL FACTS (PER MUFFIN)

Calories: 41	Fat: 0.2 g	Protein: 2.1 g
Cholesterol: 0 mg	Fiber: 1.1 g	Sodium: 67 mg

Black Magic Cake

1. In a large bowl, combine the flours, sugar, cocoa, baking soda, and salt, if desired, and stir to mix well. In a small bowl, combine the water, coffee, vinegar, and vanilla extract. Add the coffee mixture to the flour mixture, and stir to mix well.

2. Coat a 9-x-13-inch pan with nonstick cooking spray. Pour the batter into the pan, and bake at 350°F for 30 to 35 minutes, or just until the top springs back when lightly touched and a wooden toothpick inserted in the center of the cake comes out clean. Be careful not to overbake. Cool the cake to room temperature.

3. To make the frosting, place the sugar, corn syrup, and water in a small, heavy saucepan. Stir until the sugar dissolves. Place the saucepan over medium heat, and bring to a boil. Continue boiling the mixture without stirring until the temperature reaches 240°F on a candy thermometer, or until a drop of syrup forms a soft ball in cold water.

4. Just before the temperature of the syrup reaches 240°F, place the egg whites in the bowl of an electric mixer, and beat until the whites form soft peaks. Add the hot syrup in a slow, thin stream while beating at high speed. Continue beating for 3 to 5 minutes, or until the icing is glossy and firm enough to spread. Beat in the vanilla extract. Finally, beat in the cocoa 1 teaspoonful at a time.

5. Immediately spread the frosting evenly over the cake. Cut into squares, and serve immediately or refrigerate.

Variation

Instead of baking the cake in one large pan, use two 9-inch round pans, and bake for only 25 minutes. Cool the cakes in the pans, and invert one layer upside down onto a serving platter. Spread the cake with a layer of icing, and top it with the second layer, placing it right side up. Complete the layer cake by frosting the sides and top, swirling the frosting with a spoon or knife.

Yield: 16 servings

2¼ cups unbleached flour

¾ cup oat flour

1½ cups sugar

½ cup cocoa powder

2 teaspoons baking soda

¼ teaspoon salt (optional)

2 cups water

¼ cup plus 2 tablespoons prepared coffee, cooled to room temperature

1 tablespoon cider vinegar

2 teaspoons vanilla extract

FLUFFY COCOA FROSTING

¾ cup sugar

¼ cup light corn syrup

¼ cup water

3 large egg whites, warmed to room temperature

1 teaspoon vanilla extract

1 tablespoon cocoa powder

NUTRITIONAL FACTS
(PER SERVING)

Calories: 216	Fiber: 2 g
Chol.: 0 mg	Protein: 3.2 g
Fat: 1 g	Sod.: 129 mg

Part Four

Festive Fat-Free Desserts and Treats

The holidays bring an abundance of delicious desserts and baked goods, some of which are unavailable at any other time of year. These sweet and savory treats are the stars of holiday parties, and are often given as gifts, as well. At other times of the year, of course, breads, muffins, and desserts are just as welcome. A spicy fruit crisp, super-moist cake, or fruit-filled bread adds that special touch to any get-together, whether an elaborate sit-down affair or a backyard barbecue.

The recipes presented in this section—as well as in the holiday and party menus found in Parts Two and Three—will allow you to serve healthful no-fat treats which taste so great, no one but you will guess just how wholesome they are. These recipes contain no butter, margarine, oil, or shortening of any kind. Instead, ingredients like fruit purées, juices, nonfat yogurt, nonfat buttermilk, and liquid sweeteners add moistness, eliminating the need for fat. In addition, these recipes contain less sugar than most dessert recipes do. Fruits and fruit juices, flavorings like vanilla extract and cinnamon, and mildly sweet flours like oat have been used to reduce the need for sugar, and to add fiber and other nutrients, as well.

Before taking out your baking pans and preheating your oven, you might wish to turn to "Getting the Fat Out of Parties," on page 3. That section will acquaint you with the whole grain flours you'll be using, and will guide you in substituting less-refined sweeteners for traditional sweeteners, if you wish to do so. Then get ready to create some of the healthiest and best-tasting desserts and snacks you've ever tasted. Even if you're short on time, these simple, easy-to-follow recipes will help make your next special-occasion gathering an event to remember.

QUICK BREADS

Whole Wheat Apricot Bread

Yield: 20 slices

1 cup chopped dried apricots

½ cup boiling water

¼ cup plus 2 tablespoons honey

2 cups whole wheat flour

¼ teaspoon baking soda

2 teaspoons baking powder

¼ cup evaporated skim milk

¼ cup plus 2 tablespoons Prune Purée (page 198)

1 teaspoon vanilla extract

¾ cup nonfat or low-fat granola cereal

1. Place the apricots in a small bowl, and pour the boiling water over the apricots. Stir in the honey, and set aside to cool.

2. In a large bowl, combine the flour, baking soda, and baking powder, and stir to mix well. Add the cooled apricot mixture and the milk, Prune Purée, and vanilla extract to the flour mixture, and stir just until the dry ingredients are moistened. Fold in the granola.

3. Coat two 5¾-x-3¼-inch loaf pans with nonstick cooking spray, and divide the batter evenly between the pans. Bake at 325°F for about 30 minutes, or just until a wooden toothpick inserted in the center of a loaf comes out clean.

4. Remove the bread from the oven, and let sit for 10 minutes. Invert the loaves onto a wire rack, turn right side up, and cool to room temperature before slicing and serving.

NUTRITIONAL FACTS (PER SLICE)

Calories: 89	Fat: 0.2 g	Protein: 2.3 g
Cholesterol: 0 mg	Fiber: 2.3 g	Sodium: 71 mg

Making Prune Purée and Prune Butter

The dessert recipes in this book use a variety of fat substitutes, including fruit purées, fruit juices, applesauce, and nonfat buttermilk. Most of these substitutes are readily available in grocery stores. Two excellent fat substitutes, however, must be made at home. Prune Purée and Prune Butter will allow you to make moist and flavorful baked goods with little or no fat, and will add fiber and nutrients as well. Simply follow the recipes provided below, and keep these ingredients on hand for use in many holiday recipes.

Prune Purée

Yield: 1½ cups

3 ounces pitted prunes (about ½ cup)

1 cup water or fruit juice

2 teaspoons lecithin granules*

1. Place all ingredients in a blender or food processor, and process at high speed until the mixture is smooth.

2. Use immediately, or place in an airtight container and store for up to 3 weeks in the refrigerator.

Prune Butter

Yield: 1 cup

8 ounces pitted prunes (about 1⅓ cups)

6 tablespoons water or fruit juice

1. Place both ingredients in a food processor, and process at high speed until the mixture is a smooth paste. (Note that this mixture is too thick to be made in a blender.)

2. Use immediately, or place in an airtight container and store for up to 3 weeks in the refrigerator.

*Lecithin, which is derived from soybeans, improves the texture of baked goods. You'll find lecithin granules in health foods stores, where they're sold as a supplement.

Fresh Pear Bread

1. In a large bowl, combine the flour, sugar, baking soda, baking powder, nutmeg, and cinnamon, and stir to mix well. Add the pear nectar and chopped pear, and stir just until the dry ingredients are moistened. Fold in the currants or raisins.

2. Coat an 8-x-4-inch loaf pan with cooking spray. Spread the batter in the pan, and bake at 350°F for 45 minutes, or until a wooden toothpick inserted in the center comes out clean.

3. Remove the bread from the oven, and let sit for 10 minutes. Invert the loaf onto a wire rack, turn right side up, and cool to room temperature before slicing and serving.

Yield: 16 slices

2 cups whole wheat flour

½ cup sugar

1 teaspoon baking soda

1 teaspoon baking powder

¼ teaspoon ground nutmeg

¼ teaspoon ground cinnamon

¾ cup pear nectar

1⅓ cups finely chopped fresh pear (about 1½ medium)

¼ cup currants or dark raisins

NUTRITIONAL FACTS (PER SLICE)		
Calories: 98	Fat: 0.3 g	Protein: 2.2 g
Cholesterol: 0 mg	Fiber: 2.4 g	Sodium: 75 mg

Pumpkin Spice Bread

1. In a large bowl, combine the flour, sugar, baking soda, baking powder, and pumpkin pie spice, and stir to mix well. Add the juice, pumpkin, and egg white, and stir just until the dry ingredients are moistened. Fold in the cranberries or pecans if desired.

2. Coat an 8-x-4-inch loaf pan with cooking spray. Spread the batter in the pan, and bake at 350°F for 40 minutes, or until a wooden toothpick inserted in the center comes out clean.

3. Remove the bread from the oven, and let sit for 10 minutes. Invert the loaf onto a wire rack, turn right side up, and cool to room temperature before slicing and serving.

Yield: 16 slices

2 cups whole wheat flour

½ cup light brown sugar

1 teaspoon baking soda

1 teaspoon baking powder

1½ teaspoons pumpkin pie spice

¾ cup plus 2 tablespoons orange juice

½ cup mashed cooked or canned pumpkin

1 egg white

⅓ cup dried cranberries or chopped pecans (optional)

NUTRITIONAL FACTS (PER SLICE)		
Calories: 78	Fat: 0.3 g	Protein: 2.5 g
Cholesterol: 0 mg	Fiber: 2.1 g	Sodium: 108 mg

Cranberry Applesauce Bread

Yield: 16 slices

1 cup unsweetened applesauce

½ cup quick-cooking oats

1⅔ cups whole wheat flour

½ cup sugar

1 teaspoon baking soda

1 teaspoon baking powder

½ teaspoon ground cinnamon

2 egg whites

¾ cup coarsely chopped fresh or
   frozen cranberries (do not thaw)

1. In a small bowl, combine the applesauce and oats. Set aside for 5 minutes.

2. In a large bowl, combine the flour, sugar, baking soda, baking powder, and cinnamon, and stir to mix well. Add the applesauce mixture and the egg whites to the flour mixture, and stir just until the dry ingredients are moistened. Fold in the cranberries.

3. Coat an 8-x-4-inch loaf pan with nonstick cooking spray. Spread the batter evenly in the pan, and bake at 350°F for about 45 minutes, or just until a wooden toothpick inserted in the center of the loaf comes out clean.

4. Remove the bread from the oven, and let sit for 10 minutes. Invert the loaf onto a wire rack, turn right side up, and cool to room temperature before slicing and serving.

NUTRITIONAL FACTS (PER SLICE)

Calories: 87	Fat: 0.4 g	Protein: 2.6 g
Cholesterol: 0 mg	Fiber: 2.1 g	Sodium: 109 mg

Orange Date Bread

1. Place the orange juice in a small saucepan, and bring to a boil over high heat. Place the dates in a small bowl, and pour the orange juice over the dates. Set aside to cool.

2. In a large bowl, combine the flour, sugar, baking soda, and baking powder, and stir to mix well. Stir the vanilla extract into the cooled date mixture, add the date mixture to the flour mixture, and stir just until the dry ingredients are moistened. Fold in the walnuts if desired.

3. Coat a 7½-x-3¾-inch loaf pan with nonstick cooking spray. Spread the batter evenly in the pan, and bake at 350°F for about 30 minutes, or just until a wooden toothpick inserted in the center of the loaf comes out clean.

4. Remove the bread from the oven, and let sit for 10 minutes. Invert the loaf onto a wire rack, turn right side up, and cool to room temperature before slicing and serving.

Yield: 15 slices

1 cup orange juice
¾ cup chopped dates
1½ cups whole wheat flour
2 tablespoons sugar
1 teaspoon baking soda
1 teaspoon baking powder
1 teaspoon vanilla extract
¼ cup chopped walnuts (optional)

NUTRITIONAL FACTS (PER SLICE)

Calories: 79	Fiber: 2.3 g
Cholesterol: 0 mg	Protein: 2 g
Fat: 0.3 g	Sodium: 78 mg

Spiced Apple Brown Bread

1. In a large bowl, combine the flour, cornmeal, and baking soda, and stir to mix well. Add the apple butter and buttermilk, and stir just until the dry ingredients are moistened. Fold in the currants or raisins.

2. Coat four 1-pound cans with nonstick cooking spray. Divide the batter evenly among the cans, and bake at 300°F for about 45 minutes, or just until a wooden toothpick inserted in the center of a loaf comes out clean.

3. Remove the bread from the oven, and let sit for 10 minutes. Invert the loaves onto a wire rack, turn right side up, and cool before slicing and serving.

Yield: 32 slices

2 cups whole wheat flour
1 cup whole grain cornmeal
1 teaspoon baking soda
1½ cups apple butter
1½ cups nonfat buttermilk
¾ cup currants or dark raisins

NUTRITIONAL FACTS (PER SLICE)

Calories: 78	Fiber: 1.7 g
Cholesterol: 0 mg	Protein: 1.9 g
Fat: 0.4 g	Sodium: 40 mg

Whole Wheat Banana Bread

Yield: 16 slices

2 cups whole wheat flour

1/4 cup sugar

1 teaspoon baking soda

1 teaspoon baking powder

2 cups mashed very ripe banana (about 4 large)

1/4 cup skim milk

1 teaspoon vanilla extract

1/3 cup chopped walnuts (optional)

1. In a large bowl, combine the flour, sugar, baking soda, and baking powder, and stir to mix well. In a small bowl, combine the banana, milk, and vanilla extract. Add the banana mixture to the flour mixture, and stir just until the dry ingredients are moistened. Fold in the walnuts if desired.

2. Coat an 8-x-4-inch loaf pan with cooking spray. Spread the batter in the pan, and bake at 350°F for 45 minutes, or until a wooden toothpick inserted in the center comes out clean.

3. Remove the bread from the oven, and let sit for 10 minutes. Invert the loaf onto a wire rack, turn right side up, and cool to room temperature before slicing and serving.

NUTRITIONAL FACTS (PER SLICE)

Calories: 91	Fat: 0.5 g	Protein: 2.4 g
Cholesterol: 0 mg	Fiber: 2.5 g	Sodium: 75 mg

Tropical Fruitcake

Yield: 20 slices

1 cup plus 2 tablespoons whole wheat flour

1/2 teaspoon baking powder

1 cup mashed very ripe banana (about 2 large)

2 egg whites

1 cup dried mango or papaya, cut into 1-inch pieces

1 cup dried pineapple chunks

1/2 cup dark raisins or chopped Brazil nuts

1/2 cup whole pitted dates, cut in half lengthwise

1. In a large bowl, combine the flour and baking powder, and stir to mix well. Add the banana and egg whites, and stir just until the dry ingredients are moistened. Fold in the fruit.

2. Coat two 5¾-x-3¼-inch loaf pans with cooking spray. Divide batter between the pans, and bake at 325°F for 45 minutes, or until a wooden toothpick inserted in the center comes out clean.

3. Remove the loaves from the oven, and let sit for 10 minutes. Invert the loaves onto a wire rack, turn right side up, and cool to room temperature. Wrap in aluminum foil and refrigerate overnight before slicing and serving.

NUTRITIONAL FACTS (PER SLICE)

Calories: 109	Fat: 0.3 g	Protein: 2.1 g
Cholesterol: 0 mg	Fiber: 2.5 g	Sodium: 17 mg

Very Best Fruitcake

Even people who don't like fruitcake will like this one. Real dried fruits replace the processed candied fruits used in traditional fruitcakes for a taste that's truly irresistible.

1. In a large bowl, combine the flour, baking powder, nutmeg, and ginger, and stir to mix well. Add the honey, egg substitute, and vanilla extract, and stir just until the dry ingredients are moistened. Fold in the fruit.

2. Coat two 5¾-x-3¼-inch loaf pans with nonstick cooking spray. Divide the batter evenly between the pans, and bake at 325°F for about 45 minutes, or just until a wooden toothpick inserted in the center of a loaf comes out clean.

3. Remove the bread from the oven, and let sit for 10 minutes. Invert the loaves onto a wire rack, turn right side up, and cool to room temperature. Wrap in aluminum foil and refrigerate overnight before slicing and serving.

Yield: 20 slices

1¼ cups whole wheat flour

½ teaspoon baking powder

½ teaspoon ground nutmeg

¼ teaspoon ground ginger

½ cup honey

½ cup plus 2 tablespoons fat-free egg substitute

2 teaspoons vanilla extract

1 cup chopped dried pineapple

1 cup dried apricot halves (leave whole)

½ cup dark raisins, or ½ cup whole pitted dates, cut in half lengthwise

½ cup golden raisins

½ cup dried cranberries or dried pitted cherries

NUTRITIONAL FACTS (PER SLICE)

Calories: 123	Fat: 0.3 g	Protein: 3 g
Cholesterol: 0 mg	Fiber: 2.6 g	Sodium: 28 mg

Fruitful Brown Bread

Yield: 32 slices

2 cups whole wheat flour

1 cup whole grain cornmeal

1 teaspoon baking soda

1 can (8 ounces) crushed pineapple
in juice, undrained

½ cup mashed very ripe banana
(about 1 large)

1 cup nonfat buttermilk

½ cup molasses

¾ cup chopped dried apricots

½ cup chopped pecans (optional)

1. In a large bowl, combine the flour, cornmeal, and baking soda, and stir to mix well. Add the pineapple, including the juice, and the banana, buttermilk, and molasses, and stir just until the dry ingredients are moistened. Fold in the apricots and, if desired, the pecans.

2. Coat four 1-pound cans with nonstick cooking spray. Divide the batter evenly among the cans, and bake at 300°F for about 45 minutes, or just until a wooden toothpick inserted in the center of a loaf comes out clean.

3. Remove the bread from the oven, and let sit for 10 minutes. Invert the loaves onto a wire rack, turn right side up, and cool before slicing and serving.

NUTRITIONAL FACTS (PER SLICE)

Calories: 68	Fat: 0.4 g	Protein: 1.8 g
Cholesterol: 0 mg	Fiber: 1.7 g	Sodium: 37 mg

Sweet Potato Gingerbread

1. In a large bowl, combine the flour, cornmeal, baking soda, ginger, and allspice, and stir to mix well. Add the sweet potato or pumpkin, apple or orange juice, and honey or molasses, and stir just until the dry ingredients are moistened. Fold in the raisins if desired.

2. Coat four 1-pound cans with nonstick cooking spray. Divide the batter evenly among the cans, and bake at 300°F for 40 to 45 minutes, or until a wooden toothpick inserted in the center of a loaf comes out clean.

3. Remove the bread from the oven, and let sit for 10 minutes. Invert the loaves onto a wire rack, turn right side up, and cool before slicing and serving.

Yield: 32 slices

2 cups whole wheat flour

1 cup whole grain cornmeal

1 teaspoon baking soda

2 teaspoons ground ginger

1 teaspoon ground allspice

1 cup mashed cooked sweet potato
 or pumpkin

1¼ cups apple or orange juice

¾ cup honey or molasses

¾ cup golden raisins (optional)

NUTRITIONAL FACTS (PER SLICE)

Calories: 83	Fat: 0.3 g	Protein: 1.7 g
Cholesterol: 0 mg	Fiber: 1.7 g	Sodium: 34 mg

A Festive Touch

Any quick bread recipe can be used to make festive round loaves by baking the batter in cans instead of loaf pans. These loaves can be wrapped in colored plastic wrap, tied on top with a ribbon, and given as gifts during the holiday season or at any time of the year.

Simply spray three or four 1-pound food cans with nonstick cooking spray, and divide the batter evenly among the cans, filling each half full. Bake at 300°F for about 45 minutes, or just until a wooden toothpick inserted in the center of a loaf comes out clean. Cool the bread in the cans for 10 minutes, remove the loaves from the cans, and cool completely before wrapping.

A word of caution is in order regarding the cans used to make these loaves. When choosing cans for baking, be sure to avoid those that have been lead-soldered. Lead is a toxic metal that can leach into foods during baking. Food cans produced in this country do not contain lead solder, as the United States canning industry eliminated this process in 1991. Some labels even state that the can is lead-free. Imported foods, however, may still be packaged in soldered cans. To be safe, avoid baking bread in all cans with pronounced seams—a sign of lead soldering—and in all imported food cans. You will then be sure that the festive breads you make are as healthy as they are delicious.

MUFFINS

Cranberry Almond Muffins

Yield: 12 muffins

1¼ cups whole wheat flour

½ cup whole grain cornmeal

½ cup sugar

1 tablespoon baking powder

1 cup plus 2 tablespoons nonfat
buttermilk

2 egg whites

1 teaspoon almond extract

1 cup fresh or frozen cranberries (do
not thaw), coarsely chopped

TOPPING

1 tablespoon finely ground almonds

1 teaspoon sugar

1. To make the topping, combine the almonds and sugar in a small bowl. Set aside.

2. In a large bowl, combine the flour, cornmeal, sugar, and baking powder, and stir to mix well. Add the buttermilk, egg whites, and almond extract, and stir just until the dry ingredients are moistened. Fold in the cranberries.

3. Coat muffin cups with nonstick cooking spray, and fill ¾ full with the batter. Sprinkle the topping over the batter, and bake at 350°F for about 18 minutes, or just until a wooden toothpick inserted in the center of a muffin comes out clean.

4. Remove the muffin tin from the oven, and allow it to sit for 5 minutes before removing the muffins. Serve warm or at room temperature.

NUTRITIONAL FACTS (PER MUFFIN)

Calories: 115	Fat: 0.9 g	Protein: 3.6 g
Cholesterol: 0 mg	Fiber: 2.5 g	Sodium: 118 mg

A Sizzling Fourth of July Cookout
Center Left: Salsa Burgers (page 173)
Center Right: Fresh Tomato Salad (page 175)
Bottom: All-American Potato Salad (page 175)

A Caribbean-Style Labor Day Cookout
Top: Zesty Coleslaw (page 186)
Center Left: Baked Plantain (page 186)
Center Right: Jamaican Red Beans and Rice (page 184)
Bottom: Caribbean Shrimp on a Stick (page 183)

A Haunting Halloween Buffet
Top Left: Hot Apple Cider (page 63)
Top Right: Mini Mexican Corn Muffins (page 192)
Center Left: Two-Bean Chili (page 191)
Center Right: Black Olive Dip (page 52)

A Sumptuous Selection of Sinless Desserts
Top: Fresh Fruit Trifle (page 240)
Bottom Left: Cranberry Upside-Down Cake (page 231)
Bottom Right: Chocolate-Almond Cannoli Cake (page 233)

Harvest Pumpkin Muffins

Yield: 12 muffins

1. To make the topping, combine the brown sugar and wheat germ in a small bowl. Set aside.

2. In a large bowl, combine the flour, brown sugar, baking powder, and pumpkin pie spice, and stir to mix well. Add the pumpkin, apple juice, and egg whites, and stir just until the dry ingredients are moistened. Fold in the apple.

3. Coat muffin cups with nonstick cooking spray, and fill ¾ full with the batter. Sprinkle the topping over the batter, and bake at 350°F for 16 to 18 minutes, or just until a wooden toothpick inserted in the center of a muffin comes out clean.

4. Remove the muffin tin from the oven, and allow it to sit for 5 minutes before removing the muffins. Serve warm or at room temperature.

2 cups whole wheat flour

½ cup light brown sugar

1 tablespoon plus 1 teaspoon baking powder

1¼ teaspoons pumpkin pie spice

⅔ cup mashed cooked or canned pumpkin

½ cup plus 1 tablespoon apple juice

2 egg whites

1¼ cups finely chopped apple (about 1½ medium)

TOPPING

1 tablespoon light brown sugar

1 tablespoon toasted wheat germ

NUTRITIONAL FACTS (PER MUFFIN)		
Calories: 116	Fat: 0.5 g	Protein: 3.5 g
Cholesterol: 0 mg	Fiber: 3 g	Sodium: 135 mg

Holiday Banana Muffins

Yield: 12 muffins

2 cups whole wheat flour

¼ cup light brown sugar

1 tablespoon baking powder

1 cup mashed very ripe banana
   (about 2 large)

⅓ cup orange juice

2 egg whites

1 teaspoon vanilla extract

⅓ cup dried cranberries or golden
   raisins

TOPPING

1 tablespoon light brown sugar

1 tablespoon finely ground pecans

1. To make the topping, combine the brown sugar and pecans in a small bowl. Set aside.

2. In a large bowl, combine the flour, brown sugar, and baking powder, and stir to mix well. Add the banana, orange juice, egg whites, and vanilla extract, and stir just until the dry ingredients are moistened. Fold in the cranberries or raisins.

3. Coat muffin cups with nonstick cooking spray, and fill ¾ full with the batter. Sprinkle the topping over the batter, and bake at 350°F for 14 to 16 minutes, or just until a wooden toothpick inserted in the center of a muffin comes out clean.

4. Remove muffin tin from oven, and allow it to sit for 5 minutes before removing muffins. Serve warm or at room temperature.

NUTRITIONAL FACTS (PER MUFFIN)		
Calories: 131	Fat: 0.9 g	Protein: 3.8 g
Cholesterol: 0 mg	Fiber: 3.1 g	Sodium: 95 mg

Apple Butter Bran Muffins

Yield: 12 muffins

1 cup whole wheat flour

1 cup wheat bran

½ cup oat bran

1 teaspoon baking soda

½ teaspoon ground cinnamon

1 cup apple butter

1 cup nonfat buttermilk

2 egg whites

½ cup dark raisins

1. Combine the flour, wheat bran, oat bran, baking soda, and cinnamon, and stir to mix well. Add the apple butter, buttermilk, and egg whites, and stir just until the dry ingredients are moistened. Fold in the raisins.

2. Coat muffin cups with cooking spray, and fill ¾ full with batter. Bake at 350°F for 15 to 18 minutes, or until a wooden toothpick inserted in the center of a muffin comes out clean.

3. Remove muffin tin from oven, and allow it to sit for 5 minutes before removing muffins. Serve warm or at room temperature.

NUTRITIONAL FACTS (PER MUFFIN)		
Calories: 123	Fat: 0.9 g	Protein: 4.1 g
Cholesterol: 0 mg	Fiber: 3.8 g	Sodium: 101 mg

Cocoa Banana Muffins

1. In a large bowl, combine the flours, sugar, cocoa, and baking powder, and stir to mix well. Add the banana, milk, egg whites, and vanilla extract, and stir just until the dry ingredients are moistened. Fold in the walnuts if desired.

2. Coat muffin cups with nonstick cooking spray, and fill ¾ full with the batter. Sprinkle the sugar over the batter if desired. Bake at 350°F for 14 to 16 minutes, or just until a wooden toothpick inserted in the center of a muffin comes out clean.

3. Remove the muffin tin from the oven, and allow it to sit for 5 minutes before removing the muffins. Serve warm or at room temperature.

Yield: 12 muffins

1¼ cups whole wheat flour

½ cup oat flour

½ cup sugar

¼ cup plus 2 tablespoons cocoa powder

1 tablespoon baking powder

1 cup very ripe mashed banana (about 2 large)

¾ cup skim milk

2 egg whites

1 teaspoon vanilla extract

¼ cup chopped walnuts (optional)

TOPPING

4 teaspoons sugar (optional)

NUTRITIONAL FACTS (PER MUFFIN)

Calories: 120	Fat: 0.6 g	Protein: 3.8 g
Cholesterol: 0 mg	Fiber: 2.4 g	Sodium: 182 mg

COOKIES AND BROWNIES

Mint Chocolate Chippers

Yield: 30 cookies

¾ cup whole wheat flour

½ cup unbleached flour

⅔ cup light brown sugar

¾ teaspoon baking soda

¼ cup Prune Purée (page 198)

2 tablespoons honey

1 teaspoon vanilla extract

⅓ cup mint chocolate chips

¼ cup chopped walnuts (optional)

1. In a large bowl, combine the flours, brown sugar, and baking soda, and stir to mix well. Add the Prune Purée, honey, and vanilla extract, and stir to mix well. (Note that the dough will seem dry at first. Keep stirring until it holds together.) Fold in the mint chocolate chips and, if desired, the walnuts.

2. Coat a baking sheet with nonstick cooking spray. Drop rounded teaspoonfuls of dough onto the baking sheet, placing them 1½ inches apart. Slightly flatten each cookie with the tip of a spoon.

3. Bake at 350°F for 9 to 10 minutes, or until lightly browned. Cool the cookies on the pan for 1 minute. Then transfer the cookies to wire racks, and cool completely. Serve immediately, or transfer to an airtight container and arrange in single layers separated by sheets of waxed paper.

NUTRITIONAL FACTS (PER COOKIE)

Calories: 49	Fat: 0.7 g	Protein: 0.7 g
Cholesterol: 0 mg	Fiber: 0.5 g	Sodium: 21 mg

Mocha Pecan Drops

Yield: 34 cookies

1. In a large bowl, combine the flour, sugar, cocoa, coffee granules, and baking soda, and stir to mix well. Add the Prune Purée, chocolate syrup, and vanilla extract, and stir to mix well. (Note that the dough will seem dry at first. Keep stirring until it holds together.) Fold in the pecans.

2. Coat a baking sheet with nonstick cooking spray. Drop rounded teaspoonfuls of dough onto the baking sheet, placing them 1½ inches apart. Slightly flatten each cookie with the tip of a spoon.

3. Bake at 350°F for 9 to 10 minutes, or until lightly browned. Cool the cookies on the pan for 1 minute. Then transfer the cookies to wire racks, and cool completely. Serve immediately, or transfer to an airtight container and arrange in single layers separated by sheets of waxed paper.

1 cup plus 2 tablespoons whole wheat flour

⅔ cup sugar

2 tablespoons cocoa powder

½ teaspoon instant coffee granules

¾ teaspoon baking soda

¼ cup Prune Purée (page 198)

3 tablespoons chocolate syrup

1 teaspoon vanilla extract

⅓ cup chopped pecans

NUTRITIONAL FACTS (PER COOKIE)

Calories: 42	Fat: 0.9 g	Protein: 0.7 g
Cholesterol: 0 mg	Fiber: 0.7 g	Sodium: 30 mg

Fruitcake Cookies

Yield: 40 cookies

1 cup plus 2 tablespoons whole wheat flour

¾ cup sugar

1 teaspoon baking soda

¼ cup Prune Purée (page 198)

3 tablespoons honey

1 teaspoon vanilla extract

2 cups bran flake-and-raisin cereal

¼ cup chopped dried apricots

¼ cup chopped dried pineapple

¼ cup dried cranberries or golden raisins

1. In a large bowl, combine the flour, sugar, and baking soda, and stir to mix well. Add the Prune Purée, honey, and vanilla extract, and stir to mix well. Fold in the cereal and dried fruits.

2. Coat a baking sheet with nonstick cooking spray. Drop rounded teaspoonfuls of dough onto the baking sheet, placing them 1½ inches apart. Slightly flatten each cookie with the tip of a spoon. (Note that the dough will be slightly crumbly, so that you may have to press it together lightly to make it hold its shape.)

3. Bake at 350°F for 9 to 10 minutes, or until lightly browned. Cool the cookies on the pan for 1 minute. Then transfer the cookies to wire racks, and cool completely. Serve immediately, or transfer to an airtight container and arrange in single layers separated by sheets of waxed paper.

NUTRITIONAL FACTS (PER COOKIE)

Calories: 47	Fat: 0.1 g	Protein: 0.8 g
Cholesterol: 0 mg	Fiber: 0.9 g	Sodium: 39 mg

Lebkuchen

These chewy spice cookies are a traditional German holiday treat.

1. In a large bowl, combine the flours, brown sugar, baking soda, spices, and orange rind, and stir to mix well. Add the honey and orange juice, and stir to mix well. Add the almonds and dried fruit, and stir to mix.

2. Coat a baking sheet with nonstick cooking spray. Roll the dough into 1-inch balls, and place 1½ inches apart on the baking sheet. Using the bottom of a glass dipped in sugar, flatten the cookies to ¼-inch thickness.

3. Bake at 275°F for about 18 minutes, or until golden brown. Cool the cookies on the pan for 1 minute. Then transfer the cookies to wire racks, and cool completely. Serve immediately, or transfer to an airtight container, and arrange in single layers separated by sheets of waxed paper.

Yield: 34 cookies

1 cup whole wheat flour

¾ cup unbleached flour

¼ cup plus 2 tablespoons brown sugar

¾ teaspoon baking soda

¾ teaspoon ground cinnamon

¼ teaspoon ground nutmeg

¼ teaspoon ground cloves

½ teaspoon dried grated orange rind

¼ cup plus 2 tablespoons honey

3 tablespoons plus 2 teaspoons orange juice

¼ cup finely chopped almonds

⅓ cup finely chopped mixed dried fruit

NUTRITIONAL FACTS (PER COOKIE)

Calories: 50	Fat: 0.6 g	Protein: 1.0 g
Cholesterol: 0 mg	Fiber: 0.7 g	Sodium: 29 mg

Crispy Meringues

Yield: 48 cookies

4 egg whites, warmed to room
temperature

$\frac{1}{4}$ teaspoon cream of tartar

$\frac{1}{4}$ teaspoon salt

$\frac{3}{4}$ cup sugar

1 teaspoon vanilla extract

$1\frac{1}{2}$ cups Rice Krispies cereal

For best results, make these light-as-air treats on a dry day. Also be careful to prevent any egg yolk from getting mixed in with the whites, or the whites will not whip properly.

1. Place the egg whites in the bowl of an electric mixer, and beat on high until foamy. Add the cream of tartar and salt, and continue beating until soft peaks form. Still beating, slowly add first the sugar, and then the vanilla extract. Remove the beaters and fold in the cereal.

2. Line a large baking sheet with aluminum foil. (Do not grease the sheet or coat it with cooking spray.) Drop heaping teaspoonfuls of the meringue onto the baking sheet, placing them $1\frac{1}{2}$ inches apart.

3. Bake at 250°F for 45 to 50 minutes, or until firm and creamy white. Turn the oven off, and let the meringues cool in the oven for at least 2 hours with the door closed. Remove the pans from the oven and peel the meringues from the foil. Serve immediately, or transfer to an airtight container.

NUTRITIONAL FACTS (PER COOKIE)		
Calories: 17	Fat: 0 g	Protein: 0.3 g
Cholesterol: 0 mg	Fiber: 0 g	Sodium: 26 mg

Variations

To make Chocolate Chip Meringues, fold in $\frac{3}{4}$ cup of chocolate chips—semi-sweet chocolate, milk chocolate, or chocolate mint—along with the cereal.

NUTRITIONAL FACTS (PER COOKIE)		
Calories: 30	Fat: 0.9 g	Protein: 0.4 g
Cholesterol: 0 mg	Fiber: 0.1 g	Sodium: 26 mg

To make Almond Meringues, substitute almond extract for the vanilla extract, and fold in $\frac{3}{4}$ cup of slivered almonds along with the cereal.

NUTRITIONAL FACTS (PER COOKIE)		
Calories: 26	Fat: 0.8 g	Protein: 0.6 g
Cholesterol: 0 mg	Fiber: 0.2 g	Sodium: 27 mg

To make Coconut Meringues, add $\frac{1}{2}$ teaspoon of coconut-flavored extract along with the vanilla extract, and fold in $\frac{1}{2}$ cup of sweetened shredded or flaked coconut along with the cereal.

NUTRITIONAL FACTS (PER COOKIE)		
Calories: 22	Fat: 0.4 g	Protein: 0.4 g
Cholesterol: 0 mg	Fiber: 0.1 g	Sodium: 28 mg

To make Lemon Meringues, fold in the grated zest of 1 lemon and substitute lemon extract for the vanilla.

NUTRITIONAL FACTS (PER COOKIE)		
Calories: 18	Fat: 0 g	Protein: 0.3 g
Cholesterol: 0 mg	Fiber: 0.2 g	Sodium: 26 mg

To make Minty Meringues, add $\frac{1}{4}$ teaspoon of peppermint extract along with the vanilla. If desired, use food coloring to tint the meringues green or pink.

NUTRITIONAL FACTS (PER COOKIE)		
Calories: 17	Fat: 0 g	Protein: 0.3 g
Cholesterol: 0 mg	Fiber: 0.2 g	Sodium: 26 mg

To make Cocoa Meringues, beat in 4 tablespoons of cocoa powder, 1 tablespoon at a time, right after the sugar has been added.

NUTRITIONAL FACTS (PER COOKIE)		
Calories: 18	Fat: 0 g	Protein: 0.4 g
Cholesterol: 0 mg	Fiber: 0.1 g	Sodium: 26 mg

Pfeffernüsse

Yield: 30 cookies

¾ cup whole wheat flour

¾ cup unbleached flour

¼ cup plus 2 tablespoons sugar

¾ teaspoon baking soda

½ teaspoon ground cinnamon

⅛ teaspoon ground cloves

⅛ teaspoon ground white pepper

¼ cup molasses

3 tablespoons plus 1 teaspoon apple juice

3 tablespoons finely chopped walnuts

¼ cup finely chopped golden raisins

Like Lebkuchen, German "Peppernuts" are traditional holiday fare.

1. In a large bowl, combine the flours, sugar, baking soda, and spices, and stir to mix well. Add the molasses and apple juice, and stir to mix well. Stir in the walnuts and raisins.

2. Coat a baking sheet with nonstick cooking spray. Roll the dough into 1-inch balls, and place 1½ inches apart on the baking sheet. Bake at 275°F for about 18 minutes, or until lightly browned. Cool the cookies on the pan for 1 minute. Then transfer the cookies to wire racks, and cool completely. Serve immediately, or transfer to an airtight container, and arrange in single layers separated by sheets of waxed paper.

NUTRITIONAL FACTS (PER COOKIE)

Calories: 47	Fat: 0.5 g	Protein: 1 g
Cholesterol: 0 mg	Fiber: 0.6 g	Sodium: 32 mg

Pumpkin Pecan Bites

1. In a large bowl, combine the flour, oat bran, brown sugar, baking soda, and pumpkin pie spice, and stir to mix well. Add the pumpkin and the honey or molasses, and stir to mix well.

2. Coat a baking sheet with cooking spray. Roll the dough into 1-inch balls, and place 1½ inches apart on the sheet. Press a pecan half in the center of each cookie to flatten the dough.

3. Bake at 300°F for 15 minutes, or until lightly browned. Cool the cookies on the pan for 1 minute. Then transfer to racks, and cool completely. Serve immediately, or transfer to an airtight container, and arrange in single layers separated by waxed paper.

Yield: 40 cookies

1 cup whole wheat flour

1 cup oat bran

¾ cup brown sugar

¾ teaspoon baking soda

2–3 teaspoons pumpkin pie spice

½ cup mashed cooked or canned pumpkin

¼ cup honey or molasses

40 small pecan halves

NUTRITIONAL FACTS (PER COOKIE)		
Calories: 49	Fat: 1.2 g	Protein: 1 g
Cholesterol: 0 mg	Fiber: 1 g	Sodium: 17 mg

Maple Spice Drops

1. In a large bowl, combine the flour, oats, sugar, baking soda, cinnamon, and nutmeg, and stir to mix well. Add the maple syrup, water, and vanilla extract, and stir to mix well. Fold in the raisins.

2. Coat a baking sheet with cooking spray. Drop rounded teaspoonfuls of dough onto the baking sheet, placing them 1½ inches apart. Slightly flatten each cookie with the tip of a spoon.

3. Bake at 275°F for 18 minutes, or until lightly browned. Cool the cookies on the pan for 1 minute. Then transfer to racks, and cool completely. Serve immediately, or transfer to an airtight container and arrange in single layers separated by waxed paper.

Yield: 36 cookies

1 cup whole wheat flour

1 cup quick-cooking oats

⅔ cup sugar

¾ teaspoon baking soda

½ teaspoon ground cinnamon

½ teaspoon ground nutmeg

¼ cup maple syrup

¼ cup water

1 teaspoon vanilla extract

½ cup dark raisins

NUTRITIONAL FACTS (PER COOKIE)		
Calories: 47	Fat: 0.2 g	Protein: 0.9 g
Cholesterol: 0 mg	Fiber: 0.8 g	Sodium: 27 mg

Honey Orange Biscotti

Yield: 24 biscotti

1 cup whole wheat flour

1 cup unbleached flour

⅓ cup sugar

2 teaspoons baking powder

1 teaspoon dried grated orange rind

⅓ cup chopped pecans or currants (optional)

¼ cup plus 2 tablespoons fat-free egg substitute

2 tablespoons honey

2 tablespoons frozen orange juice concentrate, thawed

1. In a large bowl, combine the flours, sugar, baking powder, and orange rind, and stir to mix well. Add the pecans or currants if desired, and stir to mix. Add the remaining ingredients, and stir just until the dough holds together.

2. Turn the dough onto a lightly floured surface, and shape into two 8-x-2-inch logs. (If the dough is too sticky to handle, knead in a little more flour.) Coat a baking sheet with nonstick cooking spray, and place the logs on the sheet. Bake at 350°F for about 23 minutes, or until lightly browned. Transfer the logs to a wire rack, and allow to cool for 10 minutes.

3. Place the logs on a cutting board, and use a serrated knife to slice the logs diagonally into ½-inch-thick slices. Place the slices on a baking sheet, and bake at 300°F for 20 minutes, or until lightly browned, turning after 10 minutes.

4. Transfer the biscotti to wire racks, and cool completely. Serve immediately or store in an airtight container.

NUTRITIONAL FACTS (PER BISCOTTI)		
Calories: 56	Fat: 0.1 g	Protein: 1.6 g
Cholesterol: 0 mg	Fiber: 0.8 g	Sodium: 19 mg

Cocoa Almond Biscotti

Yield: 24 biscotti

1. In a large bowl, combine the flour, sugar, cocoa, and baking powder, and stir to mix well. Add the almonds if desired, and stir to mix. Add the remaining ingredients, and stir just until the dough holds together.

2. Turn the dough onto a lightly floured surface, and shape into two 8-x-2-inch logs. (If the dough is too sticky to handle, knead in a little more flour.) Coat a baking sheet with nonstick cooking spray, and place the logs on the sheet. Bake at 350°F for about 23 minutes, or until lightly browned. Transfer the logs to a wire rack, and allow to cool for 10 minutes.

3. Place the logs on a cutting board, and use a serrated knife to slice the logs diagonally into ½-inch-thick slices. Place the slices on a baking sheet, and bake at 300°F for 20 minutes, or until lightly browned, turning after 10 minutes.

4. Transfer the biscotti to wire racks, and cool completely. Serve immediately or store in an airtight container.

1⅔ cups whole wheat flour

⅔ cup sugar

¼ cup cocoa powder

2 teaspoons baking powder

⅓ cup chopped almonds (optional)

¼ cup plus 2 tablespoons fat-free egg substitute

¼ cup chocolate syrup

2 teaspoons almond extract

NUTRITIONAL FACTS (PER BISCOTTI)		
Calories: 60	Fat: 0.3 g	Protein: 1.7 g
Cholesterol: 0 mg	Fiber: 1.4 g	Sodium: 29 mg

Peppermint Brownies

Yield: 36 servings

4 squares (1 ounce each) unsweetened baking chocolate

1½ cups sugar

½ cup plus 1 tablespoon egg substitute

¾ cup Prune Butter (page 198)

2 teaspoons vanilla extract

1½ cups unbleached flour

¼ teaspoon salt (optional)

½ cup skim milk

¾ cup chopped walnuts (optional)

GLAZE

1 cup confectioners' sugar

1 teaspoon vanilla extract

4 drops peppermint extract

2 drops green food coloring

4–5 teaspoons skim milk

1. If using a microwave oven to melt the chocolate, place the chocolate in a small bowl and microwave uncovered at high power for 3 to 4 minutes, or until almost melted. Remove the bowl from the oven and stir the chocolate until completely melted. If melting the chocolate on the stove top, place the chocolate in a small saucepan and cook over low heat, stirring constantly, until melted.

2. Place the melted chocolate in a large bowl, and stir in first the sugar, and then the egg substitute, Prune Butter, and vanilla extract. Stir to mix well. Stir in the flour, the salt, if desired, and the milk. Fold in the walnuts if desired.

3. Coat a 9-x-13-inch pan with nonstick cooking spray. Spread the batter evenly in the pan, and bake at 325°F for 35 to 40 minutes, or just until the center springs back when lightly touched. Be careful not to overbake. Cool to room temperature.

4. To make the glaze, combine the glaze ingredients in a small bowl. If using a microwave oven, microwave the glaze uncovered at high power for 20 seconds, or until runny. If using a conventional stove top, transfer the glaze to a small saucepan and place over medium heat for 30 seconds, stirring constantly. Drizzle the glaze over the brownies, and let harden before cutting into squares and serving.

NUTRITIONAL FACTS (PER SERVING)		
Calories: 99	Fat: 1.5 g	Protein: 1.6 g
Cholesterol: 0 mg	Fiber: 1.3 g	Sodium: 28 mg

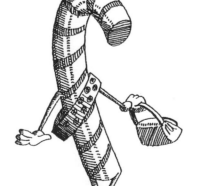

FINGER-FOOD TREATS

Flaky Phyllo Pastries

Phyllo dough makes a simple fat-free pastry.

1. Place the apples, raisins, $\frac{1}{3}$ cup of apple juice, maple syrup or honey, cinnamon, and nutmeg in a medium-sized pot, and stir to combine. Place the pot over high heat and bring to a boil. Reduce the heat to low, cover, and simmer for about 8 minutes, or until the apples are tender.

2. In a small bowl, stir together the 4 teaspoons of apple juice and the cornstarch. Add to the cooked apple mixture, and stir over low heat for about 30 seconds, or until thickened. Set aside to cool.

3. Spread the phyllo dough out on a clean dry surface. You should have a 14-x-18-inch sheet that is 20 layers thick. Cut the dough lengthwise into 4 long strips. Cover the dough with plastic wrap to prevent it from drying out as you work. (Remove strips as you need them, being sure to recover the remaining dough.)

4. Remove 1 strip of phyllo dough, and lay it flat on a clean dry surface. Spray the strip lightly with cooking spray. Top with another phyllo strip, and spray lightly with cooking spray. Spread 1 teaspoon of the apple filling over the bottom right-hand corner of the double phyllo strip. Fold the filled corner up and over to the left, so that the corner meets the left side of the strip. (See the figure on page 26 for clarification.) Continue folding in this manner until you form a triangle of dough. Repeat with the remaining dough and filling.

5. Coat a baking sheet with nonstick cooking spray. Place the pastries seam side down on the sheet. Spray the tops lightly with cooking spray, and sprinkle with cinnamon sugar if desired.

$3\frac{1}{2}$ cups finely chopped apples (about 5 medium)

$\frac{2}{3}$ cup dark raisins

$\frac{1}{3}$ cup apple juice

$\frac{1}{3}$ cup maple syrup or honey

$\frac{3}{4}$ teaspoon ground cinnamon

$\frac{1}{4}$ teaspoon ground nutmeg

4 teaspoons apple juice

4 teaspoons cornstarch

20 sheets phyllo dough (1 pound)

Cinnamon sugar (optional)

6. Bake at 375°F for 15 to 20 minutes, or until nicely browned. Cool to room temperature, and serve.

NUTRITIONAL FACTS (PER PASTRY)		
Calories: 54	Fat: 0.3 g	Protein: 1.3 g
Cholesterol: 0 mg	Fiber: 0.5 g	Sodium: 41 mg

Time-Saving Tip

When you have time, prepare the pastries to the point of baking, and arrange them in single layers in airtight containers, separating the layers with waxed paper. Freeze until the day of the party. Then arrange the frozen pastries on a coated baking sheet, and allow them to sit at room temperature for 45 minutes before baking.

Tips for Super-Moist Fat-Free Baking

The most common complaint people have about fat-free baked goods is that they are too dry. The good news is that it is possible to produce deliciously moist fat-free cakes, cookies, muffins, quick breads, and brownies. Here are some important tips that you should keep in mind as you follow the recipes in this section.

❑ *Avoid overbaking.* Fat-free treats bake more quickly than do those made with fat. Baked at too high a temperature or left in the oven too long, they will become dry. That's why the recipes in this book use lower-than-standard oven temperatures and shorter-than-standard baking times. Use the suggested baking temperatures and times as guidelines, keeping in mind that ovens do vary.

❑ *Use the toothpick test or another test of doneness.* The best way to check fat-free cakes, muffins, and quick breads for doneness is to use the toothpick test. Simply insert a wooden toothpick in the center of the product. As soon as the toothpick comes out clean, the product should be removed from the oven. Remove fat-free brownies from the oven as soon as the edges are firm and the center is almost set.

❑ *Keep your baked goods moist and fresh.* Fat-free baked goods made with the natural fat substitutes used in this book will have a high moisture content and no preservatives. To keep your fat-free cookies at their freshest, place them in an airtight container and arrange them in single layers separated by sheets of waxed paper. To keep your muffins, cakes, and other baked treats moist, wrap them carefully in plastic wrap, or place them in airtight containers. Any leftovers not eaten within twenty-four hours should be refrigerated for maximum freshness.

Hot Chocolate Dip

1. Place all of the ingredients except for the vanilla extract in a small nonstick saucepan. Place over medium heat and cook, stirring constantly, until the mixture is thickened and bubbly. Stir in the vanilla.

2. Transfer the mixture to a chafing dish or Crock-Pot heated casserole to keep warm. Serve with squares of angel food cake and sponge cake, whole fresh strawberries, and chunks of banana and fresh pineapple.

Yield: 2 cups

½ cup cocoa powder

1 cup light brown sugar

4 teaspoons cornstarch

1½ cups skim milk

2 teaspoons vanilla extract

NUTRITIONAL FACTS (PER TABLESPOON)

Calories: 28	Fat: 0.3 g	Protein: 0.6 g
Cholesterol: 0 mg	Fiber: 0.4 g	Sodium: 6 mg

Strawberry-Cheese Bites

1. Place the cream cheese or farmer cheese, sugar, and vanilla extract in a food processor or blender. Process until smooth.

2. Place 1 rounded teaspoonful of the cheese mixture in the center of each cookie, and press a strawberry half into the cheese. Arrange on a serving plate and serve immediately.

Yield: 36 servings

1 cup nonfat cream cheese, reduced-fat cream cheese, or soft curd farmer cheese

3–4 tablespoons sugar

¾ teaspoon vanilla extract

36 vanilla wafers or lemon snaps

18 large strawberries, halved

NUTRITIONAL FACTS (PER SERVING)

Calories: 32	Fat: 0.6 g	Protein: 1.6 g
Cholesterol: 2 mg	Fiber: 0.2 g	Sodium: 54 mg

Caramel Apple Dip

Yield: 1⅛ cups

1 cup nonfat or reduced-fat cream cheese, softened to room temperature

¼ cup light brown sugar

¼ teaspoon vanilla extract

1. Place the cream cheese, brown sugar, and vanilla extract in the bowl of a food processor. Process until smooth.

2. Transfer the dip to a serving dish, and serve at room temperature, or warm in a microwave oven for 40 seconds at high power. (If you choose to warm the dip on a conventional stove top, transfer the mixture to a small saucepan and place over low heat until warm.) Serve with apple slices that have been dipped in pineapple juice to prevent browning.

NUTRITIONAL FACTS (PER TABLESPOON)

Calories: 24	Fat: 0 g	Protein: 2.7 g
Cholesterol: 1 mg	Fiber: 0 g	Sodium: 67 mg

Chocolate Cannoli Treats

Yield: 36 servings

1½ cups nonfat ricotta cheese

¼ cup confectioners' sugar

½ teaspoon vanilla extract

36 fat-free chocolate wafer cookies or chocolate snaps

18 large strawberries, halved

1. Place the ricotta cheese, sugar, and vanilla extract in a food processor or blender. Process until light and creamy.

2. Place 1 heaping teaspoonful of the cheese mixture in the center of each cookie, and press a strawberry half into the cheese. Arrange on a serving plate and serve immediately.

NUTRITIONAL FACTS (PER SERVING)

Calories: 40	Fat: 0 g	Protein: 1.6 g
Cholesterol: 1 mg	Fiber: 0.2 g	Sodium: 22 mg

Mini Cherry Cheesecakes

If you are unable to locate fat-free graham crackers, just use regular graham crackers. They, too, are low in fat.

1. Break the crackers into pieces, and place in the bowl of a food processor or in a blender. Process into fine crumbs. Measure the crumbs. There should be $1\frac{1}{4}$ cups. (Adjust the amount if necessary.)

2. Return the crumbs to the food processor, and add the sugar and egg substitute. Process until the mixture resembles moist crumbs.

3. Coat nonstick mini-muffin tins with nonstick cooking spray. Place $1\frac{1}{2}$ teaspoons of the graham cracker mixture in the bottom of each muffin cup, and use a pastry press or small spoon to push the mixture over the bottom and $\frac{1}{4}$ inch up the sides of each cup. (Periodically dip the pastry press or spoon in sugar to prevent sticking).

4. Bake the crusts at 350°F for 5 to 6 minutes, or until they feel firm and dry. Remove from the oven and set aside to cool.

5. Place all of the filling ingredients in a food processor or blender, and process until smooth. Place 1 tablespoon of filling in each graham cracker shell, and bake at 300°F for 25 minutes, or until the filling is puffed and lightly browned around the edges. Turn the oven off, and let the cheesecakes cool in the oven with the door ajar for 1 hour.

6. Top each cheesecake with 1 teaspoon of cherry filling. Chill for several hours or overnight before serving.

Yield: 40 servings

CRUST

8 large ($2\frac{1}{2}$-x-5-inch) fat-free graham crackers

2 tablespoons sugar

2 tablespoons fat-free egg substitute

FILLING

$1\frac{1}{2}$ cups nonfat or reduced-fat cream cheese

1 cup dry curd or nonfat cottage cheese

$\frac{1}{2}$ cup fat-free egg substitute

$\frac{1}{2}$ cup sugar

$2\frac{1}{2}$ tablespoons unbleached flour

2 teaspoons vanilla extract

TOPPING

$\frac{3}{4}$ cup plus 2 tablespoons canned light (low-sugar) cherry pie filling

---

NUTRITIONAL FACTS (PER SERVING)

Calories: 45	Fat: 0.3 g	Protein: 3.1 g
Cholesterol: 2 mg	Fiber: 0.2 g	Sodium: 89 mg

CAKES, PIES, AND CRISPS

Apricot Kuchen Cake

Yield: 10 servings

2 cans (1 pound each) apricot halves
   in juice, undrained

¾ cup unbleached flour

½ cup whole wheat flour

¾ cup sugar

1½ teaspoons baking powder

¼ cup plain nonfat yogurt

3 tablespoons fat-free egg substitute

1 teaspoon vanilla extract

½ teaspoon almond extract

TOPPING

1 tablespoon plus 1½ teaspoons
   finely ground almonds

2 tablespoons sugar

1. To make the topping, combine the almonds and sugar in a small bowl. Set aside.

2. Drain the juice from the apricots, reserving ¼ cup of the juice to use in the cake batter. Set aside.

3. In a large bowl, combine the flours, sugar, and baking powder, and stir to mix well. Add the reserved apricot juice and the yogurt, egg substitute, and extracts, and stir just until well mixed.

4. Coat a 10-inch round cake pan with nonstick cooking spray, and spread the batter evenly in the pan. Place 1 apricot half, cut side down, over the center of the batter. Then arrange the remaining apricot halves, barely touching, in concentric circles around the center. (The apricots will partially sink into the batter during baking.) Sprinkle the topping over the batter and fruit.

5. Bake at 350°F for about 35 minutes, or until the top is golden brown and a wooden toothpick inserted near the center comes out clean. Let sit for at least 20 minutes before cutting into wedges and serving.

NUTRITIONAL FACTS (PER SERVING)

Calories: 157	Fat: 1 g	Protein: 2.8 g
Cholesterol: 0 mg	Fiber: 2.1 g	Sodium: 56 mg

Mocha Carrot Cake

1. In a large bowl, combine the flour, sugar, cocoa, and baking soda, and stir to mix well. Add the coffee, egg whites, and vanilla extract, and stir to mix well. Stir in the carrots, the raisins, and, if desired, the walnuts.

2. Coat a 9-x-13-inch pan with nonstick cooking spray, and spread the batter evenly in the pan. Bake at 325°F for about 40 minutes, or just until a wooden toothpick inserted in the center of the cake comes out clean. Cool to room temperature.

3. To make the icing, place the cream cheese and ricotta in a food processor or blender, and process until smooth. Add the confectioners' sugar and vanilla extract, and process to mix well. Spread the icing over the cooled cake, and serve immediately or refrigerate.

Yield: 16 servings

2 cups unbleached flour

1 1/4 cups sugar

1/2 cup cocoa powder

2 teaspoons baking soda

3/4 cup plus 2 tablespoons coffee, cooled to room temperature

4 egg whites

2 teaspoons vanilla extract

3 cups grated carrots (about 6 medium)

1/2 cup dark raisins

1/2 cup chopped walnuts (optional)

CREAM CHEESE ICING

1 cup nonfat or reduced-fat cream cheese

1 cup nonfat ricotta cheese

1/2 cup confectioners' sugar

1 teaspoon vanilla extract

NUTRITIONAL FACTS (PER SERVING)

Calories: 192	Fat: 0.7 g	Protein: 8.3 g
Cholesterol: 0 mg	Fiber: 2.2 g	Sodium: 237 mg

Golden Pear Cake

Yield: 8 servings

¾ cup unbleached flour

½ cup whole wheat flour

½ cup light brown sugar

¾ teaspoon baking soda

⅛ teaspoon ground cardamom or nutmeg

½ cup plain nonfat yogurt

2 egg whites

2 cups chopped peeled fresh pears (about 2½ medium)

¼ cup golden raisins

TOPPING

1 tablespoon light brown sugar

1 tablespoon toasted wheat germ

1. To make the topping, combine the light brown sugar and wheat germ in a small bowl. Set aside.

2. In a large bowl, combine the flours, brown sugar, baking soda, and cardamom or nutmeg, and stir to mix well. Add the yogurt and egg whites, and stir to mix well. Fold in the pears and raisins.

3. Coat an 8-inch square pan with nonstick cooking spray. Spread the batter evenly in the pan, and sprinkle with the topping. Bake at 350°F for 30 to 35 minutes, or just until a wooden toothpick inserted in the center of the cake comes out clean.

4. Cool the cake to room temperature, cut into squares, and serve.

NUTRITIONAL FACTS (PER SERVING)

Calories: 162	Fat: 0.5 g	Protein: 4.6 g
Cholesterol: 0 mg	Fiber: 2.7 g	Sodium: 149 mg

Strawberry-Coconut Coffee Cake

1. To make the topping, combine all of the topping ingredients in a small bowl until moist and crumbly. Set aside.

2. Place the skim milk and the ¼ cup of coconut in a food processor or blender, and blend at high speed for one minute, or until creamy. Set aside.

3. Place the egg whites in the bowl of an electric mixer, and beat to form soft peaks. Set aside.

4. In a large bowl, combine the flours, sugar, and baking powder, and stir to mix well. Add the coconut mixture, mashed strawberries, and vanilla extract, and stir just enough to mix well. Gently fold in the egg whites.

5. Coat a 9-inch round cake pan with nonstick cooking spray, and spread the batter evenly in the pan. Sprinkle the topping over the batter, and bake at 350°F for 25 to 30 minutes, or just until a wooden toothpick inserted in the center of the cake comes out clean. Cool to room temperature.

6. To make the glaze, combine the glaze ingredients in a small bowl, and stir until smooth. Drizzle the glaze over the cake, and let sit for at least 15 minutes before cutting into wedges and serving.

Yield: 10 servings

¼ cup plus 2 tablespoons skim milk

¼ cup shredded unsweetened coconut

2 egg whites

1 cup unbleached flour

⅓ cup whole wheat flour

¾ cup sugar

1 tablespoon plus 1½ teaspoons baking powder

½ cup mashed strawberries

1 teaspoon vanilla extract

TOPPING

¼ cup plus 2 tablespoons quick-cooking oats

1 tablespoon plus 1½ teaspoons whole wheat flour

2 tablespoons sugar

2 tablespoons shredded unsweetened coconut

1 tablespoon strawberry fruit spread or jam

GLAZE

¼ cup confectioners' sugar

1⅛ teaspoons skim milk

¼ teaspoon coconut extract

NUTRITIONAL FACTS (PER SERVING)		
Calories: 177	Fat: 1.4 g	Protein: 3.7 g
Cholesterol: 0 mg	Fiber: 1.9 g	Sodium: 67 mg

Applesauce Gingerbread

Yield: 16 servings

1½ cups unbleached flour

1 cup whole wheat flour

⅔ cup sugar

2½ teaspoons baking soda

1 teaspoon ground ginger

1 teaspoon ground cinnamon

1 teaspoon ground allspice

1½ cups unsweetened applesauce

1 cup molasses

3 egg whites

1½ cups light whipped topping
   (optional)

1. In a large bowl, combine the flours, sugar, baking soda, and spices, and stir to mix well. Add the applesauce, molasses, and egg whites, and stir to mix well.

2. Coat a 9-x-13-inch pan with cooking spray, and spread the batter in the pan. Bake at 325°F for 40 minutes, or just until a wooden toothpick inserted in the center comes out clean.

3. Cool the cake to room temperature, cut into squares, and serve, topping each serving with a dollop of light whipped topping, if desired.

NUTRITIONAL FACTS (PER SERVING)

Calories: 157	Fat: 0.3 g	Protein: 3.1 g
Cholesterol: 0 mg	Fiber: 1.6 g	Sodium: 146 mg

Pear-Maple Crisp

Yield: 6 servings

FRUIT FILLING

6 cups sliced fresh pears (about 6 medium)

1 tablespoon cornstarch

¼ teaspoon ground cinnamon

2 tablespoons maple syrup

¼ cup dark raisins or chopped walnuts (optional)

TOPPING

½ cup quick-cooking oats

3 tablespoons whole wheat flour

3 tablespoons light brown sugar

2 tablespoons maple syrup

1. To make the topping, combine the oats, flour, and brown sugar in a small bowl, and stir to mix. Add the maple syrup, and stir until the mixture is moist and crumbly. Set aside.

2. In a large bowl, combine the pears, cornstarch, and cinnamon, and toss to mix well. Drizzle the maple syrup over the pears, and toss gently. Toss in the raisins or walnuts if desired. Place the mixture in a 9-inch deep dish pie pan, and sprinkle with the topping.

3. Bake at 350°F for 35 to 40 minutes, or until the filling is bubbly and the topping is nicely browned. If the topping starts to brown too quickly, cover the dish loosely with aluminum foil during the last 10 minutes of baking. Serve warm.

NUTRITIONAL FACTS (PER SERVING)

Calories: 185	Fat: 0.9 g	Protein: 2.1 g
Cholesterol: 0 mg	Fiber: 4.8 g	Sodium: 4 mg

Cranberry Upside-Down Cake

While this cake is baking, the cranberries float up into the batter, leaving an orange glaze that forms a festive topping when the cake is turned upside down.

1. Coat an 8-inch square pan with nonstick cooking spray. Combine the orange juice concentrate and water in a small bowl, and spread the mixture over the bottom of the pan. Sprinkle the brown sugar over the concentrate, and arrange the cranberries over the sugar. Set aside.

2. In a large bowl, combine the flours, baking powder, and sugar, and stir to mix well. Add the milk, honey, egg whites, and vanilla extract, and stir to mix well. Pour the batter over the cranberries.

3. Bake at 350°F for 35 to 40 minutes, or just until a wooden toothpick inserted in the center of the cake comes out clean. Loosen the sides of the cake by running a knife around each edge, and *immediately* invert onto a serving platter. If any glaze remains in the pan, spread the glaze over the top of the cake. Let sit for at least 20 minutes before cutting into squares and serving.

Yield: 9 servings

2 tablespoons frozen orange juice concentrate, thawed

1 tablespoon water

⅓ cup brown sugar

1 cup plus 2 tablespoons fresh or frozen cranberries (do not thaw)

1¼ cups unbleached flour

⅓ cup oat flour

1½ teaspoons baking powder

½ cup sugar

⅔ cup skim milk

⅓ cup honey

2 egg whites

1 teaspoon vanilla extract

NUTRITIONAL FACTS (PER SERVING)		
Calories: 210	Fat: 0.4 g	Protein: 4 g
Cholesterol: 0 mg	Fiber: 1.4 g	Sodium: 110 mg

Pineapple Upside-Down Cake

Yield: 8 servings

1 can (20 ounces) sliced pineapple in juice, undrained

1/3 cup brown sugar

10–12 frozen pitted sweet cherries, cut in half (do not thaw)

1 cup unbleached flour

2/3 cup whole wheat flour

1/3 cup sugar

1 teaspoon baking soda

1 teaspoon baking powder

1/3 cup honey

2 egg whites

1/2 teaspoon almond extract

1. Drain the pineapple, reserving the juice.

2. Coat a 12-inch ovenproof skillet with nonstick cooking spray. Place 1 tablespoon of the reserved pineapple juice in the bottom of the skillet and distribute evenly. Sprinkle the brown sugar evenly over the juice. Place 1 pineapple ring in the center of the skillet, and arrange 8 more slices around it. Fill in the spaces with the cherry halves.

3. In a large bowl, combine the flours, sugar, baking soda, and baking powder, and stir to mix well. Stir in $\frac{3}{4}$ cup of the reserved pineapple juice and the honey, egg whites, and almond extract. Pour the batter over the pineapple slices.

4. Bake at 350°F for 25 to 30 minutes, or just until a wooden toothpick inserted in the center of the cake comes out clean. Let cool in the skillet for 15 minutes; then invert onto a serving platter. Cut into wedges and serve warm or at room temperature.

NUTRITIONAL FACTS (PER SERVING)

Calories: 228	Fat: 0.5 g	Protein: 4.2 g
Cholesterol: 0 mg	Fiber: 2.3 g	Sodium: 221 mg

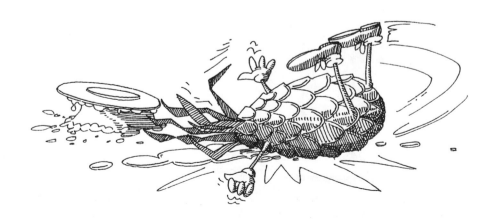

Chocolate-Almond Cannoli Cake

This cake is made in a flan or tiara pan. The bottom of the pan has a raised center that makes an ideal place to put the filling after the cake has been baked, cooled, and inverted.

1. In a large bowl, combine the flours, sugar, cocoa, baking soda, and salt, if desired, and stir to mix well. In a small bowl, combine the water, vinegar, liqueur, and vanilla extract. Add the vinegar mixture to the flour mixture, and stir to mix well.

2. Coat a 10-inch flan pan with nonstick cooking spray. Spread the batter evenly in the pan, and bake at 350°F for about 15 minutes, or just until a wooden toothpick inserted in the center of the cake comes out clean. Let the cake cool to room temperature in the pan. Then invert onto a serving platter.

3. To make the filling, place the ricotta cheese, confectioners' sugar, and almond extract in the bowl of a food processor or in a blender, and process until smooth. (Do not add more sugar, as this will make the filling too thin.) Fill the depression in the top of the cake with the filling. Arrange the strawberries around the edge of the filling and, if desired, sprinkle the almonds over the top.

4. Chill the cake for several hours, cut into wedges, and serve.

Yield: 10 servings

1 cup unbleached flour

½ cup oat flour

½ cup plus 2 tablespoons sugar

¼ cup cocoa powder

1 teaspoon baking soda

⅛ teaspoon salt (optional)

1 cup water

1½ teaspoons white wine or cider vinegar

¼ cup amaretto liqueur

1 teaspoon vanilla extract

FILLING

15 ounces nonfat ricotta cheese

⅓ cup confectioners' sugar

½ teaspoon almond extract

2 cups sliced fresh strawberries

2 tablespoons toasted sliced almonds (optional)

NUTRITIONAL FACTS (PER SERVING)

| Calories: 198 | Fat: 0.6 g | Protein: 8.6 g |
| Cholesterol: 0 mg | Fiber: 2.5 g | Sodium: 158 mg |

Strawberry-Banana Pie

Yield: 8 servings

CRUST

8 large (2½-x-5-inch) fat-free or
  regular graham crackers

3 tablespoons strawberry fruit spread

GLAZE

⅓ cup sugar

3 tablespoons cornstarch

1½ cups cran-strawberry juice or
  other strawberry juice blend

FILLING

2 cups fresh strawberries, cut in half

2 cups sliced fresh bananas

1. To make the crust, break the crackers into pieces, and place in the bowl of a food processor or blender. Process into fine crumbs. Measure the crumbs. There should be 1¼ cups. (Adjust the amount if necessary.)

2. Return the crumbs to the food processor. Add the fruit spread, and process until the mixture is moist and crumbly.

3. Coat a 9-inch pie pan with nonstick cooking spray, and use the back of a spoon to press the crumbs against the sides and bottom of the pan, forming an even crust. (Periodically dip the spoon in sugar, if necessary, to prevent sticking.) Bake at 350°F for 10 minutes, or until the edges feel firm and dry. Set aside to cool.

4. To make the glaze, place the sugar and cornstarch in a small saucepan, and stir to mix well. Slowly stir in the juice. Place the saucepan over medium heat, and bring the mixture to a boil, stirring constantly. Reduce the heat to low, and cook and stir for another minute. Remove the saucepan from the heat, and set aside for 15 minutes.

5. To assemble the pie, stir the glaze and spoon a thin layer over the bottom of the crust. Arrange half of the strawberries and half of the bananas over the glaze, and top with half of the remaining glaze. Repeat the layers. Chill for several hours, or until the glaze is set. Cut into wedges and serve cold.

NUTRITIONAL FACTS (PER SERVING)

Calories: 208	Fat: 0.4 g	Protein: 2.2 g
Cholesterol: 0 mg	Fiber: 2.2 g	Sodium: 128 mg

Peach Pizzaz Pie

1. To make the crust, place the cereal in the bowl of a food processor or blender, and process into fine crumbs. Measure the crumbs. There should be 1¼ cups. (Adjust the amount if necessary.)

2. Return the crumbs to the food processor. Add the fruit spread, and process until the mixture is moist and crumbly.

3. Coat a 9-inch pie pan with nonstick cooking spray, and use the back of a spoon to press the crumbs against the sides and bottom of the pan, forming an even crust. (Periodically dip the spoon in sugar, if necessary, to prevent sticking.) Bake at 350°F for 10 minutes, or until the edges feel firm and dry. Set aside to cool.

4. To make the glaze, place the sugar and cornstarch in a small saucepan, and stir to mix well. Slowly stir in the nectar. Place the saucepan over medium heat, and bring the mixture to a boil, stirring constantly. Reduce the heat to low, and cook and stir for another minute. Remove the saucepan from the heat, and set aside for 15 minutes.

5. To assemble the pie, stir the glaze and spoon a thin layer over the bottom of the crust. Arrange half of the peach slices in a circular pattern over the glaze. Top with the blueberries or raspberries and half of the remaining glaze. Arrange the rest of the peaches over the glaze, and top with the remaining glaze. Chill for several hours, or until the glaze is set. Cut into wedges and serve cold.

Yield: 8 servings

CRUST
5 ounces (about 2½ cups) oat flakes or oat flakes with almonds ready-to-eat cereal

3 tablespoons peach fruit spread

GLAZE
⅓ cup sugar

3 tablespoons cornstarch

1½ cups peach nectar

FILLING
3 cups sliced fresh peaches (about 4 medium)

1 cup fresh blueberries or raspberries

NUTRITIONAL FACTS (PER SERVING)		
Calories: 193	Fat: 0.3 g	Protein: 2.7 g
Cholesterol: 0 mg	Fiber: 3.1 g	Sodium: 111 mg

Pumpkin Roll

Yield: 10 servings

¾ cup unbleached flour

¾ cup sugar

1⅛ teaspoons baking powder

1 tablespoon pumpkin pie spice

⅔ cup mashed cooked or canned pumpkin

½ cup plus 1 tablespoon fat-free egg substitute

6 tablespoons confectioners' sugar

FILLING

1 cup plus 2 tablespoons nonfat ricotta cheese, soft curd farmer cheese, or reduced-fat cream cheese

¼ cup confectioners' sugar

1 teaspoon vanilla extract

1. Combine the flour, sugar, baking powder, and pumpkin pie spice in a medium-sized bowl, and stir to mix well. Add the pumpkin and egg substitute, and stir to mix well.

2. Line a 15¼-x-10¼-inch jelly roll pan with waxed paper by laying a 16-inch piece of waxed paper in the pan, and folding up the sides so that the paper covers the bottom and sides of the pan. Spray the waxed paper with nonfat cooking spray, and spread the batter evenly in the pan. Bake at 350°F for about 12 minutes, or just until the cake springs back when lightly touched.

3. While the cake is baking, sift ¼ cup of the confectioners' sugar over a clean kitchen towel. Remove the cake from the oven, and immediately invert it onto the towel. Peel off the waxed paper. Starting at the short end, roll the cake and towel up together. Place on a wire rack to cool completely.

4. To make the filling, place the filling ingredients in the bowl of a food processor or blender, and process until smooth. Gently unroll the cooled cake, and spread the filling over the cake to within ½ inch of each edge. Roll the cake up, and transfer to a serving platter. Cover and chill for several hours or overnight.

5. Sift the remaining 2 tablespoons of confectioners' sugar over the top of the roll. Trim ½ inch off of each end, and slice and serve.

NUTRITIONAL FACTS (PER SERVING)

Calories: 111	Fat: 0.1 g	Protein: 5.2 g
Cholesterol: 3 mg	Fiber: 0.6 g	Sodium: 92 mg

PUDDINGS AND TRIFLES

Golden Indian Pudding

Yield: 8 servings

1 cup mashed cooked sweet potato

1 cup fat-free egg substitute

$\frac{2}{3}$ cup molasses, honey, or maple syrup

2 teaspoons pumpkin pie spice

3 cups skim milk

$\frac{1}{2}$ cup whole grain cornmeal

1. Combine the sweet potato, egg substitute, molasses or other sweetener, and pumpkin pie spice in a blender, and blend until smooth. Leave in the blender and set aside.

2. Combine the milk and cornmeal in a $2\frac{1}{2}$-quart pot, and stir to mix well. Place over medium heat, and cook, stirring constantly, for 12 to 15 minutes, or until the mixture is thickened and bubbly. Reduce the heat to low. Add 1 cup of the hot cornmeal mixture to the sweet potato mixture, and blend at low speed with the lid slightly ajar until well mixed. Then stir all of the sweet potato mixture into the cornmeal mixture. Cook and stir for 2 to 3 minutes, or until the mixture thickens slightly. Remove the pot from the heat.

3. Coat a 2-quart round casserole dish with nonstick cooking spray. Pour the pudding mixture into the dish, and place the dish in a pan filled with 1 inch of hot water.

4. Bake uncovered at 350°F for 1 hour and 30 minutes, or until set. When done, a sharp knife inserted midway between the center of the pudding and the rim of the dish should come out clean. Remove the pudding from the oven, and let sit for 30 minutes. Serve warm, or refrigerate for several hours and serve chilled.

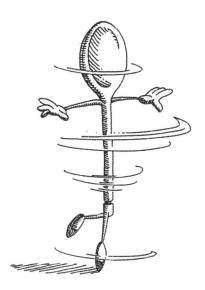

NUTRITIONAL FACTS (PER $\frac{2}{3}$-CUP SERVING)		
Calories: 143	Fat: 0.5 g	Protein: 5 g
Cholesterol: 0 mg	Fiber: 1.4 g	Sodium: 66 mg

Creamy Baked Custard

Yield: 6 servings

2 cups skim milk

1 cup evaporated skim milk

1 cup fat-free egg substitute

½ cup sugar

2 teaspoons vanilla extract

Ground nutmeg

1. Place all of the ingredients except for the nutmeg in the bowl of a food processor or in a blender, and process for 30 seconds to mix well.

2. Coat a 1½-quart baking dish with nonstick cooking spray. Pour the custard mixture into the dish, and sprinkle with the nutmeg. Place the dish in a pan filled with 1 inch of hot water.

3. Bake uncovered at 350°F for 1 hour and 20 minutes, or until set. When done, a sharp knife inserted midway between the center of the custard and the rim of the dish should come out clean. Cover and chill for several hours or overnight before serving.

NUTRITIONAL FACTS (PER ⅔-CUP SERVING)

Calories: 214	Fat: 0.3 g	Protein: 14 g
Cholesterol: 4 mg	Fiber: 0 g	Sodium: 216 mg

Raspberry Bread Pudding

Yield: 8 servings

1. Place the bread cubes in a large bowl. In a medium-sized bowl, combine the milk, egg substitute, sugar, vanilla extract, and lemon rind, and pour over the bread cubes. Set aside for 10 minutes.

2. Coat a 1½-quart casserole dish with nonstick cooking spray. Place the bread cube mixture in the dish, and bake uncovered at 350°F for about 40 minutes, or until set. When done, a sharp knife inserted midway between the center of the pudding and the rim of the dish should come out clean.

3. While the casserole is baking, soften the jam. If using a microwave oven, place the jam in a microwave-safe bowl, and microwave uncovered at 50-percent power for 2 minutes or until runny. If using a conventional stove top, place the jam in a small saucepan over low heat and cook, stirring constantly, until runny. Remove the pudding from the oven, and spread the jam over the pudding.

4. To make the meringue, place the egg whites and the cream of tartar in the bowl of an electric mixer, and beat on high until soft peaks form when the beaters are removed. Beat in the sugar 1 tablespoon at a time, and continue beating until stiff peaks form. Swirl the meringue over the jam, and return the pudding to the oven. Bake for 10 additional minutes, or until the meringue is lightly browned.

5. Remove the pudding from the oven, and let sit for 15 minutes. Serve warm.

5 cups French bread cubes

2 cups skim milk

1 cup fat-free egg substitute

¼ cup sugar

1 teaspoon vanilla extract

1½ teaspoons freshly grated lemon rind, or ½ teaspoon dried

½ cup raspberry jam or fruit spread

MERINGUE TOPPING

2 egg whites, warmed to room temperature

⅛ teaspoon cream of tartar

¼ cup sugar

NUTRITIONAL FACTS (PER ¾-CUP SERVING)		
Calories: 192	Fat: 0.6 g	Protein: 7.2 g
Cholesterol: 1 mg	Fiber: 0.5 g	Sodium: 189 mg

Fresh Fruit Trifle

Yield: 12 servings

1 fat-free pound or angel food cake (12 ounces)

⅓ cup raspberry jam or fruit spread

1 tablespoon amaretto or chambord liqueur

4 cups mixed fresh fruit

3 cups vanilla pudding made with skim milk

TOPPING

1 cup light whipped topping

1 cup nonfat vanilla yogurt

1 cup mixed fresh fruit (optional)

Use your choice of seasonal fresh fruit to make this beautiful layered dessert. Strawberries, kiwis, bananas, peaches, raspberries, blueberries, and seedless green grapes all yield delicious results.

1. Slice the cake into ¾-inch slices, and spread each piece with jam on one side. Set aside.

2. Drizzle the liqueur over the sides and bottom of a 3-quart trifle bowl or other decorative glass bowl. Arrange half of the cake slices over the bottom of the bowl. Top with half of the fruit, and then half of the pudding. Repeat the cake, fruit, and pudding layers.

3. Place the whipped topping in a small bowl, and fold the yogurt into the topping. Swirl the mixture over the top of the trifle, and garnish with fresh fruit, if desired. Cover and chill for at least 2 hours before serving.

NUTRITIONAL FACTS (PER 1-CUP SERVING)		
Calories: 209	Fat: 1 g	Protein: 5.5 g
Cholesterol: 0 mg	Fiber: 1.5 g	Sodium: 165 mg

Resource List

Most of the ingredients used in the recipes in this book are readily available in any supermarket, or can be found in your local health foods or gourmet store. But if you are unable to locate what you're looking for, the following list should guide you to a manufacturer who can either sell the desired product to you directly or inform you of the nearest retail outlet.

Meat Substitutes

Harvest Direct, Inc.
PO Box 4514
Decatur, IL 62525-4514
(800) 835-2867

Harvest Burger mixes, and texturized vegetable protein (TVP).

Nondairy Cheeses

Sharon's Finest
PO Box 5020
Santa Rosa, CA 95402
(800) 6569669

Almondrella Cheese, Tofurella Cheese, and Veganrella Cheese.

Sweeteners

Fruit Source
1803 Mission Street, Suite 401
Santa Cruz, CA 95060
(408) 457-1136

Fruit Source granulated and liquid sweeteners.

Lundberg Family Farms
PO Box 369
Richvale, CA 95974-0369
(916) 882-4551

Brown rice syrup.

NutraCane, Inc.
5 Meadowbrook Parkway
Milford, NH 03055
(603) 672-2801

Sucanat granulated sweetener.

Vermont Country Maple, Inc.
PO Box 53
Jericho Center, VT 05465
(800) 528–7021

Maple sugar, maple syrup, and other maple products.

Westbrae Natural Foods
1065 East Walnut
Carson, CA 90746
(310) 886–8200

Brown rice syrup and other natural foods.

Whole Grains and Flours

Arrowhead Mills, Inc.
Box 2059
Hereford, TX 79045
(800) 749–0730

Whole wheat pastry flour, oat flour, and other flours and whole grains.

King Arthur Flour
PO Box 876
Norwich, VT 05055
(800) 827–6836

White whole wheat flour and other flours, whole grains, and baking products.

Mountain Ark Trading Company
PO Box 3170
Fayetteville, AR 72702
(800) 643–8909

Whole grains and flours, unrefined sweeteners, dried fruits, fruit spreads, and a wide variety of other natural foods.

Walnut Acres
Walnut Acres Road
Penns Creek, PA 17862
(800) 433–3998
(717) 837–0601

Baking and cooking aids, whole grains and flours, unrefined sweeteners, dried fruits, and a wide variety of other natural foods.

Index